Willie Stargell

AN AUTOBIOGRAPHY
by Willie Stargell and Tom Bird

ONONDAGA COMMUNITY COLLEGE
LIBRARY BLDG.
SYRACUSE, NEW YORK 13215

1817

HARPER & ROW, PUBLISHERS, New York
Cambridge, Philadelphia, San Francisco, London
Mexico City, São Paulo, Sydney

Photographs follow pages 120 and 184.

WILLIE STARGELL: AN AUTOBIOGRAPHY. Copyright © 1984 by Willie Stargell and Tom Bird. All rights reserved. Printed in the United States of America. No part of this book may be used or reproduced in any manner whatsoever without written permission except in the case of brief quotations embodied in critical articles and reviews. For information address Harper & Row, Publishers, Inc., 10 East 53rd Street, New York, N.Y. 10022. Published simultaneously in Canada by Fitzhenry & Whiteside Limited, Toronto.

FIRST EDITION

Designer: Lydia Link

Library of Congress Cataloging in Publication Data
Stargell, Willie, 1941–
  Willie Stargell : an autobiography.

  1. Stargell, Willie, 1941– . 2. Baseball players
—United States—Biography.   3. Pittsburgh Pirates
(Baseball team) I. Bird, Tom.   II. Title.
GV865.S76A38 1984   796.357′092′4 [B]   83-48387
ISBN 0-06-015238-9

---

84 85 86 87 88 10 9 8 7 6 5 4 3 2 1

Willie Stargell

ACKNOWLEDGMENTS

I'D ALWAYS WANTED TO WRITE A BOOK ON MY LIFE BUT I was always skeptical about choosing the correct writer to help me. Over the years, I'd turned down dozens of writers who asked to help me with my story. Then Tom Bird, a good friend of mine who was also the assistant publicist for the Pirates, told me that he had a secret ambition of becoming a writer. I could always trust Tom as a loyal friend. Because of that fact, Tom and I decided to collaborate on my autobiography shortly afterward.

What you will find on the following pages is an extensive portrayal of myself, a story that I could not have written without Tom. He is a talented writer and a close and dear friend. Working with him made writing this book not only a very rewarding experience but also fun. We entered this project as friends, and after completing the book we were even closer friends. I guess that's what I was looking for all along, a person who was my friend first and a writer second.

But Tom and I couldn't have written this book without the help of dozens of other people. Most of the credit for the detailing of my ancestry and the early years of my life goes to my mother, Gladys Russell. She spent hundreds of hours on the telephone with both Tom and me, answering all the questions we could muster. She told me a lot of things about myself that I didn't even know.

When we stumped my mom, we usually turned to either Joe Stargell or Bobby Mays, two of my uncles who are familiar with my ancestry. Both were very patient with our inquiries, as was my stepfather Percy Russell, who also helped a tremendous amount. Two books that I read during the construction of my autobiography also helped me better understand the plight of my Seminole ancestors—*Fearless and Free,* by George Walton, and *Seminoles,* by Edwin Reynolds. I would also like to thank the Oklahoma Historical Society for their direction and guidance.

Further into the book, George Reed, Bob Zuk, Carl McKane, Tommy Harper, Bob Clear and Al Kupski helped me jar my memory for information I may not have been able to recall without them.

Joe Morgan, Rich Hebner, Bill Madlock, Bob Prince, Tony Bartirome, Jack Berger, Manny Sanguillen, Joe Lonnett, Dave Parker, Lanny Frattare, Al Monchak, Harvey Haddix, Bob Skinner, John "Hully" Hallahan and Chuck Tanner also deserve my thanks for all their help with the facts concerning my years as a major-leaguer.

Other special thanks go to Ed Wade and Sally O'Leary of the Pirates, who were always of valuable assistance; Linda Reed (George Reed's daughter) and Robert Krause of the Eastman School of Music for their help in securing some valuable photographs; to my sister Sandrus for her constant support and guidance; our typist Marilyn Gomrick; my agent and close friend David Litman and his associate David Brown; our literary agents Scott Meredith and Russ Galen, whose patience kept us on an even keel; to Don Klein, a close and personal friend who also has a finely tuned mind for recall; to Doug Looney, a senior writer with *Sports Illustrated,* whose friendship and knowledge helped to make this book a reality; to our family and friends, who supported both of us wholeheartedly; to Larry Ashmead and Craig Nelson, of Harper & Row, who patiently worked our material into shape; and finally to Tom's wife, Amy, who gave him the love, encouragement, understanding and patience he needed through all the hours of work this project handed him.

Without the help of the people mentioned above, writing this book would have been a hassle rather than a pleasure. Thank you.

Willie Stargell

"Simple pleasures were all the pleasures I knew as a child."

1 FEW PEOPLE KNOW anything about my heritage. That's a shame, for I'm extremely proud of my forefathers. I became known for my home runs and my accomplishments in the big leagues. But my ancestors are the roots of those accomplishments and they deserve some of the credit. They are responsible for what I am today.

I was raised in both a Negro and Seminole Indian environment. The Seminole in my blood runs way back before the founding of North America to the Mayan Indians of Central America. The Creek Indians were direct descendants of the Mayans, and the Seminoles eventually descended from the Creeks, but not without a battle.

The Seminoles, who established their homes in southern Georgia and all throughout Florida, were a much more advanced tribe than the Creeks. They were also more liberal and were known for the clean, friendly atmosphere of their tribes. The Creeks resented the Seminoles for separating and they were also jealous of the Seminoles' superiority.

One area in which they were advanced was a liberal acceptance of Negroes into their tribe. At this time, the early 1800s, the Seminoles were the only people on the face of the earth that accepted Negroes as equals. Hearing this news, hundreds of Negro slaves from

1

the south escaped and fled in droves to Seminole camps. The Seminoles offered the fleeing slaves immediate access and fiercely guarded their escape route.

Once within the Seminole compound, the Negroes were given their own plot of land in the Negro side of camp. They became known as Seminole slaves—though in contrast to the white man's treatment, the Indians' treatment was exceptionally good. The Negroes were only responsible for providing the Seminoles with a small percentage of their harvest each season or a minute portion of their slaughtered livestock. Otherwise, they were left alone.

Like no other civilization at that time, the Seminoles permitted slaves to intermarry into their tribe. This is what eventually happened with my great-grandparents, the Brunners. Once married to a Seminole, a Negro became a full member of the Seminole tribe. No ifs, ands or buts—he or she was accepted.

This relationship worked well for both parties for quite some time until the white slave owners began fearing a general slave revolt. That was when all the action started. The slave owners' fear eventually caused a war between the U.S. Government and the Seminoles.

All would have been fine if the loyal Seminoles had surrendered the runaways. But they didn't. Because of political pressure from the slave owners, war became imminent, and my distant ancestor, War Chief Osceola, ignited the fighting by killing an Indian agent named Wiley Thompson after the agent had betrayed him.

Other incidents fed the fire of the war, and the Seminoles were way ahead on all scorecards in the early going. That's when the army, which was terribly embarrassed by being beaten by the red man, turned to treachery. Osceola, who was eventually taken prisoner while standing under a white flag, became a victim of the government's cheating ways. But because of his heroism on the field of battle, Osceola became known as a war hero, not only to his Seminole tribesmen but to the white man as well. After his death, twenty-three towns, three counties, two lakes, two mountains and a national forest all carried the name Osceola. My ancestor did even more for his tribesmen after his capture than he had done on the battlefield.

The war dragged on for over a decade. The Negroes were said to be the fiercest of warriors. With vengeance in their eyes, they attacked the white soldiers. The Seminole and the Negro established

2

an extremely close relationship on the field of battle. Never had one people fought so fiercely to preserve the rights of another.

The war eventually ended with the government losing 1466 soldiers and spending approximately $40 million. The Seminoles, though depleted significantly in numbers, emerged the winner. The war may have ended but the spirit of the Seminole lives in me today. Though I consider myself a leader like Osceola, I utilize the smile as my weapon instead of the rifle. I'd rather make a friend than shoot an enemy any day.

As I think back to my ancestors, several aspects of my own nature can be traced to the Seminoles. For one, I value my solitude. Literally, the word "Seminole" means "those who camp at a distance." That phrase describes me perfectly. I value my time alone.

Also, like the Seminoles, I value the beauty of nature.

And like the Seminoles, I greet each person and each day with an open heart. I believe that only a free spirit allows a person to become him or herself in the presence of another person. Thus, I allow a person to approach me in whatever shape, color or form he or she may desire.

I believe that my open-heart philosophy is the key to my popularity. I love and accept all people for what they are. I never expect them to live up to my expectations, only their own. But like that of my Seminole ancestors, my trusting disposition leaves me open to attack. I'm ready to be bruised, so the wound is easily healed. But the Seminoles relied on the white man's word and eventually became pawns in the white man's political game.

Though the exact date is unknown, my Seminole/Negro ancestors were eventually shipped to an Oklahoma reservation. The trek, which started in Tampa and continued by boat to New Orleans, then up the Arkansas River by riverboat and by foot the last 250 miles, became known as the Trail of Tears. Thousands of Seminoles either starved, were stricken with disease, famine or exhaustion, or were stolen by slave traders along the route. Brave warriors and squaws were said to have dropped dead at every step along the way.

But the Seminole tribe survived and was joined with four other Indian nations—the Creek, the Cherokee, the Shawnee and the Cheyenne—in Oklahoma, which had become a national dumping ground for the red man.

My great-grandparents arrived at the reservations sometime in the mid-1840s. My great-grandfather, Tom Brunner, had been a

Negro slave. My great-grandmother was a Seminole squaw.

The Seminoles immediately ran into trouble with the Creeks and other envious Indian nations who sought to steal their slaves. But several decades later, and after the Seminoles' significant contribution to the war effort on the side of the Union Army in the Civil War, conditions improved immensely.

On April 22, 1889, and September 22, 1891, Oklahoma was opened up to settlers in two frantic drives for homesteads. During this time, the Brunners gave birth to a daughter named Nora, who eventually became my grandmother.

In 1898, Seminole courts were dissolved and placed under the jurisdiction of the U.S. Government. The country was preparing the Seminoles to become American citizens. Shortly after this time, Nora met and married my grandfather, Wil Stargell, a son of a Negro farmer named Henry, who'd migrated from Georgia to Oklahoma.

On November 16, 1907, and approximately a year before Oklahoma was officially named a state, land was surveyed and allotted to all members of the five tribes. The Negro was given the worst land whenever possible. Wil and Nora were given a dusty patch of land in a region called Turkey Creek.

The couple gave birth to four boys, one of which was William, who later became my father. My grandparents later separated and married other people. Nora retained the homestead. She remained stone broke until the Great Seminole Oil Boom struck in the early 1920s.

The poor land given to the Negro flowed with oil. The once poverty-stricken Negro was rich until the local white attorneys developed illegal methods for stealing the Indians' money. Nora's land looked like a forest of oil wells, but she, too, was cheated back into poverty and eventually moved to Tulsa, where she died, leaving behind her only real possession, a chicken restaurant commonly referred to as a chicken shack.

Though the Boom wasn't as beneficial to my ancestors as it could have been, it did provide my father with my lovely mother, Gladys, whose family had migrated west from Georgia to join in the hunt for riches.

My mom and dad became sweethearts in their early teens. They'd met in elementary school, and at the age of fifteen they were going steady. At eighteen, they married. It appeared as the perfect relationship until my father left my mother, who was pregnant with me, to return to high school in Tulsa. My father never returned to my mom, and I never met him until about nineteen years later.

I was born on March 7, 1941, on a cold, windy day, just outside of Earlsboro, Oklahoma, in the home of my grandfather, Wil Stargell.

My mother had entered labor at eleven o'clock on the morning of March 6. Late the next day, on March 7, she still hadn't delivered. I was not making this an easy time for her. My grandfather began to worry. He soon summoned onto the scene a specialist, Mrs. Armstrong, a midwife, and the local specialist on birth. After one entire day of labor, I was finally born at 11:27 A.M. on the seventh.

I was a hefty baby, weighing in at eight pounds even. I was also nineteen inches long. I was tagged Wilver, a combination of my father's first name, William, and my mom's middle name, Vernell. But for no designated reason I was given the middle name Dornell.

My mother, Gladys, had been absorbed into the Stargell clan after my father had left her, a Seminole custom prevalent in the war years a century before. Gladys had been alone in the world. Both her parents had died, but she immediately became a part of the close-knit Stargell household.

Earlsboro seems so long ago and so far away. But I smile each time I try to relive my childhood. Earlsboro was not much more than a roadside stop. There was no airport, one main highway, one post office, a grocery store and a bank. We liked to keep things simple then, and Earlsboro was the simplest of all things. But it was home. At that time, the one set of railroad tracks, the main way in and out of town, regulated Earlsboro's travel schedule through a small variety of infrequent stops.

I would like to say that I was the most famous athlete ever to emerge from Oklahoma, but I'd be lying. For the greatest athlete of all time, Jim Thorpe, was born only sixteen miles northwest of Earlsboro in a town named Shawnee. Thorpe, who was a full-blooded Shawnee Indian, later became a gold-medal winner in track and field, capturing both the pentathlon and decathlon—an outstanding collegian athlete, a major-leaguer and a professional football player.

Like myself, Thorpe had a prestigious Indian background. His great-grandfather, a Shawnee chief named Black Hawk, had been the most famous of all Shawnee warriors. Thorpe later rose from the reservation to achieve his greatness in Pennsylvania. He soon be-

5

came a legend at the Carlisle Indian School in Carlisle, Pennsylvania, which is located approximately four hours east of Pittsburgh, my mecca of fortune and fame.

Thorpe later died on March 28, 1953, when I was twelve years old. He was buried along the Lehigh River in Pennsylvania in between two towns—Mauch Chunk and East Maunch Chunk. The towns later merged and changed their names to Jim Thorpe, Pennsylvania, in hopes of attracting tourists, even though Thorpe never had any connection with the towns while alive.

Thorpe was responsible for opening the door of professional sports to the red man. No Indian would ever, or will ever, create more clout in the world of sports for his people than Thorpe had.

Besides Thorpe, another well-known figure who was better known by his accomplishments than his name, Brewster Higley, a physician, a Shawnee native and the author of the song "Home on the Range," died nearly forty years before my birth, in Oklahoma. But his song lives on as the most accurate illustration of how the West really had been.

But the best-remembered Oklahoman of my life, Johnny Ray, did not appear on the national scene until 1981. Johnny, a talented young second-baseman of both Negro and Cherokee descent, was acquired by the Pittsburgh Pirates from the Houston Astros in my second-to-last season. J-Ray (as I called him) and I immediately became close friends. I don't know if it was our Indian blood that tied us together but we immediately became close friends. I referred to him as my favorite Bucco.

Johnny was always eager to listen and learn. I liked that most about him, for I always considered myself a good teacher and I enjoyed sharing my experience with others. He was extremely mature for his young age. I was as proud as anyone when J-Ray was named as *Sporting News* Rookie of the Year in 1982. I only hope that some of my experience helped.

I suppose the most dominating factor concerning my childhood was not the desolation of Oklahoma but the fact that I was born fatherless. That's where my grandfather enters the scene. Were it not for him, I believe the chances of my living a normal life today would be minute.

But fortunately Wil Stargell picked up where his son had left off and saved me from all that. He was a tall, well-built man who loved me like a son. Though it's tough for me to remember so far back, I would have to say that he was my original role model for manhood. In recognition of his time and love and attention, my first word spoken as a child was "Da-Da."

My grandfather was more than just a grandfather to me. He was also a father figure to my mother, who saw in Wil the type of father she wished she'd been born to. Wil was hardworking and sincere and a close friend to his deserted daughter-in-law.

With the exception of my mother, no person meant more to me than my grandfather in the early years of my life. Though I was too young to remember everything about him, my mother told me as much as she could remember. "He'd wear a path straight to your crib," she always said, and he'd often spend hours looking over the crib, making funny faces and strange noises, attempting to make me smile.

The thought of such scenes still sends tickles around my heart. Maybe it was knowing that my grandfather had cared so much, I'm not sure, but I still feel something today.

Though I eventually understood my father's reason for leaving, my mother never did. Her disgust caused her to love my grandfather even more. He's the only one that she recognizes for helping us when we needed help. Wil gave us everything we both needed during some very difficult early years.

Still today, my mother tolerates, but fails to recognize, any of the so-called close relatives that appeared on the scene after I began playing professional ball. She lays claim to one person for my normal upbringing: Wil Stargell.

In retrospect, I realize the importance of my early years in the formation of my attitude. Like everyone else, I was raised among a variety of factors that greatly affected my viewpoint as an adult. The single most significant nontangible, nonhuman factor of my childhood was the Second World War. Its results adversely affected the lives of Americans everywhere. To shelter themselves from the pain, individuals banded together for support. As a result, the World War II generation became a product of this togetherness. Thus, togetherness became, and still is, the most important aspect of my life. While other generations value the worth of gold or silver, nothing is more precious to me than togetherness. There's nothing I value more than the closeness of my friends and family, a smile as I pass someone on the street, or the familiarity of an acquaintance. Without such things, I would surely perish.

People may not realize this fact about me, but all those thousands of dollars I made playing baseball never really mattered. All they were to me was a way to keep my family warm, well-fed and prosperous. I was never money made. I saw money only as a way to keep my family safe and secure—that's all.

I never allowed my life to revolve around my income. I never had any money until the Pirates signed me for $1500 and I still have the love for the simple pleasures of my youth. To me a party isn't a high-society cocktail party with invitations and all; it's a group of good friends, a bottle of Chardonnay, a handful of records and a bucket of fried chicken. I don't feel comfortable at high-society, black-tie gatherings. I appreciate the simple pleasures in everyday living more than life's big events. Clothes hanging on the line in a backyard turns me on. I also like to see chickens in a backyard. Such scenes remind me of the pleasures of Oklahoma. Unfortunately, because of automation, clotheslines and backyard chickens have all but disappeared from everyday life. But they're still in my heart and I feel a rise in my spirit whenever I see them.

Simple pleasures were all the pleasures I knew as a child. But I'm not ashamed; in fact, I'm proud. For simple pleasures are the best pleasures. My major playing area was a small dirt hill located just off our porch. I could be found there almost any time of the afternoon, digging holes with my two rusty play spoons and pushing my small toys through the dusty Oklahoma soil.

The biggest thrill of my day was when my grandfather would take me for a walk around the farm to see the animals, or when my mom led me in a game of hide-and-go-seek. I was the only child in the three-room farmhouse, so I received all the attention. In fact, I was the only child for a considerable distance, which usually meant that when my grandfather and mom weren't around, I played alone. But when they were around, I hoarded all their affection.

Grandpa also taught me how to sing, and his lessons became a "daily event." My mom told me that he loved to hear me sing. He called me Little Dumpy. When he arrived home from working on the farm each day, he'd walk over to his favorite chair and sit down. Then he'd look up at me and say, "Come along, Little Dumpy. Let's go sing." I'd run across the room as fast as I could and climb into my grandfather's lap. I loved the singing sessions. My mom said that Grandpa taught me my love for music.

My behavior as a child was about the same as any other child's, with the exception of my great love for the skills of baseball. Though I wasn't old enough at the time to realize the results of my movements, I was actually preparing for a career in the majors. It's wondrous how all the pieces fit together to form a life. I didn't even know what baseball was at the time, but the game flowed through my veins at a very young age. I flailed my arm in a throwing motion even before I could walk. I never knew why I did so. It just seemed natural, and like all other children I only did what felt good.

Nothing felt better than throwing. After I made the big leagues, my mom began telling everyone that my baseball career actually began at the age of two. But before all the pieces of the puzzle came together, my odd actions as a child made almost all my relatives, including Gladys, shake their heads. My grandfather was the only understanding one, and at times he and my mother would argue over my behavior.

My mother was always afraid that my actions would cause me to break something in the house, so she usually stood me in the center of the room to keep me away from anything breakable. But at times, when her patience didn't prevail, she'd lose her temper and spank my hands.

That's when my grandfather would enter in my defense. "You leave Little Dumpy alone," he'd say. Such scenes were common in the Stargell household, and though battles had to be fought, I kept on flailing my arm, my mom kept on scolding and my grandfather kept running to my defense.

Later in my life, I progressed to the throwing of stones or small objects. Gladys was still very confused as to the nature of her son's actions. But as time passed, she began to accept my behavior. She loved me too much to keep scolding me continually. My mom always gave me more than enough attention and affection.

While I was very young, Gladys left me in the secure hands of my grandfather and moved to Shawnee to accept a position as a cleaning lady. Unfortunately, there were no jobs open in Earlsboro, so I was forced to do without my mother during the week. But she never failed to return to Earlsboro on the weekends. I missed her, but the weekends usually made up for the loneliness I felt during the week.

For my mom, living in Shawnee wasn't any day at the beach. Though Shawnee had been the most prosperous city during the oil boom, it had become a victim of the depression. Deserted makeshift housing, formerly constructed for oil company employees, defaced the town. The population had shrunk to its pre-boom mark. Shawnee was typical of Oklahoma at this time. The racial, historical and economic makeup of the city paralleled that of the state. Both were basically depressed.

Thousands of Shawnee inhabitants had already left for other opportunities around the country, especially in California. The San Francisco Bay region, which was responsible for exporting supplies to the Pacific war front, was the most popular of job havens. Bay area dock workers became famous for their productive tendencies. The dock workers were often said to have worked around the clock loading supply ships with precious munitions and supplies. Because of these devoted dock workers, the Bay area became the essential first link in the Allies' Pacific supply lines.

During the early war years, when my mother cleaned homes in Shawnee, she rented a small house in the downtown area. It was a considerable amount of time before she met and married Lesley Bush, a soldier, and we again began to see each other on a full-time basis.

But with the good also came the bad. Unfortunately, I was unable to see my grandfather when Mom decided to move to California to live with her new in-laws. I was permanently separated from the primary father figure in my life.

The Bush family had preceded our move to California by a few months. Like thousands of others, Lesley's father had been hired as a dock worker in Alameda. He and his family had moved into an apartment on Campbell Street, which was just off the docks.

By the time my mother decided to move, she and I were the lone members of the Bush family left in Oklahoma. Impending disappointment foreshadowed our leaving, but we bit our lips and left for the promised land, regardless. Leaving was difficult for Mom. I could see it in her eyes. She'd come to love the vast Oklahoma countryside. As for me, I would follow my mother anywhere. I knew that I would miss my grandfather, but I also knew that my place was by my mother's side.

Mom and I boarded a train from Shawnee sometime in 1944. The conditions on the train were crowded at best. As is customary during wartime, military personnel were given first choice on traveling accommodations. The soldiers were packed into the passenger cars like sardines in a can. We were lucky to be sold a ticket; we didn't even ask for a seat. We were two of only a few civilians aboard.

Besides being extremely uncomfortable, the conditions soon became dangerous. In the dark of night, Mom and I were once even pushed out of the car. There we stood in the cold night air as the train sped along the tracks. We stayed outside on the narrow strip connected with the car trailing ours for hours. I don't remember, but Mom said she wrapped me in her coat and laid me along the cold steel floor. She feared for my safety as sparks flew off the spinning wheels. Luckily for me, I slept through the entire experience. I awoke back inside the crowded car. Somehow my mother had maneuvered us back inside. She told me later that we had been out in the cold night air for three hours.

The poor train ride had definitely foreshadowed the disappointment that greeted us in California. My mother looked puzzled as we walked from the train. "Where is the sun?" she thought. In all the travel brochures, California had been billed as the Sunshine State. None of the brochures had ever mentioned the cold, fog or wind that haunted Alameda year 'round.

I could see that she wished we had never left the wide open spaces of Oklahoma, especially when we moved into Bush's small, dingy apartment located above a grocery store. Mom immediately became irritated when she discovered that the only place for me to play was a small porch on the rear of the apartment. My new grandparents seemed to share her sentiments, but they remained in California for one reason—money, which was almost double what they had earned in Oklahoma.

Her disappointment with California, combined with a poor relationship with Lesley, caused my mother to file for her second divorce in 1945, after three years of marriage.

We next moved in with my step-aunt, Ozzie, who lived in the Alameda projects. My mother loved project living. The people of the projects were real people—friendly, open-hearted, good neighbors—exactly what my mom needed. The projects became the answer to Mom's homesick blues.

Mom found a job working as a cleaning lady in a men's dormitory, and it wasn't long before she met Percy Russell, a sailor who frequented our complex when on leave. Life was taking a positive swing for us. We both enjoyed our new home and new friends. Mom was dating a very caring, loving man in Percy, and we'd left the Bush experience behind us. What more could we both want?

11

The war ended soon after our move to the projects. Though it was good news for everyone, Mom had mixed emotions. Yes, she was happy that the fighting had stopped, but the end of the war also meant that she'd lose her post office job that she'd just taken. She was laid off immediately. Twenty-three years old, divorced twice, raising her son alone, and now unemployed, my mom began to sink to the bottom.

Percy came to my mother's rescue. He proved himself a knight in shining armor. Mom had found the security she so desperately needed. They were married in 1946.

We all moved into our own apartment in the projects. Since Percy had recently been discharged from the navy, he began a new career as a civil service truck driver. Unfortunately, the position didn't pay well, and with Mom out of work, we struggled to make ends meet.

Without our friends in the projects, the three of us were basically alone in the world. Neither Mom or Percy had much contact with their families. But Mom had never had much contact with her family. She was the youngest of eight children. She was just learning to talk when her brothers and sisters were setting out on their own. She'd never been provided the opportunity to become acquainted with any of them.

That's why it was so surprising when one of my mom's older sisters, Lucy, wrote and asked permission to pay us a visit. None of us fully understood her motives, but we were happy to have her come. She and my mom were little better than strangers; the two had hardly communicated at all the last twenty years, and now Lucy wanted to travel five days on a train for a visit. Something was very strange.

Mom hadn't seen Lucy since her dad had packed up the family and headed west. Lucy was on her own then, and had remained behind, eventually relocating in Orlando, Florida. She'd been married once, then divorced. Lucy now worked as a cook in an Orlando restaurant. That was about all Mom knew about her older sister. She'd never met, or even known the name of Lucy's former husband.

Questions ran through Mom's mind as we drove to the train station to meet Lucy. Why was she visiting? As Lucy stepped from the train, I glanced at Mom and then back at Lucy. There was absolutely no resemblance. No one would have ever known they were sisters.

Mom was a petite, pretty woman who wore a childish smile well. Lucy, large-boned, bowlegged and with a pinch of snuff tucked loosely inside her lower lip, carried herself awkwardly, almost like a retired cowboy. She had a strict disposition, which showed in the scowl on her face. A smile would have been an unnatural act for Lucy; she was hard as nails. We didn't know why, but for some reason we felt it: Lucy had come to California with a motive.

She stayed with us for nearly a month, and the more I got to know her, the less unattractive Lucy seemed. We all became close friends during that month. My mother began to appreciate Lucy's company. Her older sister was the first sibling who had made a genuine effort to contact her in California, and Mom appreciated that. Mom began to trust Lucy. It was obvious that she yearned for stronger family ties.

During the course of her visit, Lucy sensed the pressure Mom was under—a new marriage, no job, a pile of bills. That's when Lucy offered to take me back to Orlando with her. That way Mom and Percy could pull themselves back together financially, and Lucy also thought that the young couple needed time alone to work out some things between themselves.

Mom was surprised by my aunt's offer, but after considering it for some time, she accepted. Without a job, she was having a difficult time supporting me in a proper manner. Mom thought I might be better off with Lucy for a while. I know she was doing what she thought was best for me, but I couldn't bear the thought of leaving my mother. For such a long time, we had been the only security each other had.

I believe this was the most difficult decision of my mother's young life, but she and Percy *were* having financial troubles, so the sisters agreed on a one-year stay, maximum, which was plenty of time for the young couple to get everything together.

Only my mother could convince me of the reason for my leaving, and even she had a difficult time explaining as she fought to hold back the tears. She was still explaining as she escorted Lucy and me to the train, and I still didn't understand her reasoning—I was only five years old at the time. But I had enough faith in my mother to believe that what she was doing for me was right, though I could see that she was doing better controlling my fears than her own.

"You're going on a choo-choo ride with Aunt Lucy," she would tell me as the tears welled up in her eyes. "Don't worry, and be a good boy because I'll be coming soon to bring you back."

What I remember most about my mother at this time is seeing her break down in tears as my train pulled away from the station. What I remember most about myself is the fact that, along with the constant flailing of my arm, I also began carrying a stick wherever I went. For no specific reason, I loved to swing it through the air. I didn't know what baseball was at this time, but I did know that I loved to throw small objects and swing sticks.

The train ride with Aunt Lucy is a bit fuzzy, too, but I remember it as the longest train ride of my life—emotionally, that is. I missed my mother. That's what made it agonizing.

The highlight of the journey was when we stopped in Oklahoma to visit one of my uncles, a brother of Aunt Lucy's, and I got an opportunity to see my grandfather again. I hadn't seen him in years and I had missed him so. This was the last time I would see my grandfather alive. He died when I was about seven years old. I cried when my mother told me the news. I loved him. A very large part of him still lives in me today. Mom used to tell me that he and I were alike in many ways. I'm proud to know that I am like my grandfather.

As we reentered the train in Oklahoma, I still felt the pain of missing my mother. The train ride began to seem like an eternity. Mom and I had been everything to each other. Later in life, as a father, I would look back at this experience and remember the pain. I swore to myself there and then on that train that I would never allow anything—not money, not lack of money—to separate me from my children. I'm proud to say that I never did allow anything to keep me from my kids. They're the most important part of my life.

But on that train ride, it was only Lucy and me, and though I was hurting inside, I made the best of the situation. Lucy and I became very close friends on the journey, and by the time we arrived at Orlando, she had eased some of the hurt from my soul.

I grew to love and respect my Aunt Lucy, though my description of her may sound somewhat derogatory. But that's simply how she looked. She had several manly characteristics, including her short, bowlegs and her continual dipping of snuff. Her favorite

14

brand was Buttercup. I know, as part of my chores, she'd always send me to the store to buy it for her. Even that became routine. I was just making the best of the situation.

The longer I stayed with Lucy, the more I learned about her. But I would have only needed to be with her for one minute to realize the driving force in her life. She was very disciplined and she immediately expected me to accept her ways. Her strict approach to life was what I most remembered about Lucy. The transition from easygoing life with my mother to life with Lucy was difficult at first. But there was a switch always in sight and a scowl always on her face, and the transition began to progress more rapidly.

She was especially strict regarding chores. I must have been large for my age, because she worked me like an eighteen-year-old. She always expected me to carry more than my weight. Her house contained no luxuries—no electricity, no refrigerator, no washer, no dryer, no furnace. The house could have been a model for pioneer living. Luxury for Lucy was a nephew to do her chores.

I was constantly chopping wood, toting water, fetching ice for the icebox or kerosene for the lamps, and cleaning ashes out of the wood stove. This five-year-old's work was never done, and with all these chores, there was very little time left over for me to play. I became Lucy's Cinderella.

But I really didn't mind the chores as much as the time it took to do them. In fact, carrying the ice helped strengthen my hands later for baseball, and making soap and doing the wash—well, the strenuous work is a fond memory now.

One of the first chores Lucy taught me to do was to make lye soap. Everyone has a different way of making lye soap. Lucy would pour the ingredients into a washtub hung over an open fire and filled with boiling water. The remainder of the work was up to me. I would stir the solution for hours with a large wooden stick until the strong alkaline solution finally hardened and could be cut into squares.

Lye soap was the staple cleaning component in my Aunt Lucy's household. I fondly recall the entire process each time I see a rerun of the *Beverly Hillbillies* on TV and Granny, the show's spunky grandmother figure, is brewing a batch of her spoon-dissolving lye soap by the swimming pool, or cee-ment pond, as she called it. Even though the work was hard, I'm very proud of the accomplishments of my youth—from lye soap to the major leagues. I'll bet that when

I established myself in the big leagues that none of my fans ever thought that I had once been a perfectionist at making lye soap.

But the production of the soap was only the first step in a long afternoon of cleaning. After the soap was made, I next filled three washtubs with water; one for washing—the water brought to a boil by a fire placed under its tub—one for rinsing and one for bluing. Once the water in the washing tub reached its boiling point, I began to scrub the clothes along the rough edges of the scrub board until every inch of the clothing was clean. Lucy watched attentively. She was meticulous about washing, as she was with everything else. Once I had finished scrubbing the clothes, I dipped them in the rinsing tub and then the bluing tub before hanging them on the clothesline to dry. Nothing is cleaner than lye-scrubbed clothes and nothing fresher than clothing dried in the open air.

Hard work in those days was seen as a sign of faith in the Lord. It's said that a good Christian praises the Lord always, in good, bad and indifferent situations. A Baptist Negro's way of praising the Lord was to live life to its fullest. Negroes sang at the top of their lungs in church, they worked hard in school and they pushed their bodies to exhaustive states when doing chores. Negroes during this era praised the Lord with their lives.

Performing my strenuous daily chores was seen as a part of my religious conviction, and lazy Negroes were viewed as sinners, but working hard was also how Negroes survived. Since most, like Lucy, were poor and without modern conveniences, all family members had to pitch in to run a respectable home. Each member of the family was assigned a specific routine of chores, which were gauged to their individual abilities. Unfortunately for me, I was all the family Lucy had and I was sometimes allotted twice as many responsibilities as the average child my age. During my stay with Lucy, my heavy load of chores may have made me the most religious kid on the block.

Aunt Lucy's strictness bred determination and conviction in my life—though mostly for baseball, not chores. While I lived with Lucy, I began to think like a hitter. I didn't understand why, but I developed a fixation for tossing stones in the air and clubbing them with sticks. I knew nothing about baseball at the time. I simply loved to strike small objects with a stick and watch them fly into the distance.

And when I wasn't hitting rocks, I was throwing them. Of

course, since I'd been practicing this since before I was able to walk, the strength and accuracy of my throwing arm far outweighed that of the average child my age. Baseball for me was instinctive, born within me, given to me as a gift of God. From that experience, I began to believe that everyone is created for a specific purpose. It's up to us as individuals whether we have the courage to live out our destiny or not.

My favorite example is that of the baby kangaroo. Once born, the young kangaroo is solely responsible for its own survival. To survive, it must navigate two-thirds the length of its mother's body to her pouch, the source of its life-preserving nourishment. It's only when the baby reaches the pouch that it's fed. Quite an experience for a baby fresh from birth.

I think human instinct is as obvious as the baby kangaroo's. Human beings are pampered by the Lord. Their real tests don't come until later in life. But I believe that my instinct to hit and throw were God-given. I'm a God-fearing man who worships with my heart and with my life. I leave the decision making to the Lord and view myself as only a response mechanism who receives His messages through my heart. I never search for a reason why—why a baby kangaroo survives, why I loved to hit and throw. Such questions don't enter my mind. I have faith in the Lord's purpose through people. I will try anything, for I know that if I'm meant to succeed, I will.

As an extension of my beliefs, I feel that great hitters are born, not bred. Hitters have a talent that no other athlete has. I consider hitting the most difficult activity to perform in sports. It takes a special eye, a rapid response mechanism and quick reflexes to make instant adjustments in the already flowing motion of one's bat.

I've witnessed thousands of superior athletes try to become hitters and fail at it, and I've seen the most nonathletic-looking creature approach the plate and beat a baseball to death, for he had the God-given talent, the gift.

Let me cite an example from a home-run hitters' contest pitting the Pirates against the Pittsburgh Steelers in 1980. It was a pre-game promotion for a Saturday afternoon game, and judging by the applause it was obvious that the Steelers were the crowd's favorite to win. The audience roared each time one of the massive Steelers strolled to home plate to take his swings. Though the men of steel, as they are referred to by Pittsburghers, looked awesome with their bulging muscles, they disappointed their fans that afternoon by driving only a few balls to the warning track between them.

The Pirates, on the other hand, who were half the size of their opponents, swatted every third pitch out of the park for a home run. Of course, there is something to be said for practice, but the Pirates had the gift of the hitter. The extremely athletic-looking Steelers fell like Goliaths next to their David-like foes.

Few people but brave and self-satisfied individuals understand what I'm speaking about in God-given ability. But imagine my philosophy through my eyes. You step into the batter's box. You have a bat in your hand, its weight and size specifically fitted to your size and strength. You have only one purpose in mind: hit the ball hard. It doesn't matter where, just anywhere.

The pitcher winds and throws his first pitch. It zooms by you, nothing but a blur. You begin to laugh. You didn't even see the pitch, and yet you're supposed to hit it. All you saw was a swerving white streak. You begin to concentrate harder. It makes sense that to hit the ball hard, one must hit it squarely. The task can be completed only when you strike your round bat against the round ball, approaching you at over ninety miles an hour, squarely. Now that's absurd. Round on round never equals square. But that's the dilemma of the hitter.

Because of the absurdity of the task involved, baseball is the only sport that recognizes its players as heros if they fail only two-thirds of the time. That's what a .333 hitter does, and if a player fails only two-thirds of the time over a long period of time, he's a shoo-in for the Hall of Fame.

The magic cutoff point for a great season is usually the .300 mark, or a 70 percent failure ratio. But even some hitters who hit less than .300 are inducted into the Hall of Fame. Their contributions may have been of a different variety. They may have been pitchers, power hitters or defensive whizzes. I had a lifetime average in the high .280s, and I'm very proud to have done that well. Ted Williams was the last man to hit .400 for a season. He was a rare breed and I don't place myself in the same category as him as far as hitting for average. Heck, he only failed 60 percent of the time.

Baseball, as a profession, is so built around failure that the large-egoed, insecure players, no matter how talented, rarely advance through the ranks to the big leagues. Pride and judgment usually stand in their way. Baseball taught me to be modest but durable. A good major-league hitter is a humbled but persistent hitter. He's usually realistic enough to realize that failure is a big part of the game, and of life. Those hitters who've learned and accepted this fact will go far, both on the diamond and in life.

Sometimes you're sure of yourself and other times you're forced to be a good guesser. When a job needs to be done, but you don't have all the answers, you guess. Good hitters are usually educated guessers. I must admit that several of my 475 career homers were hit with my eyes closed. But I wasn't afraid to take a chance. I gambled and had confidence in my estimation of the situation.

I simply guessed what pitch the pitcher was going to throw, where he was going to throw it, fed the info into my mind, timed his delivery and swung in the pre-chosen location. Bingo—home run. But only an educated guesser, a wise gambler, could have made such estimation. There is skill in prediction and estimation. I've spent most of my life guessing.

Not all hitters admit to guesswork. My boyhood hero, Stan Musial, who played for the Cardinals, actually claimed that he could pick up changes in the rotation of a pitched ball. And who's to question his results—a lifetime .331 average and over 470 home-runs? Hitters like Musical are supermen born under the guidance of the supernatural.

Though baseball fans follow different players and the game for a variety of reasons, I believe that the top players are attracted to the game instinctively. For me, baseball became an outlet for my fixation with hitting and throwing, my God-given talents. My belief that each person is created for a specific purpose flows over to every person I meet.

I once saw a young boy squatting down by the edge of a road beating a stick against a rock. He never seemed to stop. Whenever I saw him, he'd be beating rocks with sticks. I don't believe he understood the purpose of his actions. He simply liked what he was doing. When I saw him, I thought of myself throwing stones and swinging sticks. I didn't know why I was doing it either. I just liked to throw rocks and swing sticks.

Now when I see the boy, I think of a future sculptor or a carpenter, someone who likes to work with his hands, and I think of myself and how my fixation with hitting and throwing led me to the major leagues.

I see a lot of people who love their jobs. I see some garbage collectors smiling as they go about their work. But then I see some highly placed executives dreading the start of each day. All people are obligated to live their own lives and do their own thing, but you must be honest enough with yourself to realize what your role really is. That's the only way you'll ever be truly happy.

How do we find what we were meant to be? You simply follow your body's guidance system. It's called your heart, the control panel of your emotions. I believe that one was installed in each of us to guide us through life. If you listen to and follow the guidance of your heart, you'll discover the true meaning of your life. But when people second-guess their guidance system, all types of dangerous side effects may result—ulcers, depression, frustration.

I've always been a slave to my heart. I've never doubted its ways, and look what it's done for me. I'm emotionally and spiritually fulfilled. I have lived my dream. No emotionally fulfilled individual has ever suffered from an ulcer or depression. The work may snowball at times and we may become physically fatigued, but the enthusiasm is always there if we listen to our hearts.

Unfortunately, innate feelings and potential are often stunted by our parents, relatives or peers. Such was the case with my Aunt Lucy. She was a strict advocate of my devotion to my daily chores. A lot of her dependence on me had to do with her being lonely. She had no one else in the world and she demanded that I remain alongside her at all times. She may have been tough on the outside, but like all of us she looked to love someone from the inside.

Even though Aunt Lucy did restrict most of my free time, I always managed enough time to sneak away for a few swings. I played most of my baseball during summer vacation while Lucy was at work. She usually left the house at eight o'clock. I'd walk her to the door and watch her climb aboard the bus, then I'd head for the ballfield, leaving an extensive list of chores behind.

My first stop each morning was at the local soda shop for a chocolate milkshake. After that, with my shake in my hand, I'd stroll over to the corner of Beramore and West Washington Streets to Jones High School where most of the boys met each day to play ball —wiffle ball, fast pitch, home-run derby, softball, a straight game of hardball, single-double-triple—we played it all, and I was always assured of company. There were always more than enough kids gathered at the school.

But like me, most of the boys were poor Negro kids who

couldn't afford bats, gloves or hardballs, so we improvised. Bats were often replaced by broomsticks, balls by any circular object. The games were never extravagant, but they were always fun.

One of my favorite pastimes was batting practice. Baseballs were always too rare and expensive to risk losing in practice, so again I was forced to improvise. Caps from soda bottles usually sufficed and they were very accessible. To get some caps, I only needed to empty a local soda machine of its precious caps and I could practice all day.

I would fill my pockets and swat caps with my broomstick for hours. I'd often drive them clear out of sight—over lawns, houses, garages, or whatever stood in the way. Once I had a pocketful of caps, I'd swing forever.

And when the caps weren't available, rocks or stones would do. Nothing stopped me from taking my swings. The longer I'd swing, the more my mind would begin to drift. Soon I'd be imagining myself standing at home plate in some major-league park. The broomstick would automatically change to a Louisville Slugger and my rocks and caps instantly became brand new, shiny baseballs. In my imagination, my uniform was always spotless and the game was always on the line.

I would stroll confidently to the plate. The crowd would roar as I took practice swings. Then the pitch, and—wow! I'd awake just in time to see the bottle cap fly over a neighbor's house. But then my imagination would kick in again and the ball would be sailing over an outfield fence and into a bleacher filled with cheering fans. Home run! Stargell wins the game! Tingles would roll up my spine and a smile would light up my face. I may have still been in Orlando swatting caps and stones, but my mind was in the majors, hitting homers in packed stadiums. That's the dream I was living with.

My dreaming would come to a conclusion each summer afternoon at approximately two-thirty. Reality always struck me hard. I'd race home, usually arriving about ten minutes before Aunt Lucy walked through the door. Fantasy was light-years away as I worked frantically to complete a whole day's list of chores in ten minutes to avoid the reality of being spanked. But no matter how I tried, I never finished my chores on time, and spanking became a permanent part of my late afternoon routine. I rarely completed my daily chores, and Aunt Lucy never failed to remind me.

Aunt Lucy loved me but she never understood my strange

ways. If I'd been playing doctor or lawyer, she may have forced herself to see the light, but baseball—no chance. To her, there was no sense in practicing to become a baseball player. That was a white man's sport. It had no future and was out of reach for the Negro. My behavior just wasn't practical.

Speaking from experience, I know the sacrifices one must endure to live a dream. But I never allowed anything to stand in my way. The spankings I took taught me to budget my time better for baseball. I learned that whatever you need is worth being spanked for.

I also learned from Aunt Lucy's spankings that any dream can be accomplished if a person is willing to give it what it takes, and no matter what it takes. Once you make the decision to go for it, only then do you see how much fun living a dream can be.

As each summer vacation would come to an end, I would have to readjust my playing time. With school open, I kept almost the identical hours as Aunt Lucy, and after I'd arrive home, she expected me to stay close. She didn't believe in playtime. I was the best friend my aunt had. So I had to be extra tricky during the school year to squeeze my swings in each day. I took advantage of every opportunity.

The only time Aunt Lucy allowed me to stray from her side was on errands, which became my only outlet for playtime. I made the most out of each errand I ran. Fortunately, she asked me to run several errands daily, and I didn't fall too far out of practice; I made sure each errand took me by the high school for a few swings. Speed was the key to my success.

Upon receiving my instructions from Aunt Lucy, I'd sprint out the door in the direction of the school. By running, I usually picked up enough time to take a few swings—about ten minutes. Then it was off to the store, or wherever. After purchasing the desired goods, I'd make a quick trip back to the school for a few more swings, then run home again. Surprisingly, Aunt Lucy never suspected a thing.

I still remember my mother telling the story of my time with Aunt Lucy to the press and other people after I became a success in the big leagues. "Wherever he had to go, he had to go in a hurry so he could stop off for a while and play ball. Then he'd have to hurry home," I still remember her saying. "He still moves in a hurry today because of that experience."

Though I worked around whatever obstacles Aunt Lucy placed in my way, living in Orlando was anything but ideal. Why? The reason is obvious: I was away from the person I cared about most in my life—my mother. Mom faithfully wrote letters and sent money each month, but I don't think I received all the letters she sent. I believe Aunt Lucy intercepted a good portion of them. Aunt Lucy was so afraid of losing me.

My mother told me that Aunt Lucy wrote of various fictitious trips she and I were taking together. It all sounded too good in Florida to my mother, who only wanted the best for me. She felt ashamed to ask me to return to California, for she knew there was no way she could match all the luxuries Aunt Lucy wrote about in her letters. But after a while, Mother came to realize that she wanted me back with her anyway. Her shame at being poor finally wore off. Mom wrote to Aunt Lucy after one year away from me to inform her that she would soon be traveling to Florida to retrieve me and bring me home. In her reply, Aunt Lucy wrote and said not to bother, that she planned to return me to California while on a visit.

Mom waited patiently for my return. They passed their agreed-upon one-year deadline. She continued to wait. Six years passed and I was still living with Aunt Lucy. It finally became obvious to my mother that her sister had no intention of returning me.

"Those were the most important years of Wilver's life," Mother later admitted.

Finally, after six years of waiting, Mother became as tough as a Sherman tank. Nothing was going to keep her from seeing me. She boarded a train bound for Orlando with my newly born half-sister, Sandrus. Sandrus's presence in the family is what helped build the flame in my mother's furnace. She wanted to reunite her entire family.

As she later told me, "I made up my mind that I had to see you. I finally realized that your Aunt Lucy didn't want me to have you any more."

Over the six years that we had been apart, Gladys and Percy's financial situation had improved significantly. Mom now worked at a cannery, and paying for her journey to Florida was not a difficult task. Over the five-day train ride, she tossed around several ideas in her mind. She wondered if she was doing the right thing. Fooled by my aunt's deception, she even questioned if she could support me in the manner I'd become accustomed to.

"Maybe he wouldn't want to leave Florida," she thought. She finally decided to leave the decision up to me. She decided that her stay would only be for a visit. If I told her that I wanted to return to California with her, she'd gladly take me home, but if I wanted to remain, she'd find a way to understand. Optimistically, she carried return fare for me in her purse. If I decided to stay in Orlando, she'd use the money to buy me a gift instead.

But Aunt Lucy, not out of tricks yet, tried desperately to convince her younger sister to remain in California. When she realized that her plan had failed, Aunt Lucy informed me of my mother's impending arrival, but not until the day before she was due to arrive.

I was excited beyond belief. My life had, at best, been bleak without my mother. For six years I'd buried the pain of being apart from her deep inside myself. I tried to remain happy at all times, but my joy was superficial until this time.

All my pain dissolved when I spotted her face in the window of her passenger car. Just to see her grinning face made me happy. I no longer hid the pain. I'd been too patient for too long. I decided then and there at that train station that no one would ever keep us apart again. I didn't care where I had to go as long as I was going with her.

But the look on my mother's face scared me. She looked shocked as she stared at me through her window. What was wrong? Her anxiety was a result of my poor physical appearance. I was deathly thin. It was obvious that I hadn't been properly cared for. I could see she was worried.

She ran from the train. We met and hugged each other tightly. Tears ran from both our eyes. I was the first to speak. I told her that if she didn't take me with her, I was going to run away. My mother's decision was made for her only thirty seconds into her visit.

She later told me, "I didn't realize how unhappy you were there." She went on to tell me how she had always wanted me back but that she had gone to Florida leaving the decision up to me. The six years apart and Lucy's letters had intimidated her.

But after she spoke with me, it became obvious to her that I hadn't been properly cared for. In Aunt Lucy's letters to my mother, she'd never written about the time I blacked out from stomach cramps and was rushed to the hospital. The doctors discovered that I had eaten too many green oranges, and they pumped out my stomach. I was starving from a poor diet. I'd probably eaten the oranges in a search for nourishment.

When my mother, a strong advocate of a child's playtime, heard of the vast number of chores I was expected to do each day, she was furious. Then, remembering my deathly thin body, she began to wonder what had happened to the money for food she'd sent to Aunt Lucy.

It was obvious that my mother had been deceived in a variety of ways. There were never any vacations, no trips. The farthest I'd traveled in six years was on a bus to the restaurant where Aunt Lucy worked. As each day wore on and each argument between the two came to a close, the fact emerged that Aunt Lucy, torn apart from the pain of her broken marriage, had tried to soothe her maternal instincts by borrowing me from her younger sister.

My mother became convinced that Aunt Lucy's trip to California six years before hadn't been just a visit and that my aunt had her sights set on me all along. She'd simply stayed long enough in California to win my mother's trust. According to my mother, Aunt Lucy's misleading reports clearly substantiated her theory. Nothing would keep my mother from taking me back to California with her. In a fit of frustration, my usually quiet mother spoke, "I could never leave my son here."

But I never took part in the discussions between Aunt Lucy and Mother. I won't say that I enjoyed living with Aunt Lucy. But I will say that I thoroughly understood her situation. I realize that her efforts were awkward at times, and even detrimental, but all her actions were born out of love. I judged Aunt Lucy by her actions and not her results. She meant well. She simply wanted a child of her own. Her maternal instincts had overpowered her better judgment and led her off in errant ways.

Approximately thirty years later, Aunt Lucy was placed in a convalescent home. Senile and physically incapable of caring for herself, she was doomed to spend the remainder of her life there. Today I still feel remorse over not contributing enough time to the lady who welcomed me into her home. Though my mother and Aunt Lucy never regained a friendly relationship, I'll always hold a soft spot in my heart for the lady who tried to become the mother she thought I needed.

Some may feel that I shouldn't still love Aunt Lucy and that I should dislike her for keeping me away from my mother, but that's not my style. I feel that I can better understand individuals when I don't judge but try to understand their position instead.

My mother says that I try too hard to please everyone, but that's not true. I don't adjust myself to anyone else's life; I just don't expect them to adjust themselves to mine. I believe that in this way I can constantly please people in nonjudgmental ways that they'll understand. This way of treating people breeds acceptance and confidence among individuals.

My formula for building relationships with others is easy. First, I allow people to show me what they're all about. I don't ask anything of them but to be themselves. I don't listen to rumors or stories about their past. That's behind them. As far as I'm concerned, they're exactly what they decide to show me and only that. This philosophy has built hundreds of very close relationships for me. It's easy, just don't be judgmental and be a little more patient and open-hearted. It's worked for me.

No matter how good a friend I tried to be, I found it impossible to lessen the guilt that Mother was feeling. Each time she looked at my deathly thin body, I knew that inside she was kicking herself. She never forgave herself for being what she thought herself to be—less than a mother. I wished that she would only have realized that in sending me to Aunt Lucy's she was trying to be more than a mother.

Soon our goodbyes were said and Mom loaded Sandrus and me aboard the train. After our tickets had been purchased, Mom had $25 left in her purse, our meal money. Under her guidance, I began a gain-weight diet that day. Her major concern was seeing that I was properly fed, and she worried that the $25 wouldn't be enough money for the entire five-day journey.

Fortunately, a Negro conductor who was familiar with the train's route helped stretch our meal money by directing Gladys to the most reasonably priced restaurants in each town we stopped at. With his help, the money stretched all the way from Florida to California. Every few stops, my mother, with directions from the conductor, would scamper from the train and return with two hot meals—one for her and Sandrus and one for me. The conductor was even nice enough at times to fetch the meals for us.

The train ride back to California wasn't anything like the journey I'd taken with Lucy six years before. It seemed shorter because I was happy to be going home. I was with my mother again, but I'd changed considerably in those six years. At the age of eleven, I feel, I was basically the product of six factors.

First, like my grandfather and father, I'd grown tall and very thin. By that time, I'd accumulated enough height that it was obvious that I was going to be larger than the average man. Though my frame needed padding, I had plenty of room to expand.

My mom told me that I resembled my grandfather in a lot of ways. She said that I was a kind, sensitive, loving person out of the mold of Grandad, who could love a stone. Though I was too young to remember exactly all the influence he had on me, Mother still sees Grandad's tune being played in my heart, and her word is good enough for me.

Lucy had also made her mark on my life. She taught me discipline. As a result, I strove more efficiently toward my goal. Because of her, I learned to extract the most from each moment, a habit I still carry with me today.

My mother is the person responsible for teaching me to allow my heart to be my guide. Like her, I feel instead of think.

I was also a product of my race. I was bred as an outcast, part Negro and part Seminole, in my early years raised as an Indian. Like a Seminole, I'd also never been a member of a conventional family. Being a Negro, I was also trapped within the confines of societal prejudice.

My family had become an extension of this prejudice. We were poor and misled. My mother, an energetic and hard worker, barely made enough money to finance the train ride to Florida. At the age of eleven, I was making an upward economical climb from a shack in Florida to the projects of Alameda. Gladys and Percy were viewed as well-to-do Negroes.

I was also a product of my generation. Togetherness had been the theme of my generation and it was also what I cared most about. There wasn't anything that I valued more than my family and friends. Feeling for togetherness was the most outstanding factor in my makeup. That's why I understood Aunt Lucy's situation so well. Because for me, the main result of any relationship is friendship. At times, as in situations with Lucy, I gave more than my share, but my extra effort is what made the relationship work.

At age eleven, my love for hitting baseballs was also a large part of my life. On the train ride back to California, I swung at imaginary baseballs in the air. I fantasized about hitting home runs in the majors. I'd progressed significantly as a hitter since my mother had last seen me. I had only begun carrying around a stick then. But at this point in my life, the stick was a permanent fixture in my hand.

Though I didn't realize it then, were it not for my love of hitting and throwing I may have become just another talented, lonely person trapped within the confines of society's ghetto.

"Never had I had so many friends and so much fun as I did in the projects."

---

2 THE TRAIN ARRIVED IN ALAMEDA a few days before Christmas, 1951. I instantly felt at home.

I found Percy there, a friend and a father. He was also exactly what my mother had needed after two divorces. He was loving and dependable. He accepted me immediately. He became the father figure that I had needed. He was a strict disciplinarian when he had to be, but he was also soft-hearted at the right times.

Like my mother, Percy was astounded when he saw how thin I had become. He, too, began to force food down my throat. It was obvious that he cared about me. Eventually, eating became a common line of communication between my stepfather and me. Every Friday night, his weekly evening out, I'd wait up late for him to arrive home. At that time, Percy would cook up one of his greasy, gravy-soaked meals. He was a gourmet at such treats. I was not only a loyal son but an educated eater.

Percy and I also shared a common love for sports, one of his soft spots. Percy had been raised in a mining town in Alabama. Working was the major pastime in such places. But once a week the entire population of the tiny town would turn out for the Sunday afternoon baseball game. It was the social event of the week. Family get-togethers and picnics were scheduled around the ball game.

Baseball was the highlight of Percy's life as a boy. He loved to play each Sunday. And now when he thinks back to his childhood, he always remembers his days on the dusty diamond in Alabama before anything else.

His fond memories often caused him to soften as a parent. I could go to Percy with permission slips to play sports that I knew he would sign even after my mother had vetoed my request only minutes before. Like our Friday night meals, his signature on the permission slips became our secret.

In Alameda, and the projects, I found a home. Originally constructed as makeshift housing for persons working for the government during the Second World War, the projects weren't stylish or pretty. They were plain, unattractive, long, rectangular buildings housing apartments of no more than two bedrooms. Each building was characterized by four subdivisions of four apartments each, two on the ground floor, two on the second, which shared the same entranceway.

The exterior of the projects was covered with some sort of sheetrock that could be forced to break away into chunks. The projects were always constructed near playgrounds, conveniently located for the use of the tenants' children. A few buildings had driveways, but the majority of the tenants were forced to park their cars in the streets.

After the war ended, the projects were retitled low-income housing units. They were perfect living quarters for my parents and other young couples like them, who needed a place to live while saving for a house.

The projects became a comfortable holding bin. They weren't attractive but they were comfortable. We lived at 965A Thou Way in a one-bedroom apartment. Percy, Gladys and Sandrus all slept in the apartment's one bedroom while I slept on a rollaway bed in the living room. I, more than anyone else, was inconvenienced by the small apartment. My sleeping schedule revolved around the stay of each evening's guests and the arrival of my mother's first customer each Saturday morning.

Besides working at the cannery, my mother also worked out of our apartment as a beautician. Her salon was our kitchen, which offered a clear view into my sleeping quarters. Thus, Mom always roused me out of bed before her first customer arrived. But I never minded the inconvenience. I was just happy to be home with my family.

The projects were often wrongly associated with crime and corruption. Unfortunately, poor people are often misread as criminals. But there were no criminals in the projects. We never locked our doors or windows at night. We always felt safe. Project families watched out for each other. I loved living in the projects. I thought that it was the perfect environment in which to be raised.

There weren't any economic barriers. Each family was on the same level. There were dozens of different races and nationalities represented, but because we were all on the same economic plane, there wasn't any prejudice. We all struggled together. My mother termed our neighborhood "the family"—different households were that close with one another.

Because of the open-hearted attitude of the project people, I made friends instantly. Though I was initially kidded about being so skinny, my bony physique was soon overlooked. I made friends of all races and colors—red, black, yellow, brown and white. There was a Chinese kid named Allen, a Mexican named Sanchez, and a Caucasian named John Ford, plus the Mays and Epps who were Negroes, and X. L. Davis, and Willie Ford.

My idol in those days was a teenager named Marlon Mays, who was a few years older than I. He was the president of his high school class and one of the finest athletes in the area. I dreamed of being like Marlon when I was very young.

Never had I had so many friends and so much fun as I did in the projects. Before this time, I'd been starved for peer attention. I had been isolated in Oklahoma as an only child and surrounded by kids in Orlando but prohibited from playing with them by Aunt Lucy.

My friends were more important to me at this time than ever before in my life. With my mother working two jobs and Percy extra hours, I was left to fend for myself a good part of the time. That's why I was so dependent on my friends. Because I did a lot of my growing up on the streets, one might guess that I caused a lot of trouble, but I was usually a very good, obedient child who rarely ever gave his mother cause to worry.

There were a few instances when I made my parents mad. And though they were very few, they were the most frightening times of my youth. As I grew older, they became the most vivid of all my memories.

One such incident occurred on one of those hot summer days when a young man's mind turns to thoughts of swimming. Some of the boys and I headed for a nearby beach on the Pacific. The area wasn't too far from the projects and I'd become quite familiar with it since moving back to Alameda. It had the basics—the ocean, a beach, hot dogs and a Boy's Club. What more could a group of fun-loving, overheated boys want?

Normally, nothing more, but this day was unusual. On the way to the ocean, we spotted a large, private swimming pool that belonged to the navy. Its clear, glimmering water drew us like a magnet. To a poor boy from the projects, nothing could be more inviting. It could easily attract even the most law-abiding youngster over the surrounding fence and into its crystal-blue waters, or so I told myself as I prepared to aid my friends in their assault. But first we decided to stall momentarily to get together an alibi, just in case something went wrong.

I worked the hardest at preconditioning my conscience. Lying was the most difficult task in the world for me. I realized that what I was about to do was wrong. No one needed to tell me. But my buddies presented a better case. And after a good strong convincing, I became a part of the venture the entire way. My alternative was not to reason why, but either to swim or walk home alone. I chose to swim.

After an in-depth discussion we chose the old, reliable we're-just-here-to-fetch-our-baseball alibi. Of all of us, the pill was the hardest for me to swallow. I repeated the alibi over and over again to myself, trying to ram home its authenticity into my subconscious. I was still practicing the alibi when we approached the fence. Face down toward the ground, I walked softly, muttering the alibi over and over again to myself. My lips moved slightly as some of the words slipped out of my mouth.

One by one, we ascended the silver, chain-link fence that surrounded the government's pool. I was still practicing the alibi. The toughest part of this venture was convincing myself why I was doing it.

Each of us slipped slowly into the pool. Not a single drop of water was spilled. I was still rehearsing. At first, I felt more guilty than ever as my body entered the pool, but that soon changed. My psyche became a slave to the refreshing powers of the water. I soon relaxed and simply allowed my body to float in the water as I clung onto one side of the pool. No poor boy from the projects could ever experience a richer feeling. This was ecstasy.

Soon my eyes began to close, though I wasn't sleeping, only relaxing. Who knows where my mind was as my buddies slowly slipped out of the pool and scurried back over the fence. I unknowingly was left alone to face the wrath of the pool's guard. I was probably dreaming of baseball, approaching the plate in a packed stadium, bases loaded, two out in the ninth, my team down by three runs, a homer would win it, when the large hand clamped onto my right shoulder.

I screamed as much of the alibi as I could remember. But even with all my practicing, I still hadn't executed it properly. Obviously, the guard didn't fall for my weak excuse. He hauled me inside a nearby building and telephoned the police.

I was shaking like a leaf as the squad car pulled up. I considered making a break for it but my legs never responded to my call. They were too frightened to move. My parents would never tolerate my being driven home in a squad car. That's when I decided to give the officers a phony address, in hopes that we'd avoid my parents by dropping me off at another home.

Three phony addresses later, I was still riding in the back seat of the squad car. Obviously my plan had failed. The officers wanted to speak with at least one of my parents. Completely out of lectures, they were becoming irritated. I finally broke down and gave them my correct address.

After the officers' explanation of what I had done, but before I could conjure up a reasonable excuse, my mother gave me one of the most impressive whippings of my childhood. She didn't do that often, but when she did the effect lasted forever, or at least until another hot day, a few years later.

It was one of those days when only two things could save a person from the heat of the day—a dip in a pool, though that suggestion had been ruled out years ago, and ice cream.

I was a student in junior high school at the time. Such hot days always brought out the best and worst in me. Later, when I became a major-leaguer, I had my best days on hot afternoons. But as a youth, the heat always brought out my most devious ways, as it did on this one very memorable afternoon.

On the route home from school, my friends and I always passed by the local drugstore. It was really just an old soda shop that specialized more in phosphates than prescriptions. Behind its counters were neatly tucked away several flavors of ice cream, ready and waiting to be served in a variety of styles: single, double and triple scoops. But on this one afternoon, the boys and I decided to go for the works.

Though it was extremely hot, I was wearing a new rain slicker that my mother had just bought for me. Even though the slicker added a few extra degrees to the already rising temperature around my body, I didn't consider it a bother to wear. Instead, I was proud to have it on. Poor boys from the projects often make big issues out of small purchases.

As we approached the drugstore, we spotted an ice cream delivery truck parked outside. The driver was unloading five-gallon cartons of ice cream, one by one. He stacked the containers one on top of another on the sidewalk. After he had piled the entire week's worth of ice cream on the sidewalk, he began to carry one container into the drugstore at a time.

Our minds clicked with ideas but our pockets were bare. None of us had enough money to purchase a single scoop of ice cream, let alone enough for all of us. Surely, the deliveryman wouldn't miss one five-gallon container from his huge pile.

Our idea was instantaneous but simple. As the delivery man carried the containers into the drugstore, one of us would sneak by and snatch one. Unfortunately, because of my raincoat, I was chosen to heist the loot. After a short pep talk from my peers, I timed the entrance of the delivery man and then swiftly breezed by the containers and slipped one under my new rain slicker. I casually strolled offstage to meet my colleagues, who were waiting in the wings.

My cohorts escorted me, with the five-gallon container tucked securely beneath my rain garment, to a set of nearby railroad tracks. The tracks had become a familiar meeting place, an area to play and other times hide.

David Hughes, a close childhood friend of mine, had lost a leg crawling under a train only a few years before. Since then, a city ordinance prohibiting such acts had been instituted. But the boys and I never changed our ways. To us it made perfectly good sense to perform a single illegal act each day rather than walk several blocks out of our way. Even Hughes still crawled under trains, wooden leg and all.

The tracks hold very fond memories for me; they became my

practice area, my dream place, my zone of solitude. I would often walk over to the tracks with a friend or two, and after a while I'd begin tossing stones in the air and hitting them with sticks. My friends would soon become bored with the activity and would leave, but I would stand alone for hours, swatting stones and dreaming of someday playing in the big leagues.

At a stretch of auxiliary tracks, on an old flatbed railroad car, I was unloaded of my precious cargo. We were all smiles as we slipped the five-gallon container from beneath my new rain slicker. There was no stopping us now. Soon the lid was off and hungry hands gouged into their icy prey.

We used no spoons, no bowls, no scoop and no manners. Our hands were good enough. And though each of us hurried our hands into the container, there would be plenty of ice cream for all of us and too much for a few.

Like my experience with a dip in the pool, the ice cream was a project boy's dream come true. The ice cream was our caviar, and the pool had been the French Riviera. Nothing could be better, and we consumed all the evidence. With our stomachs bulging with ice cream, each of us began on our separate treks home. None of us expected to be caught; if we had been spotted, we thought, we would have been stopped at the drugstore.

But the scowl on my mother's face as I entered our apartment immediately soured the fine-tasting ice cream in my stomach. She confronted me instantly. Someone had seen me swipe the ice cream and had telephoned my school, and the school had just contacted her. I was unable to lie and I quickly confessed. Though she was furious initially, she calmed quickly, understanding the temptations of a poor child. But she knew that it was her duty to punish me, and so she gave me a spanking to serve as a reminder of what I had done wrong.

With her maternal obligations out of the way, soon all was forgotten. The owner of the drugstore was very understanding. He only asked that we reimburse him for the cost of the ice cream. Each boy was expected to submit one equal share. But not having any money was the reason we had swiped the ice cream in the first place. If we could have afforded it, we would not have stolen it.

Somehow my mother scraped up my share and paid the drugstore owner, but not all my friends were quite as fortunate. In fact, my Mexican friend, Sanchez, telephoned me to ask if he could borrow the money. I listened as his mother issued instructions to him in Spanish in the background. Sanchez then interpreted his mother's requests into English for me.

Looking for a laugh to ease my mother's sorrow, I turned to her and retranslated Sanchez's request from English to Spanish. Instantly, she exploded with laughter, shaking her head from side to side. I told Sanchez we didn't have any money and hung up the telephone.

I was punished only once more as a child and that was the worst whipping of my life, because Percy gave it to me. Back then, Sandrus was approximately three years old. My parents were going out one evening and I was left in charge of the apartment and my baby sister. I was attentively watching Sandrus play in our front yard when some boys began choosing sides for a baseball game across the street. Never one able to resist an urge to play, I raced across the street to join in, leaving my responsibilities and Sandrus behind.

As usual, I became completely engrossed in the game and lost all conception of time and responsibility. The game must have gone into extra innings or we must have played a triple-header, for I didn't return to Sandrus until a considerable time later. Fortunately, when I finally returned to her my parents hadn't arrived home yet.

But one of our neighbors, watching out for Sandrus' safety, reported my lack of responsibility to Percy, who, when he arrived home at 2 A.M., grabbed the nearest object, the cord of an electric iron, and began whipping some sense into me. He did make sense though. Yes, sir, he sure did make sense. That was the worst whipping I ever took.

Only three miscues in my stay at the projects, that's not bad. In fact, it may have been a record for the neighborhood. I was a good boy. I always tried to be considerate and polite. But oddly enough, I was sometimes too honest.

I was always swinging at tennis balls, rubber balls, baseballs, softballs, rocks or any small object with my broomstick or bat. I would drive the objects to various parts of the neighborhood, sometimes over the project houses and sometimes—accidentally, mind you—through the windows of neighboring apartments.

Though my control with a broomstick or bat was perhaps better than any other kid's in the neighborhood, it was far from perfect and I usually shattered at least one window every other day. I even drove a ball through a double set of windows once. Unfortunately, the windows belonged to the neighborhood grouch, who made it seem that I had aimed at her apartment.

But my mother, who was working two jobs and fighting to save money to buy a house, reluctantly paid for the replacement of the double sliding glass doors, just as she had paid for all the others. A good portion of Mom's hard-earned money each week was devoted to my window-breaking service. And often when she had just finished unloading a fistful of dollars to cover my miscues, I would honestly remind her that she hadn't paid for them all. That's what I mean when I say that sometimes I was too honest.

And shortly after she'd completed her payments for each broken window, the vicious cycle would begin again with me hammering objects through another neighbor's window. She never asked me to stop playing baseball, though at times she would question me concerning the lack of practicality in my future. But I loved baseball and that's all I knew. I never worried about the future, only thought about the next game. During my years in Alameda, only a handful of Negro players had made it as far as the major leagues. My chances seemed slim at best.

At times, she sought the power of my reasoning. "Boy, what you going to do for a living?" she'd ask me.

"Play ball," I'd always reply.

"I'd say that you'd better rid your mind of this ball-playing idea," she'd respond, obviously trying to save me from a long painful career in organized baseball.

But I'd answer that playing ball was what I wanted to do. I think in the beginning she thought I was fooling her. But when my answer never changed, she finally realized that I was serious. She loved me too much to try to separate my heart from my dream. So she just kept working hard, paying for windows, shaking her head in disgust and hoping for the best. On the other hand, I kept resisting attempts by other people to sway me away from my dream and continued to hit baseballs, stones, whatever, sometimes over the projects and sometimes through windows.

With my sights set on the major leagues, I practiced daily. But I must admit that playing was a lot more fun. I received my initial opportunity to play organized baseball in Alameda. Until then, I'd become more or less a master at pickup baseball, home-run derby, fast pitch and several other impromptu games.

Washington Park became the center of my baseball career

while I was in the projects. It was a large, spacious park, a few blocks in diameter, decorated with finely trimmed grass and attractively spaced trees. It was a public park individually maintained by Lil Aldrich. I admired Lil for the beauty he added to the surroundings, and we became very close friends after only a short period of time.

Aldrich was especially an artist with the park's baseball field. He kept the field smooth and fast. The all-dirt infield was always raked, the playing surface always lightning fast. There were never any rocks on the field that could alter the angle of an innocent grounder. Every ball bounced true on Aldrich's infield, he saw to that.

The outfield grass was always cut short and nicely tailored. The outfield area was lined with a short cyclone fence, which helped to keep the vastness of the park from being exaggerated. Hitting a ball out of Washington Park was quite a task. But I must admit that I accomplished the feat more often than any other kid my age.

In fact, I became so proficient at the art of the long ball that I'd often even name my target. A tall oak tree that shadowed the right center-field wall was my favorite sight. Each time I strolled to the plate, I dreamed of launching a ball over the giant oak. In most cases, my aim was perfect but I never possessed enough strength (of course, neither did anyone else). Though I launched several balls into the leafy center of the tree, I found it impossible to clear its entire height.

Monumental blasts later became a major part of my career and I'm proud of my tape-measure homers. I'm especially proud of the fact that I'm the only player to hit a ball completely out of Dodger Stadium. In fact, I hit two balls completely out of the Dodgers' home arena.

The Dodger organization arranged a reenactment of the two homers on my final trip as a player into Dodger Stadium. A beach-ball painted like a giant baseball was attached to a fishing line that was connected to a palm tree outside the right-field fence. A gentle touch from my bat and the beachball was on its route out of the stadium, as recordings of the original play-by-play burst from the PA system in the background. Tears formed in my eyes during this momentous reenactment.

I hit several memorable blasts in other stadiums too. In Forbes Field, I once hit a homer 542 feet to right center field. I also hit more homers onto or over the right-field roof of Forbes Field than any other player in history. In Three Rivers Stadium, Forbes Field's replacement, I was responsible for four of the six upper-deck homers hit in the stadium. In the old Park Gerry in Montreal my target was a swimming pool outside the right center-field fence. I used to love to send the swimmers scattering as my ball splashed into the pool.

And I can't forget Portland, Oregon, where one of my favorite obstacles was located in that city's ball park. The right-field wall was the rear wall of an athletic club. Approximately 40 feet from the ground, a porch used for entertaining athletic club guests juts out from the wall. The porch is approximately 500 feet from home plate.

The Pirates' AAA minor-league affiliate, the Portland Beavers, were stationed in the stadium, and annually the Buccos were invited to play an exhibition game there. A home-run hitters' contest always preceded the exhibition game, and I always zeroed in on the porch as my target.

On my last trip to Portland, in 1981, I drove a ball through a pouring rain and onto the porch on my twenty-sixth swing. That blast ranks high on my list of most memorable homers.

And twenty-five years later, the people living in the Washington Park area still speak of the crushing blasts I hit there as a teenager, over fences, trees, houses. My most memorable shot at Washington Park was a homer that easily cleared the fence, flew over the street and landed in the front yard of a house with a blue picture window. Even the major-leaguers, who played winter league baseball in the off-season at Washington Park, never hit a ball that far.

I was the most powerful lefthanded hitter in the Alameda area, but then my competition was almost nonexistent, for most of the area's other players were righthanded. Being lefthanded gained a considerable amount of notoriety for me but it also caused early coordination and fielding problems for me as a youngster.

For one, I used the same grip as a righthanded batter—right hand on top, left hand on the bottom—but from the opposite side of the plate, which meant that I hit cross-handed. But I was extremely stubborn about changing. I thought they were trying to sabotage my style. I'd been swinging bats, branches and broomsticks since I was two years old and I wasn't going to change; I'd been too successful.

Finally, one of my friends decided to try a soft approach. He told me that Hank Aaron, an idol of mine who would someday be the all-time major-league home-run king, had once hit cross-handed, but for several reasons he switched his style. I changed the position of my hands immediately. If that's what Hank Aaron did to become a better hitter, I knew that it would work for me, too.

Being a southpaw also caused considerable problems with my fielding. First of all, I received the impression from my friends, all of whom were righthanded, that I was some sort of freak as a leftie. Secondly, I didn't have enough money to buy my own baseball mitt and I was always forced to borrow one of theirs. And since all my friends were righties, I was forced to wear a righthander's mitt, forcing me to field balls with my throwing hand.

I was extremely naive at this time, and I played for several years before discovering that gloves had been specifically designed for players with a problem such as mine. My friends had actually convinced me that being lefthanded was a deformity. But finally after fielding thousands of balls with a borrowed mitt on my throwing hand, I met a man who was selling a lefthander's mitt. It was the first such glove I'd ever seen. In it, I saw an opportunity to rid myself of a vast amount of confusion. Somehow I gathered together the three dollars the man was asking for it.

After several embarrassing years, the glove helped me become a fine fielder. I never allowed the glove to stray from my side. It was my most valuable possession. I kept it with me always. I considered it a stroke of genius, the finest of all manufactured products.

No longer embarrassed by my unorthodox fielding style, I eventually wore the glove down to a soft piece of stitched leather. But I always carried it around as my security, even after replacing it with another glove, before finally misplacing it somewhere along the way.

From my early days at Washington Park, I gradually progressed to my initial trial in organized baseball. I became a member of the Encinal Project Team, which represented the subdivision of the projects I lived in. But the team was far from being organized as boys' teams are today. There were very few coaches and very little equipment, and the only requirement to become a member was that a boy had to be under sixteen years of age. Boys over sixteen were expected to play either American Legion ball, high school ball, or sometimes even both.

The Encinal team would have been extremely primitive by middle-class baseball standards. We didn't have any uniforms, we weren't tagged with a pet name such as the Cubs or the Indians, we weren't given complimentary sodas and ice cream by sponsors after each game and there wasn't any annual year-end banquet held in our honor featuring a big-name sports celebrity as the main speaker. We were there to play ball and that's all. No frills, only thrills and chills, for all our games were exciting as any.

To middle-class parents, the project team may have seemed unfit for their children, but it was exactly what I needed. The competition was stiff and the games were adventurous. Fierce internal rivalries existed between Encinal and the other project teams—the Webster Project and the Estuary Project teams. The rivalries were present even before the teams ever took the field.

As I think back, I always remember how fiercely my friends and I patrolled our neighborhood. We were like militia. It wasn't that we were afraid of intruders, we simply played the heavies for fun. Youngsters respond to the same innate territorial protection mechanism as their parents. Being known as a guardian of your neighborhood was prestigious. But we played the role in a very easygoing manner. We never hurt anyone. We just acted mean and wrestled around with kids from opposing neighborhoods. No one was ever injured past a slight bump or a small bruise.

And whenever my friends and I entered a foreign neighborhood, we could expect the same treatment that we put upon strangers in our area. One group would chase another group off their streets, and the group being chased would turn around and run their pursuers off their turf. It was all a game.

But back then we took such games very seriously. We actually saw ourselves as enemies of injustice and we were always leery of wandering alone through any neighborhood but our own. The Estuary projects were considered a natural trap. It was known as Tin Pan Alley and it had a one-road-in-and-the-same-road-out arrangement. It was a natural ambush. Chills of fear hurried up my spine each time I thought of entering Estuary alone after dark.

The Webster projects weren't much safer. Though not as suited as Estuary for an ambush, Webster had a branch of protection all its own: its fierce fighting youths. Webster was always known for its stiff competitors both on and off the field. Like Estuary, Webster after dark struck its own type of fear creeping up my spine. I would never enter either of their boundaries after dark without at least a small army of friends.

On the more mellow side, Encinal was known for its good-looking women. No wonder we were such fierce warriors. But Encinal was also known for its rotten ball field.

Unlike the site of my early trials as a player, Washington Park, the Encinal project field was a complete disaster. It was totally unmaintained, and grass grew freely in between the scattered rocks and stones. Holes of various diameters and depths littered the infield and rippled even the smoothest of one-hoppers. There wasn't a square inch of playing surface that hadn't been polluted by either stones or holes. It was a typical project field.

Because of the Baja-type conditions, fielding became the most unpredictable factor of our games. No matter how soft and agile a fielder's hands were, the adverse conditions were always responsible for mystical hops which caused every fielder to look foolish.

Unlike middle-class parents, our parents rarely if ever attended our games. But it wasn't because they didn't prefer to see us play; there simply weren't any satisfactory seating arrangements. Few bleachers, no benches, a lack of organization and an absence of uniforms made our games extremely boring from a spectator's point of view.

But on the field, a stout battle was being waged. We didn't have the color, glamour or organization of leagues in wealthier neighborhoods but we did have spirit. Baseball was our only true pastime. White boys from richer families were given other alternatives such as the Boy Scouts, family vacations and field trips. We relied solely on baseball for entertainment. Baseball was all we had.

But I didn't mind, because baseball was all that I wanted anyway. I wasn't even upset when my mother didn't come to see me play. She worked constantly and I understood. In fact, often Gladys would become so engrossed in her work that she'd forget when I had a game scheduled and would mistakenly accuse me of tardiness.

But I always understood Mom's situation and I'd repeatedly explain that I was playing ball and offer the telephone number of the coach as proof. She never accepted my offer to telephone my coach, she never doubted me, but then I rarely gave her reason to.

The finest moment of my young career came while I was on the Encinal team. I was a pitcher and a pretty good one at that. Our team had a good amount of spirit, but without uniforms we at best resembled a ragtag team. The varying styles and degrees of dress for each team member symbolized confusion rather than unity, an unfair impression for such a proud squad.

But out of the clear blue sky our image problem was solved. Early one evening a local police officer, who worked the Encinal beat, drove up to our field and tossed open the trunk of his car. Inside lay dozens of uniforms. He began handing them to us. We couldn't believe this was really happening. We couldn't believe that someone cared enough to give us uniforms.

We were so impressed with his gift that we never even noticed their dingy, white color. They were obviously used uniforms. But we didn't care. Boys from the projects are rarely given the opportunity to distinguish between new and used. We only knew that we now had uniforms. Never in my life was I so proud.

Though it resembled a burlap bag around my ultrathin body, I loved my uniform almost as much as my mitt. I was skinny where the uniform was fat. It was long where I was short. The pants hung limp to each side, kept in place only by the pressure of the over-tightened belt around my waist. The sleeves of the jersey hung almost to my wrists, but I loved it just the same.

In my first game in the uniform, I don't remember the pitch, the swing or the reason I ran so swiftly down the first-base line. But I do recall proudly gazing down at my new uniform as I ran, watching the giant pant legs balloon around my pencil-thin thighs. It wasn't the fit I was concerned about but instead the effect.

The adversity and challenge one experiences on the playing field breed champions. They transform good athletes into greats and average players into good ones. The competition between project teams during my era was fierce. Boys from the projects lived to play baseball. And over the years, several players emerged from the rubble of the projects to gain stardom. During my era, a bumper crop was harvested as in no other period before.

Fresh from boot camp on the Encinal diamond, I advanced to the Encinal high school team in 1954. Encinal was a melting pot for all the great athletes of the projects. At Encinal, we stopped fighting each other and began competing together toward a common goal. I was one of my class's better athletes but I was far from the best. That distinction went to Tommy Harper, bred in the Webster projects. He's remembered as the finest athlete to ever attend Encinal.

Tommy and I entered Encinal in the same freshman class but we were worlds apart athletically. He was chosen for the varsity baseball squad his freshman year while I played junior varsity. Tommy was also a point guard and the leading scorer on the basketball team, and he led Encinal to the Tournament of Champions competition in the Bay area. I was a substitute on the basketball squad and known as the hatchet man.

Harp was also the quarterback for the Encinal football team and he ran track whenever time permitted. I was also fleet of foot and began running track early in my high school days. But I quit early into my career, when in one of my first dual meets, an opposing runner crossed into my lane in front of me. I accidentally knocked the runner to the ground. Obviously, the accident wasn't my fault but I felt guilty anyway, especially after I learned that the runner had broken his leg. I retired from the sport soon after.

I couldn't match Tommy on the gridiron either, though I tried. After he and I became close friends, Harp convinced me, though I wasn't interested at all, in trying out for the football team. He felt that my size and speed would make me a perfect target for his aerials. I was reluctant but encouraged by his enthusiastic manner. He finally persuaded me to try out for the squad.

I survived the first practice unscratched. But for the second scrimmage, the team pulled on their pads for some heavy hitting and I was one of the first casualties. On one of my first plays from scrimmage, Harp sent me down the right sideline on a medium-range buttonhook pattern. I turned back to Tommy and watched the ball sail gently into my hands. Though I caught the ball, I failed to notice the defender approaching swiftly from the rear. I was flattened immediately. My knee hurt all the way up to my chest. I rolled from side to side in pain. The team didn't have a doctor or a stretcher, so a few of my teammates volunteered to carry me into the dressing room.

A shocked look ran across my mother's face as she peered through the front door window at me when I hobbled up the side-walk to the house. Percy had signed the permission slip for me to play football without Gladys knowing—the reason behind the shocked look on her face. My proneness to injuries was exactly why she had prohibited me from playing football.

The injury was so serious that a cast had to be put on the knee for it to heal properly. The cast placed on my leg was a constant reminder of my football-playing days. I would always remember my short but valiant football career and so would Harp, who later claimed partial responsibility for transforming me from an out-fielder into a first baseman.

But I never blamed my injury on Tommy and he never flaunted his superior athletic prowess in front of me. We remained very close friends the entire way through high school. During this time, I felt he knew me as well as anyone and he saw a side of me that my parents had missed.

Being the fine mother that she was, Gladys was ashamed that she couldn't save more time for me and my activities. But with both her and Percy working extra hours, there never seemed to be enough time. Gladys found a side of me in my high school yearbook that she had never known before.

"In your yearbook, you were described as the clown of the class," she later said. "I didn't believe it at first but then I began noticing that you were. You were the clown of them all."

I think Harp was the first person to actually give me credit for being a potential major-leaguer. Though he received most of the publicity because he was a far superior athlete, I instead became associated with hitting the long ball, a trait most major-league scouts search for.

Tommy, who stood 5'10" and weighed 160 pounds, had reached full physical maturity at an early age. He never grew any larger. I also stood about 5'10", but my weight was deathly insignificant. I was too skinny, although I had acres of space to expand. As a result of my slow physical development, my talent was still in an infancy stage. Harp realized this, and I always knew he felt I would be in the majors one day.

The Estuary projects were also athletically represented by a great athlete, Curt Motton, who, like Harp, lettered in four sports. Curt was easily the most intellectual of us three and he used this superior intelligence to boost himself to the office of class president.

Physically, Curt could run stride for stride with Tommy. But like me, he matured slowly. His talent still hadn't been perfected and he had a lot of room to grow.

The three of us graduated together from Encinal and eventually progressed to the majors. In fact, we are the only Encinal athletes to ever reach the big leagues in the history of the school. No Encinal athlete has come close since.

Harp, who was the most widely recruited of us three, initially chose a career in football but changed his plans after a few brutal practices. On the advice of several people, he chose Santa Rosa Junior College to begin his collegiate career. After a successful two years at Santa Rosa, Tommy graduated to San Francisco State College. After graduation from San Francisco, he was immediately signed with the Cincinnati Reds. And in only a few seasons of minor-league baseball, the talented Harper emerged in the big leagues with Cincinnati in 1962.

After a slow start, he became a permanent fixture in the Reds' lineup, playing a variety of positions, third base, second base, or center field. He was always a constant threat to steal a base, but initially he possessed very little power as a hitter. His finest season as a Red was in 1965, when he hit .257, with 18 homers, 64 RBIs and 35 stolen bases.

From the Reds, Harp was traded to the Cleveland Indians in 1968. After a season in Cleveland, he was chosen by the Seattle Pilots in the 1969 expansion draft. The Pilots eventually became the Milwaukee Brewers, where Tommy acquired most of his notoriety with 23 stolen bases in 1969 and uncharacteristically hit 31 homers and drove in 82 runs in 1970.

Slowing at the age of thirty-one, Harp was traded to the Boston Red Sox. He was chosen as Boston's regular center fielder and lead-off hitter. In the twilight of his career, he won the American League stolen-base title with 54 thefts in 1973.

Tommy played a few more years with the Sox before signing with the Baltimore Orioles in the final year of his career. Though his size, strength and speed hadn't changed much since his days at Encinal, Tommy was a fine major-leaguer. He made the most of every bit of talent he was given. Harp remained in baseball and later returned to Boston, where he is currently the Red Sox's first-base coach.

Curt never achieved quite as much esteem as Tommy. Like me, he was a slow starter and a late bloomer. He wasn't serious about a career in baseball until he attended California University. Curt played baseball at Cal but never graduated. He signed with the Chicago White Sox in 1962.

Curt hit .291 in his first season in the minors, before being drafted and signed by the Baltimore Orioles later that off-season. After two years in the military, he returned to the minors in 1965, and two years later he was in the big leagues with Baltimore.

He was used exclusively as a pinch-hitter by the Orioles. Tags are very prevalent in professional sports. Once a player is given a tag, it becomes very difficult to shake the reputation. Curt was

46

known as a pinch-hitter, that's all. His other talents were never appreciated. But he adjusted to his role and became the Orioles' best righthanded pinch-hitter. Players of great intelligence always possess the ability to adjust.

Both the Orioles and the Pirates were perennial league champions when the two powers collided in the 1971 World Series. The Series marked the first time since Encinal that Curt and I had been on the same field together.

I had just completed the finest season of my career by hitting 48 homers and driving in 125 runs. My first World Series was 1971. I was living a dream, but I may have lived it too hard. Though I scored the deciding run in the seventh and final game, I hit a lowly .208 in the Series.

I was disappointed with my performance but not as disappointed as Curt had been with his season. He hit only .189 in his usual pinch-hitting role during '71 and never left the bench in the Series. As he watched his teammates struggle against a tough Pirate team, I'm sure he would have given anything for the opportunity I was given to play.

Two months after we beat Baltimore in the Series, Curt was traded to Milwaukee, narrowly missing an opportunity to team up with Tommy, who was traded to Boston the very same year. Curt spent the remainder of his career as a pinch-hitter. He'd gone to the World Series three different years with the Orioles. He batted only once and grounded out.

But the finest athlete at Encinal in my opinion never even received an opportunity to ground-out in the majors. His name was Robert Earl Davis. Like Curt a product of the Estuary projects, Robert Earl, as we called him, was a master of all sports but a fan of none. He shadowed Harper on both the gridiron and basketball court and could outrun almost anyone.

On the diamond, he created his own style. He was our third-baseman, but not your ordinary block-the-ball-with-your-shins high school third-sacker. The hot corner was his domain, and he ruled it with grace, style and elegance.

Few third-basemen are capable of guarding the foul line without cheating toward their right. Most shade a few steps toward the foul line in the later innings of a game to protect against extra base hits. But Robert Earl never shaded.

A few graceful steps were all he needed. After a couple of

crossovers, he'd trap the ball neatly in the webbing of his glove then turn and throw a strike to me at first base. Few if any balls ever squeezed by Robert Earl at third. I admired his athletic ability even more than Tommy's, Curt's or my own. To me, he was the finest high school athlete I'd ever seen.

But the difference between Robert Earl and us three was that he never seemed to have a true love for any one sport. He played only for the fun of it. There was never any love involved and he never possessed the competitive flame needed to progress. Robert Earl still lives in Oakland and plays tennis regularly, and I'm still his biggest fan.

My junior year at Encinal was a turning point in my life for a number of reasons. To begin with, Gladys and Percy had finally saved enough money to buy their dream house. They purchased a home in East Oakland. I feared for my life.

For several years I and some of my buddies had terrorized the youth of East Oakland. We had always been a boastful bunch, and making fun of and playing pranks on the young males of East Oakland became our favorite pastime. And because we were always larger in numbers, we always walked away untouched while the East Oakland youth were left to clean up the remains and mend their bruised egos.

Over the years, we had scuffled over women, territory or any other knightly possession we could conjure. We were frequent but unwanted fixtures in East Oakland. We were known by both name and reputation. Were it not for the size of our group, we would never have ventured into East Oakland in the first place.

That's why an expression of terror appeared on my face when my parents made the announcement about our move to East Oakland. I felt as if I was James Bond and I'd just been moved into a suite at the Kremlin. Obviously, I wasn't nearly as excited as my parents.

We moved into a house on Eighty-second Avenue in East Oakland. Our new house provided each of us with our own bedroom, and I decided to use the extra space for hiding. Fortunately, I avoided being totally annihilated by convincing my parents to allow me to continue attending Encinal. But unfortunately, I was forced to catch the bus to Encinal each morning alone, with no buddies left to absorb the punishment for the abuse all of us had laid down. I was a sitting duck. The confrontation was still there, but the odds had changed: one versus the entire neighborhood.

On my lonely trip to the bus stop each morning, I was as casual yet as sly as possible. I would inconspiculously hurry to the bus stop and pray that the bus was only just around the corner. But I was always a few minutes early, and I received my paybacks from the East Oakland boys in stages each morning.

Finally, after several embarrassing confrontations, I was saved by Robert Earl, whose family had also moved to East Oakland. Earl lived only two blocks from our house. The Lord could not have sent any better reinforcement. Together we held off the attacks until we could befriend our ex-enemies. One fact about youngsters is that they forgive and forget easy. Both Robert Earl and I were thankful for that.

The highlight of my junior year wasn't sports but my love life. Until that time, I dated frequently but I had never had a steady girlfriend. It wasn't that I didn't want one—I had just never found the right girl.

I had always had a natural attraction to older girls in my younger years. Elder sisters of close friends were usually my prime targets, though I never had the courage to admit it. I was too worried about being shut down. Andrea Hughes was the brightest flame in my life but I never told her. I hadn't been schooled in the gentle flow of passion and I usually found myself to be awkward and clumsy in such situations. I usually admired from a distance.

Then I spied Lois Beard. Petite with a shapely figure and a radiant smile, that was Lois. And since she was an innocent freshman and I was a worldly junior, I was neither intimidated nor inhibited. She looked up to me as the older man in her life. I needed that.

But what most attracted me to Lois was the manner in which she was raised. Her family was strict with her. I liked the idea that she wasn't permitted to hang out with the rest of the kids. Her parents expected her to report home early each evening. When it comes to relationships, I've always been old-fashioned. I believed in courting, chivalry and being open and honest in a relationship. I don't play games with another person's feelings.

Lois and I soon became a permanent fixture at Encinal. If I wasn't playing baseball or out running with the boys, I could always be found with Lois. We had a nice relationship. We saw each other a lot but not too much. We always reserved time for our friends.

Besides Lois, two other people made my senior year a success.

My high school baseball coach, George Reed, was one and Pittsburgh Pirate Scout Bob Zuk was the other.

Reed, a native of Parish, Texas, was a first-year coach at Encinal when I was a senior. Though he wasn't born in Alameda, he'd been raised there. His family had been among the thousands who had relocated in the area during the Second World War. His father had been a mechanic at a naval air station.

Coach Reed graduated from Alameda High School, where he'd played baseball. After graduation, he attended Santa Rosa Junior College, where he played under former Brooklyn Dodger Dolph Camilli. Santa Rosa captured the State Junior College Championship in his second season.

From Santa Rosa, Reed attended Fresno State, and he said he learned more about baseball there than he ever knew existed. Fresno captured plenty of victories during Reed's stay, but the team could never overtake their archrival, the University of Southern California. The Trojans were always all that stood in the way of Fresno winning national exposure.

Shortly after his senior season, Reed was hired to coach Encinal's baseball team. Initially, he was hired as the junior varsity coach. But because his predecessor at the varsity level had accepted a job elsewhere, Reed was given his position. The young coach was surprised but pleased.

Little did Reed know that he had inherited one of the best, if not *the* best, crop of high school baseball players on any single team. Motton, Harper, Davis and I were primed and ready for our grand finale. Fresh from college and in his first coaching position, Reed didn't realize the gold mine that lay beneath him.

I remember him telling me later, "I was immediately spoiled, but I didn't realize it until you guys left."

His evaluation was correct. He initially rated the four of us slightly below college-level players, talent-wise. But what he didn't realize was how rare such potential is at the high school level and especially on the same team.

"I don't ever remember three major-leaguers graduating from the same class and team," said Zuk later, after all three of us were in the bigs.

A few seasons after the four of us had graduated, Reed said of the talent on our team, "I thought that's how it was supposed to be."

Leading the freshman coach's list of inheritances was Tommy, swift of foot, agile, the best all-around athlete in the district. Coach Reed chose Harper as his center-fielder. Harp was our most awesome hitter and batted third in the lineup.

Curt was stationed in right field. Coach Reed decided that Curt's speed and power could be best utilized in the fifth spot of the lineup. Reed knew that Curt had potential, but he also knew that the young right-fielder had a considerable amount of physical maturing yet to do.

Curt's major defect was his weak throwing arm. And though right field is a strong-arm position, Coach Reed relied on Harp to execute the big plays and throw the ball back in from the outfield. He told Curt to let Tommy catch all the balls he could get to.

Coach Reed felt the same way about Robert Earl that I did. He rated Robert Earl as a potential major-league prospect. According to the freshman coach, "Robert Earl would have made it to the majors if he would have signed on to attend college. That way he would have gotten the exposure he needed." Coach Reed was a strong advocate of collegiate athletics, being a successful graduate himself. Robert Earl batted sixth in the lineup.

I was Encinal's first-baseman. Coach Reed believed in me. I was a free swinger with a lot of power. I also loved to hit with men on base and I rarely let the team down. He'd also heard of my massive clouts at various fields throughout the area. Coach Reed had seen enough baseball to realize the potential I had as a power hitter. He especially marveled at the tale of my home run into the yard of the white house with the blue window. Reed batted me fourth, in the cleanup spot in the lineup.

Coach Reed always complimented me on the strength of my throwing arm. Though he never actually saw it perform from the outfield under game conditions, he could gauge its strength during practice when I threw balls back in from the outfield. I loved to practice throwing from the outfield. I liked to show off my arm. I'd catch a fly ball during practice, imagining a real game situation, and turn and throw to a waiting fielder covering a base. My throw would zip off the outfield grass, change rotation without losing any momentum and slip directly into the fielder's glove. I loved to throw from the outfield.

And Reed would have loved to play me in the outfield, but because of my bad knee I was forced to remain at first base.

My playing ability, though better than that of most high school players, was still in its infancy stages. Unlike Harper, both Curt and I were far from full physical maturity. With my lanky body, I looked too uncoordinated to be strong. But Coach Reed studied each of us like a book. He knew our strengths, our weaknesses and our potential. He knew that I was only a few inches and a couple of dozen pounds from reaching my peak. He realized what potential I had. When others wrote me off as too awkward, Coach Reed ignored their opinions. He knew better. He knew that the real Willie Stargell had not yet grown enough to fill out his own shoes.

The only talent lacking on our team was pitching. A high school squad always looks to senior leadership, but on the mound, we had none. The closest we had was an excellent junior pitcher who hadn't yet played for the varsity squad. Because of his lack of experience, he wasn't expected to lead our pitching staff.

In desperation, Coach Reed even tried me out as a pitcher. My throws shot like rockets to home plate but my location was inconsistent. Throwing from the outfield, one never acquires the fine accuracy that is needed as a pitcher. Coach Reed felt that it was too late in my career to teach me to pitch. We began the season with what pitchers we had and hoped for the best.

Encinal hadn't fared well during our previous season. As a result, we weren't taken seriously by our opponents. Under Reed's leadership we finished undefeated in the first half of the season.

But our competition, who had been using their third-best and fourth-best pitchers against us, now saved the aces of their pitching staffs to face us. We were no longer the underdogs but the favorites. We responded well to the challenge and we remained undefeated entering the final game of the season.

San Leandro High School was our opponent in the final game face-off for the league championship. San Leandro's ace pitcher was on the mound. We countered with whatever pitcher we had available and relied on the strength of our positional players to pull us through. The old saying goes "Good pitching always beats good hitting," or vice versa. In this case, the pitching won out. We lost the league title on the final day of the season.

Never in over a quarter of a century of coaching at Encinal would Reed field a finer squad than ours. Reed only had two outstanding teams after my senior year, but neither could equal the power, style and talent that we provided him. Only then did Reed realize the strength of the team he had inherited.

But a high school coach's responsibility doesn't end with the last inning of each game. A high school coach has a responsibility to the seniors on his squad to help them establish themselves in a higher level of baseball, if they so desire. Often high school coaches are gauged more heavily on what players they place where than on how many games their teams win. In the tight financial world of both collegiate and professional baseball, winning high school games is often easier than capturing signing bonuses and scholarships for high school sports celebrities. But oddly enough, Coach Reed proved proficient at both.

Several scouts came to see our team play. As expected, Harper was our biggest draw for major-league scouts, most of whom attended our games on a regular basis. Curt also received a few rave reviews. Several scouts saw me, but few were interested. Major-league scouts gauge all prospects on the basis of becoming potential big-leaguers. In their estimations, I was far from that caliber. I wasn't worth risking their precious bonuses on. I was too far away from reaching complete physical maturity for them to take the chance.

Fortunately, Reed sensed my desire and enthusiasm. In his opinion, I was a potential major-league prospect. Although he also realized that my talent was extremely raw, his faith in me overcame my lack of playing ability, and he began a personal crusade to get me signed. He wanted to give me an opportunity to live my dream.

Later Coach Reed would say of my accomplishments in the majors, "It's easier to be a star than a good guy. I'm more proud of the person you developed into than any homers you ever hit." Reed always approached every one of his players on a personal level. To him we were always more than baseball players, we were human beings.

Initially, Reed struck out with every scout he spoke with. Most felt that I was too far away from being considered a prospect. But then Coach Reed met Bob Zuk, a West Coast scout for the Pittsburgh Pirates. Like Reed, Zuk was in the first year of his career. The young scout prided himself on being qualitative rather than quantitative. Later in his career, Zuk signed a slew of major-league all-stars from the Bay area, including Reggie Jackson, George Hendrick, Gary Carter, George Foster, Ellis Valentine and several other not so famous major-leaguers.

Zuk had been following Encinal to watch both Harper and

Motton play. But his standards were too high for the two outfielders and he finally decided not to offer either of them contracts. To Zuk, Curt was too small to become a major-leaguer and Harp's arm was too weak. He didn't even notice me until Coach Reed brought me to his attention.

By relaying descriptions of my massive homers, Reed convinced Zuk to take a look at me. Tales of some of my shots at Washington Park especially caught his attention. Zuk eventually approached me about a try-out.

Baseball try-outs are extremely casual events. No screaming fans, no distractions—just you, the ball, your glove, your bat and the scout. Most players nervously pray that their talent shows, too. But in this case, I left mine at home. The only thing that impressed Zuk about me was my cheerful personality.

"I hit you a few balls and I thought you were going to get killed out there," he later told me.

Scouts evaluate a player's mental makeup as much as his physical characteristics. But since Zuk was so unimpressed with me physically, my cheerful attitude didn't really matter. Coach Reed immediately asked Zuk to give me a second chance. He wanted the scout to judge my ability under game conditions.

Zuk watched me from the stands in our very next game. Unfortunately, it was one of the worst games in my entire high school career. I don't think I even made contact on a foul ball.

In two tries, I hadn't shown Zuk any of my natural ability. Zuk was disappointed, but Coach Reed never gave up. He had faith in my ability and was determined that Zuk was going to have faith in it, too. In a last-ditch effort, Reed asked Zuk to watch me one more time. Though Zuk rarely dealt with coaches when scouting their players, Coach Reed was too persistent for Zuk to say no. The Pirate scout hesitantly agreed to watch me for a third time. Though relatively inexperienced at his new job, Coach Reed must have known exactly what he was doing by pursuing Zuk, for most other scouts would not have exhibited such patience. Zuk was in the stands to watch me work out the next day.

The third time was the charm. I flew all my feathers. Though he felt I was physically a few years behind the other players my age, Zuk liked what he saw. I was lanky and somewhat uncoordinated, but Zuk was convinced I was worth a chance.

I was red-in-the-face happy when Zuk finally approached me.

"Have you thought about playing professional baseball?" he asked.

My dream had finally come true. Someone was actually going to pay me to do what I loved doing. Overflowing with joy, I ran home and told my mother the exciting news.

Time passed slowly as I waited for Zuk to call. Hours seemed like years. All the time I waited, Zuk was awaiting an answer from the Pirates on what amount to offer me. Little did they know that I probably would have played for my meals. In those days the highest-paid prospects were given bonuses of $4000. That was the limit. Any player signed for over $4000 had to be elevated to the major leagues within two years, a highly competitive demand in the world of slowly developing talent.

I wasn't a $4000 player. I was a shot in the dark. I had potential but it was far from being as developed as Zuk hoped it would become.

Zuk relayed an analogy to me that he felt described my situation perfectly. The story began with Zuk and his family purchasing a collie pup. Oddly enough, when the Zuks took their new dog home, they noticed that the collie had extremely large feet in comparison to his small, awkward body. Zuk originally thought about returning the dog to its original owner but decided to have it examined by a veterinarian first.

After examining the collie, the vet calmed any fears that Zuk may have had. "You're sure going to have some dog when he finally grows into those feet," he told Zuk.

Zuk later told me that the experience at the vet's paralleled exactly how he felt about me as a player. I would someday be a great player when I finally grew into my feet.

After what seemed like an eternity, Zuk called. He wanted to meet with me and my family that evening. He arrived at our home at about 7:30 P.M. Mom, a few neighbors and I joined him in the living room. Percy had not yet returned home from work and didn't know about the meeting.

Once situated, Zuk immediately got down to business. He began by discussing contract terms with me, explaining the basics. My mom listened attentively, offering no resistance. Silently, she wanted me to receive what I had always dreamed of—a career in professional baseball.

The discussions rolled along rapidly until Percy walked into the house. From that moment forward, my stepfather dominated the conversation. He wanted what was best for me, but Zuk later told me, "He really wrung me out."

Whatever Zuk would offer, Percy would challenge it. I was initially offered $1000 to sign. Percy countered by saying that no son of his would sign for anything less than $1500. I shook nervously in the background, afraid that my stepfather's stubbornness would ruin my chance at playing in the majors.

Finally, at 11:15 that evening, both parties agreed on a $1500 signing bonus. Zuk was happy with the price and Percy was happy with the offer. I was overjoyed. Mom was happy, too.

One part of the contract that we discussed stated that I would receive my bonus immediately but that I wouldn't be sent to the minors until the following season. Zuk felt that I couldn't possibly be sent to the minors so soon. I was too green. I needed more experience, more maturity. If I were sent out immediately, Zuk felt that I would surely be cut within a few weeks. For my sake, he felt that it was best that I wait a year.

I openly accepted all Zuk's plans and theories. I trusted him. I was convinced that he was doing what was best for my career.

As the final part of the agreement, I promised not to tell anyone that I'd signed a professional contract; that way I could still play amateur baseball until spring training of the following year. I never broke my promise.

But even though I didn't play baseball professionally, my year was far from uneventful. I played both American Legion and Connie Mack baseball regularly. My American Legion team was easily the better of the two. It was like an all-star team. Besides the likes of me and my former Encinal teammates, we were also teammates with all the other great athletes from the Alameda area. Our team was extremely competitive. We captured the Alameda County League Championship that season.

I also worked during the day on the assembly line at a local Chevrolet plant. The money was good, the hours were fair and the work was easy. The plant manager liked my work and offered me a position in the plant's management trainee program, a position I politely refused. I gave up the opportunity to make more per week than I would make in an entire month of minor-league baseball. But playing baseball was my dream and no amount of money could sway my opinion.

The best part of not being sent immediately to the minors was that I was given an opportunity to pursue another form of exercise —dancing. I loved to dance. Boogie was always in my shoes.

In fact, several of my friends remember me more as a dancer, the Fred Astaire of East Oakland, than as a baseball player. I was a member of the Ivy League, a social club designed to be a mockery of the Eastern Ivy League style. Each week we either held a dance at the nearby Brookfield Center or transported our members to a predetermined location in the Bay Area to party.

I knew all the dances. Clad in my required white sport coat and black tie, I would dance any number, from the mumbo to the cha-cha to the swing. I usually danced into the early hours of the morning, or until the rhythm finally left my feet.

Sometimes on weekends I'd have a baseball game scheduled. When the music finally stopped, I'd scurry home for a few hours of sleep. No matter how long or how hard I'd danced the evening before, I never missed a game. I always stored a lot of my energy away. I loved to dance, but baseball was always more important. My fellow Ivy League members were always amazed with how fresh I looked each morning before a game.

Once Zuk caught wind of my thriving social life, he began to worry about me like a den mother. He felt the late evenings would someday be the downfall of my career. Zuk immediately took steps to curb my socializing. He suggested that I realign my social life. Zuk was a good and conscientious scout. He watched all his signees like a hawk until they finally left his nest for the minor leagues.

Zuk meant well but he misinterpreted my association with the Ivy League. I wasn't out drinking and abusing my body. I simply loved to dance and socialize. What he thought to be bad for my body was doing wonders for my psyche.

I usually didn't see much of Zuk unless something went wrong or unless I stepped out of line. He always had his ears peeled for a signee in need of his assistance.

One such incident happened during the summer after my graduation. I was always a self-acclaimed poor slider but I was also a perfectionist. One afternoon, I decided to practice sliding at Santa Rosa Junior College. I had practiced for quite some time on one of my slides when my cleats accidentally caught in the grass. I fell to the ground like a rock. A tremendous pain shot throughout the middle of my body. The doctor at the emergency room told me that I had broken my pelvic bone. I was rushed immediately into surgery. A four-inch pin was inserted in my hip to hold the two separated bones together.

After surgery, the doctor told me that my career in sports was finished. He said the injury was too severe for me to risk any type of exercise. I listened and I heard all that he said. But I wasn't about to allow him to take my baseball career away from me. I'd risk another injury. I was willing to give my career whatever it needed. No prognosis could stop me. What I was going to do with my life was my own business.

By the time I was wheeled out of surgery, Zuk had caught wind of my accident and had raced over to the hospital. I greeted him with a big smile. I didn't want him to worry and spoil my chances with the team, so I tried to show him that everything was all right. I dropped a few one-liners about my inept sliding, but the worried look on his face never changed.

From this point forward, I never told anyone about the pain the pin in my pelvis caused. My pelvis continued to ache for the next three years but I never let on to anyone. I was too afraid of being taken from the lineup or being called a complainer. I always kept the pain to myself. No one ever knew about the constant ache I felt each game I played. It was my secret.

A few months after the sliding accident, Zuk discovered that I had enrolled in Santa Rosa Junior College, Coach Reed's alma mater. Before the Pirates made their initial offer, Reed had planned for Curt, Tommy and I to attend Santa Rosa. Reed felt the junior college would be the perfect choice for us. Our high school coach treated us like his sons, and at Santa Rosa we would receive the friendly family atmosphere we'd become accustomed to.

I wanted to attend Santa Rosa with Curt and Harp. It sounded like a good idea. But I let my sentiments stand in the way of my better judgment. I knew that I had committed myself to the Pirates and legally was considered a professional, no longer an amateur, but I enrolled at Santa Rosa just the same. I suppose I wanted the best of both worlds and just didn't think. I lost my head when I got too excited about playing another year with my old teammates.

The three of us separated much sooner than expected, though. Curt eventually chose California State University over Santa Rosa.

Harp was the only one who remained at Santa Rosa. Zuk saw to that. He'd heard of my miscue and went immediately to see Santa Rosa's baseball coach.

The coach perfectly understood Zuk's dilemma and agreed to drop me from his squad, even before I got a chance to play. Though the coach gave in quickly to Zuk, he was disappointed to lose me. He told Zuk that I was the finest baseball prospect he'd ever seen.

Zuk kept a close watch over me for quite some time. He monitored my presence at home and my evenings out. When I finally left for spring training, pelvis hurting and all, Zuk called my coaches on a regular basis for progress reports. After spring training ended and the season started, Zuk began writing to me on a continual basis. He realized the disappointments and dangers that I would be confronted with, and in his letters he tried to teach me to handle them as well as possible. He always told me to keep my head up no matter how stiff the competition became.

It wasn't until Zuk sensed that I was over the hump that he began to write less. Finally, after I became established, he stopped writing completely. He realized that the rest was up to me.

I couldn't have had a better friend than Zuk at the time. The scout had raised me to be a ballplayer, like a mother would raise a child. He gently nudged me over the rough areas and picked me up when I was down. Zuk definitely had faith in me—enough faith to stick with me no matter how difficult the situation or how insurmountable the odds.

Zuk signed four other players besides myself that same season, a particularly large crop for such a young scout. Of the five players he signed that season, he thought I was the least likely to succeed. But I proved him wrong. I progressed steadily, gradually hitting more homers in each of my four minor-league seasons. Finally, in 1962, I joined the Pirates.

That was the next time Zuk saw me play. At first, he couldn't believe the progress I'd made. My determination to become a major-leaguer had won out. Originally, he thought that I would be anchored at first base. When he saw me next, I was an outfielder. He thought that my bad knee would slow me down. But he was in the seats at Forbes Field to see my first major-league hit—a triple. After my swift trip around the bases, I'm sure I had him talking to himself.

But one thing about me hadn't changed: I was still a free

swinger who loved to hit with men on base. Zuk could see that, as he watched me slice into a pitch thrown by the opposing pitcher.

Zuk admitted that I had progressed more than any player he had ever signed. He told me later, remembering his analogy about his collie pup, "You sure grew into those feet."

"Though I was deeply bothered by the racism in the Sophomore League, I always hid the hurt inside and never allowed it to escape."

---

3 NOTHING ELSE dealing with either baseball or life was as difficult for me to handle as racism. Because I was raised in the projects, I grew up accepting all people as equal. But my belief was tested immediately when I entered the minor leagues.

My first spring training camp was held in Jacksonville Florida. My pelvis creaking, with its pin firmly in place, I reported to Al Kupski, a veteran minor-league player and manager and my first skipper in professional baseball. Kupski had been a baseball man all his life. He was characterized by a tough yet understanding attitude. It was his job to teach the young players the rules of the organization and the ways of the game.

The toughest coaches are often placed in the lowest ranks of the minor leagues. Because of this reason, Kupski was the breaking point for most players. Few players survive their initial taste of professional baseball. Several perish simply because of the intensity level of the game. Others fall apart because of personal, psychological or physical reasons.

I was reportedly under the danger of being released early that spring, even before I'd played in a regular season game. Apparently, some people in the Pirate organization felt that I hadn't matured enough physically to handle the strain of minor-league ball. But according to Kupski, who had taken a liking to me, I was never in any danger. Kupski had told Zuk, "That donkey has a future. I never considered releasing him."

After spring training, I was assigned to Kupski's San Angelo, Texas, club in the Class D Sophomore League, the lowest classification in baseball. The league encompassed a group of small cities located in southeastern New Mexico and midwestern Texas, areas characterized by dust, ghost towns, pueblos, plazas and a deep racial hatred toward Negroes.

Negroes were not accepted in any of the league's eight cities, including even the larger towns such as Odessa (78,000) and Midland (65,000). Approximately ninety percent of the population in each of the league's cities was Caucasian, nine percent was of Mexican descent and the last one percent was usually a mixture of foreigners, a few Negroes and a couple of non-Caucasian minorleaguers. The cities in the Sophomore League were every bit as prejudiced toward blacks as any town in Alabama, Georgia or Mississippi, reputedly the hot spots for racism.

The Sophomore League abided by the rules of racism. No more than four Negroes (a Negro was anyone without pure white skin) were permitted to play on any one of the league's teams at the same time. Latins and blacks were all lumped together in the Sophomore League's description of a Negro. They never cared to differentiate. The rule was designed to protect the cities from sagging attendance figures and small-scale riots.

For no fault of my own, San Angelo soon dropped out of the league, a result of the team's low attendance figures. The club was moved to Roswell, New Mexico, a county seat with a population of approximately 40,000, located at the southern end of the Rocky Mountains.

Roswell prided itself on its high Caucasian population. It had been claimed on March 4, 1871, by Van Smith, who named the city after his banker. The town struggled economically until 1891, when an artesian well was discovered. The well soon became the main irrigation source for all the area's crops.

John Mason, Emiliano Telleria (a Cuban who led the league with a .358 batting average that year), Julio Imbert (a Latin) and I were the club's four designated Negroes. We were segregated at all times from the white players, except when on the field. We were prohibited from living in the same section of Roswell or staying in the same motel as the white players. Usually, the Pirates, who were sympathetic to our difficult situation, took full responsibility for providing us with housing.

The Pirates arranged for me to board for $20 a week with a black air force sergeant, who lived in Roswell. I enjoyed the company of both my boarder and his family, but the conditions on the road were a strain.

Once on a road trip in Artesia, New Mexico, my three Negro teammates and I were scheduled to board at the home of a fishing bait dealer, who used her house to raise her bait—worms, grubs, etc. Her house was in the most deplorable of conditions. It had to be kept dark inside at all times for her bait to survive. Thus, every window had been boarded shut. No ventilation entered the house anywhere. The air inside was stale and muggy. My teammates and I sat outside late each evening absorbing as much fresh air as possible, before finally surrendering to fatigue and entering the smelly bait house to sleep.

Our food supply on the road was just as bad. Since we weren't permitted to eat in the dining room of any restaurants, we had to either eat in the kitchens of restaurants or depend on our boarders to feed us. On long bus rides, the team often stopped somewhere to eat. Not permitted to enter the restaurants, we were left in the bus, awaiting whatever leftovers or food our Caucasian teammates would bring out to us.

I was still a hefty eater at this time. My stomach would growl as I watched my teammates consume delicious morsels of food. But the best I was ever given to eat was greasy hamburgers that usually tied knots in my stomach on the ensuing miles of our bus ride.

After a while, I began to fend for myself. I began to buy large amounts of food at local markets and took the responsibility of feeding myself. I consumed many a Spam and salami sandwich while in the Sophomore League.

I did my best never to become a reflection of the prejudicial conditions I was living under. I was a poor man but I was always a snappy dresser. Since I only grossed $175 a month, Kupski began to question me about my wardrobe. He thought I had been moonlighting. But my clothes were never expensive, only stylish. I usually dressed in earth tones, which made mixing and matching easy. My trousers were always tightly creased and my shirts neatly pressed. I was proud to be a professional ball player and I always tried to dress the part.

Though I was deeply bothered by the racism in the Sophomore League, I always hid the hurt inside and never allowed it to escape. Like the pin in my pelvis, it was a constant source of pain, but I never spoke to anyone about it. And as I did when the doctor told me I was finished in sports, I listened to the prognosis stating what little chance I had to make it to the bigs but I never believed it.

What hurt me most were the racial insults that the Negro fans shouted. I'd grown somewhat accustomed to such racist remarks from whites, but when Negroes shouted the same slurs, I was floored. If anyone would console me, cheer me on, I thought, they would. Their insults left me with a very lonely feeling. I never felt that anyone in the grandstands was ever pulling for me. I felt so all alone, the worst possible feeling for a happy-go-lucky extrovert like myself.

No one seemed to understand how I felt, not even Kupski. I remember my initial confrontation with name-calling Negroes. Negroes were always assigned to a separate section in each ball yard. In this one instance, in Hobbs, New Mexico, the Negro section was situated behind our dugout, to the left of where I was fielding ground balls at first base during practice. Just then I heard my name called, followed by a list of racial insults. The shouting had come from the 'black section.

I walked off the field deeply hurt. I didn't know what to do. I felt so alone, so unwanted, so intimidated. Head down and confused, I walked over to Mason, who was standing by our dugout. I needed someone to talk to and Mason was the perfect one.

Just as I began to tell my teammate exactly how I felt, Kupski, from the other side of the field, began shouting at us to get back on the field. He thought we were dogging practice. Neither of us tried to explain—we knew he wouldn't listen anyway. I gutted up the pain and returned to my position on the field. That was my lone attempt of the season to tell someone how I felt.

From that point forward, I learned to grin and bear it. I knew that no one cared enough to try to understand, so there was no use complaining. Kupski doesn't remember me complaining even once. I was afraid of losing all that I had worked for. I never dared complain. I didn't want to be taken from the lineup.

Not even when my life was threatened did I complain. The crossroads of my life appeared in a little town named Plainview, Texas. Plainview, located in the upper northwest corner of Texas between Lubbock and Amarillo, like all of the Sophomore League cities, specialized in boredom. For a Negro baseball player, social life was usually a good night's sleep. There were no racial-free havens for us to frequent. Racism was with us every minute of the day. The majority of our daylight hours were spent searching for food or playing baseball.

Such was the case one afternoon in Plainview, when I decided to walk to the ball park early. I had nothing else to do, and at least there would be someone at the park that I could talk with. On that walk across Plainview, I came face to face with my life, my career and my dream.

A white man, hiding around a corner, jumped into my path. He had a shotgun in his hand. The next thing I felt was the cold metal barrels of the gun pressed tightly against my temple. Though I began to shake like a leaf, the gun-bearing bigot never flinched. He was as calm as a walk through the park.

He didn't fool too long with me. He stated his purpose up front. "Nigger," he told me, "if you play in that game tonight, I'll blow your brains out." Short and sweet, that's all he said but that was enough. He had made his point.

It wasn't long before he removed the shotgun from my temple but I'll never forget the experience. I still feel the touch of the cold barrels today. It's a feeling that has never left me.

On that afternoon in Plainview at the age of nineteen, my life was thrown into disarray. I had nowhere to go and no one to talk to. I was all alone. All I could think about was my first girlfriend. She had red hair and freckles. She was a white girl who lived in the Encinal projects. I was twelve years old at the time. I didn't know what racism was. To me, everyone was someone, no matter what the color of their skin.

The redheaded girl with the freckles and I were inseparable. We did everything together: shared lunch, dinner, went swimming. For us, life was friendship and fun. But now only six years later, I was being persecuted for something I would never understand. Until the Sophomore League, no one had ever cared that I was black. And then in Plainview, someone cared enough to threaten my life because of it.

Though I continued to shake for hours, I talked to no one about the incident—not Kupski, not Mason, not even my mother. I absorbed the problem within myself and decided to handle it in my own manner.

I believe that catalysts are presented to us in various stages throughout our lives. They force us to either go forward, change our rhythm or retreat. I believe that fear sometimes forces us to make our most monumental decisions. Such was the case with me in Plainview. I was at the crossroads of my life. Should I face the situation bravely and overlook the threat, or succumb to the fear I felt and drift slowly away from the game I loved?

After hours of deliberation, I felt the power. I had only one alternative, to keep playing. If I was going to lose my life, at least I would lose it doing what I loved doing.

My legs still wobbly, my kidneys weak, I stepped onto the field that evening to face my fears. I accepted the challenge because I wanted to play baseball. The game was inside me. To give up on it now, would be to sever my lifeline. I made the decision that afternoon not to allow anything to stop me from reaching the majors. I was willing to risk my life to live my dream. Life doesn't get any tougher than that.

With the exception of a few instances when cars backfired in the parking lot that evening, I wasn't jumpy at all. In fact, I had the finest evening of my young professional career. The incident had helped develop a sharp, competitive urge within me. I felt that there was no situation too difficult to overcome. I compared all my problems with the Plainview incident and my worries disappeared. I became a more productive player and person as a result. The shotgun to my temple had bred conviction in my life.

Our team finished in last place that season. But because of the Plainview incident I had become a winner. We only won 48 games out of 125, a lowly 38 percent winning percentage, 41½ games behind league-leading Alpine. But our team could hit and we finished second in the league, with a .282 batting average. In fact, we were such good hitters, although such a poor team, that some of my teammates' batting averages, Telleria's (.358) and Ed Montgomery's (.341), were as high or almost as high as the winning percentage of the team.

But because of the relatively light air in the region, the Sophomore League was known as a hitter's league. Balls carried well in each of the league's parks. Major-league front office personnel always took the light air in the cities into consideration when evaluating a player's production. Points were often shaved off batting averages, and earned run averages (ERAs) were lowered.

The conditions present in the Sophomore League were not accepted as an accurate gauge of major-league potential. For example, our small but fiery Mormon shortstop, Ron Brand, hit 11 homers my first season. Though only 5'8" and 170 pounds, Brand easily out-hit me in that category, a fact he would never allow me to forget. But Brand was not taken seriously as a potential power hitter. According to Kupski, a player by the name of Joe Bowman had set the Sophomore League record one season with 73 homers, 12 round-trippers more than Roger Maris's major-league work of 1961. Now he was a power hitter.

I was not yet strong enough to take advantage of the league's home-run susceptibility. Though I was known as a free, aggressive hitter, I didn't consistently pull pitches to right field. Thus, I often hit balls the opposite way to left field, sacrificing most of my power. Even though I wasn't a consistent home-run threat, Kupski liked my aggressiveness at the plate and placed me in the cleanup spot in the lineup.

Pirate scouts were impressed with my ability to hit the ball to the opposite field, a talent that most major-leaguers struggle with their entire career. Going to left field the majority of the time, I completed my initial year in professional baseball with a .274 average, including 7 homers and 87 runs batted in (RBIs).

My biggest deficiency at Roswell was my fielding. Though I was an adequate first-baseman with an ample amount of potential, Mason and I were the worst fielders of pop-up flies in the league. Kupski became furious each time Mason, who was a utility infielder, or I allowed a pop-up to drop between us, which was quite often. He'd march us out to the practice field for pop-up practice early each afternoon and he'd hit us pop-ups until our faces turned white. During the practice sessions, Mason and I caught the pop-ups with ease.

But each evening under game conditions, a pop-up in either of our directions was always an easy way to reach base safely. Kupski finally rationalized that our inability to catch pop-ups at night was locked somewhere in our genes. Eventually, the pop-up practices stopped. Kupski gave up and designed a special infield play that kept both Mason and me away from any fair fly balls.

Roswell finished in the basement in 1959 (though their poor showing was not connected with my inability to catch an infield fly). Surprisingly, a few players besides myself did rise from the rubble of Roswell to the major leagues.

One was Ron Brand, who hit .317 in '59 and eventually appeared in the majors with Pittsburgh in 1963. I best remember Ronnie for his fierce style of play. He may have been small, but what there was of him was all guts.

Punching holes in the walls of dugouts was one of Ron's fortes. My biggest laugh of the season came when Brand entered our dugout after a poor inning on the field. He immediately went through his usual rage. I could see he was preparing to punch his fist through the wall of the dugout. He reeled back, his fist aimed at the wall, but instantly he stopped his momentum in midair when he saw in front of him a concrete wall. He had been expecting either plywood or plasterboard, and all his frustration and fury were instantly replaced by fear. He stood alone staring at his almost shattered fist. I laughed until I cried.

But such belly-bending good times were few for me at Roswell, where I had been forced to face racism for the first time in my life. I learned to take out my frustrations on the ball. It became my only enemy, not the opposition, not their pitcher, not the fans of the Sophomore League, not even the shotgun-bearing bigot. I steered all my energy toward my effort on the field. I didn't want to waste any energy that wouldn't benefit me in some manner. I saw venting my frustrations in an unworthy manner as waste.

Because of the trials I faced at Roswell, I was a much wiser person at the conclusion of the season. I had learned how to handle my emotions better and how to direct my life around minor obstacles. I'd also proved to Kupski and myself that I was capable of being a good ball player. I was an honor student in the school of hard knocks.

But my hectic schedule had taken its toll. Because of my poor eating habits and the long exhausting road trips, I'd dropped about twenty pounds. I weighed only 162 when I boarded the airplane for home. In fact, I was so thin that my mother walked right by me at the San Francisco airport. She didn't even recognize me. I distinctly recognized the look on her face when I finally caught her attention. It was the exact same look I'd seen at the train station in Orlando.

She was shocked. My mother always prided herself on the healthy condition of both Sandrus and me. She hustled me right home for some fattening-up sessions. As always, I enjoyed each one.

Life settled back to normal with me at home. I began working on the assembly line again and rejoined my friends in the Ivy League. The social life was extremely welcome after six months of social stagnation in the minors. I also courted Lois and danced on the weekends.

But it wasn't long before I was yearning to play some baseball. One day, I decided to stop by the high school and take a few swings. Coach Reed was happy to see me. He hadn't seen me since I'd left for spring training and he was amazed at how much my body had matured.

Though because of racism I had almost starved, my body had progressed significantly at Roswell. I was skinny but solid. Initially, my increased power frightened Reed, who thought I would maim one of his players with a line drive. Thus, he cut the number of my swings to a minimum.

It was obvious to my family and friends that I was ready to begin playing again. I couldn't stay away—the game flowed like blood through my veins.

Fortunately, my second season in the minors wasn't as trying as the first. I reported to Jacksonville and my new manager Bob Clear in March of 1960. Clear offered me a new challenge. Pirate manager Danny Murtaugh, who was busy readying his team for the upcoming season, wanted to take advantage of my strong arm and swiftness in the outfield. He ordered Clear to convert me into a center-fielder.

At that time, twenty-nine-year-old Bill Virdon, a defensive whiz but a light hitter, was the Bucs' starting center-fielder. Murtaugh was hoping to groom me to take Virdon's place someday. I was extremely receptive to the idea. In fact, I was flattered. By the time I left Jacksonville and the strict spring training routine to head north, I had been well schooled by Clear at my new position.

The destination of our long bus ride was Grand Forks, North Dakota, a town of 43,000 inhabitants which boasted of snowy winters, rainy springs and cool summers. It was a far cry from Roswell. Though the citizens of Grand Forks and the other Northern League cities didn't fully accept Negroes, they didn't ridicule us either. They were hesitant to make friends but they weren't belligerent or ignorant either.

Clear, who spoke Spanish, was also more sympathetic to his Negro and Latin players than Kupski had been. On the trip north, he avoided segregated surroundings whenever possible, though he didn't find a restaurant that served Negroes until Illinois. The Pirates sensed Clear's sympathetic rapport with non-Caucasians, and Grand Forks thus became a dumping ground for Latins and Negroes. But Grand Forks was not a bad place to send us, because the town's citizens hadn't seen too many of us before anyway.

I chuckle when I remember the gentle but confused racial incidents I encountered in Grand Forks. One incident is one of my favorite all-time stories. Early one morning, a large group of Latin players and I entered a small café for breakfast. We all sat down on stools at the breakfast counter. I was the last to find a seat. I sat down at the far end of the counter, next to the swinging kitchen door.

The cafe's only waitress apprehensively approached us, obviously not knowing whether to serve us or not. Slightly embarrassed, she spoke to my Latin teammates as I nonchalantly listened in. "I don't think I'm allowed to serve you black people," she said, speaking to us as if we were from another planet.

My teammates, whose knowledge of the English language was limited to "nice play" and "you're out," didn't understand the waitress's request for them to leave. They just innocently held up their menus and pointed to their selections.

The waitress, who was both flustered and frightened, rushed by me and into the kitchen, where her boss was working. I listened as she described the customers. At first, she titled us Negroes, and her boss agreed that we should be asked to leave. But only a moment later she retitled us "the funny-talking ones," obviously not able to distinguish the difference between an Afro-American and a Latin.

"Oh, that's different," the café manager answered, altering his previous response, "you can go ahead and serve the funny-talking ones."

I was chuckling to myself as the waitress walked by me to go behind the counter and began taking my teammates' breakfast orders. I was starved. There was no way I was going to leave that café without breakfast.

I was the last to be served. Though able to communicate perfectly well in English, I impersonated my Latin teammates, pointing to my selection on the menu. Confused, my teammates peered down the counter at me. But the waitress never noticed the difference, such was the gentle, confused, sometimes humorous racism of the Northern League. Fans in that league felt pressured to segregate themselves from us but they weren't sure why.

The conditions in Grand Forks were also much better than they had been in Roswell, but they were far from luxurious. I was making $200 a month at the time, and the only place I could afford to stay was the YMCA. The only good factor about the Grand Forks YMCA was that it was conveniently located across the street from Don's Café, a Chinese restaurant which was also my favorite eating establishment. A running credit list at Don's was all that kept some of my teammates and me alive. We were poor boys looking for a cheap meal and we feasted regularly on Don's pork chops and fried rice.

But after we left Don's, there was rarely anywhere to go except back to our rooms. Grand Forks barely harbored any social life at all, and what there was wasn't worth looking for. But at times, I went in search of a good time anyway, only to arrive back at the YMCA a half an hour later.

I found happiness and camaraderie at the ball park each day. I began going to the park early each afternoon, a habit I carried all through my career. At the stadium, I found friends, laughter and something to do. There was never a color line on the diamond. I often used the extra time at the park to practice those of my skills that needed work. With Grand Forks' lack of available social life, I also had an excess of energy to burn off.

The Northern League had a few other drawbacks. For one, it should have been renamed the Long Bus Ride League. Hundreds of miles and several hours on a bus often separated the league's cities. It was 273 miles to Aberdeen, South Dakota; 251 to Duluth, Minnesota; 211 to Minot and 415 to Eau Claire, Minnesota. We spent most of the season busing across the half-frozen highways of the north central United States.

The cold climate of the Northern League also caused problems. Baseball is a summer game, but warm weather only visited the league for a brief couple of months. The rest of the time it was parka weather.

Clear, our player/manager, refused to risk any of his young pitchers' arms in the early going. He started the first three games himself. With the cold weather still sweeping across the prairie, Pirate general manager Joe Brown telephoned Clear and ordered him to use his young pitchers. Fortunately for everyone concerned, our next few games were snowed out and Clear didn't have to risk anyone, including himself.

Clear, who'd begun his professional career in the Cleveland Indians' minor-league system, was a baseball man, like Kupski, devoted solely to the sport. He was also the best pitcher on our team. As a pitcher in 1960, Clear led the league with a 21–6 record and an amazing 23 complete games in 27 starts. But at the age of thirty, he could have won 50 games a season and the Pirates would never have considered him a prospect. He was too old for their liking. The Pirates had given up on him as a pitcher years before.

The Pirate front office was more interested in the young stallions on our staff. Rodger Irvine, who sported a 2–7 record and a flowing but uncontrollable fast ball, was one of the top prospects. He could powder the ball with the best but he eventually dropped out of professional baseball before making it to the majors.

Ramon Hernandez, a young lefthander from Puerto Rico, was another favorite of the Pirate brass. Hernandez, who was in his second consecutive season at Grand Forks, played five more years in the minors before making the Atlanta Braves' squad in 1967. From there, he pitched for four different clubs, including the Pirates in 1971, when the Bucs won the World Series.

Larry West, like Clear another non-prospect, won 14 games for us in 1960 and was our second most productive pitcher. He and Clear captured 35 of our 61 victories that season between the two of them. But neither pitcher was ever elevated to the majors.

Grand Forks had an extremely high ratio of its players make it to the major leagues, though they weren't always the players with the best stats. Five players from the 1960 team eventually appeared in the bigs. Infielders Gene Alley and Gene Michael were our most highly acclaimed players. Clear felt that both were sure shots to make the majors.

Alley was our third-baseman at Grand Forks. He hit .280 with a surprising 14 home runs and 78 RBIs in 1960. Gene and I eventually became teammates at Pittsburgh in 1963. He became the regular Pirate shortstop from that time until he retired in 1973. Like Hernandez, Alley also played on the 1971 championship team.

Michael—or Stick, as he was referred to because of his lean, bony body—saw his first big-league action with Pittsburgh in 1966. He played for four other major-league clubs before retiring in 1976.

Stick is now best remembered for his in-and-out managerial career under New York Yankees owner George Steinbrenner.

Though he wasn't much of a hitter, Stick was a crafty shortstop at Grand Forks and led the Northern League in double plays. With Alley at third and Stick at short, the left side of our infield was secure. But on the right side, we had light-hitting Al Muench at second and a grab bag of players at first.

The final 1960 Grand Forks grad to play in the big leagues was outfielder Rex Johnston, a former University of Southern California halfback. A strapping 6'1", 202 pounds, Johnston finished tenth in the Northern League in hitting, with a .290 average. He received his chance with the Pirates in 1964, though his major-league career spanned only 14 at-bats and a lifetime .000 average.

But I was the first player off the 1960 Grand Forks squad to make it to the majors. Though I was still maturing at Grand Forks, I joined the Pirates only two years later, in 1962.

As in all my previous years in baseball, I was extremely devoted to my craft. My added maturity helped. I handled situations more easily and was less bothered by racism. As usual, I never complained. I was just happy to be playing. My pelvis still hurt but I never told Clear. I once crashed into the center-field wall trying to catch a fly ball and was badly injured. But with a bandage wrapped around my head, I continued to play. I would have gone crazy if I had ever been taken from the lineup. Baseball was all that I had to look forward to each day. Without it, I would have driven myself nuts.

Though I performed well in the outfield with Grand Forks, my biggest plus was still my hitting. Clear used to say that I left the bench swinging. He was right. I wasn't up there to walk. I wanted to hit. I felt that was my job. I once even struck out swinging at a fast ball that hit me in the chest. I was a free swinger.

Under Clear's guidance, I significantly progressed as a player. Though my average dipped to .260, I hit 11 homers and drove in 61 runs. I developed more strength and began to pull the ball toward right field. Though most of my balls were hit to center field, the deepest part of any park, my increased strength had converted me from an opposite field hitter to a straightaway hitter.

But even though I produced well at Grand Forks, I was some-what distressed at the play of our team. It wasn't playing in front of tiny crowds of cowboys and farmers that bothered me, or even the trace of racism. What bothered me was that we didn't win. My individual stats never mattered one-tenth as much as how we produced as a team. I considered myself only a small cog in a large machine. But at Grand Forks, we won less than half our games, 61 out of 123, good enough for only a lowly fifth-place finish.

Even though the constant offensive threat was always there in Alley, Johnston and myself, we didn't have any consistent pitching outside Clear and West. It doesn't matter how many runs a team scores if they can't hold down the opposition—this was the story of my first two years in the minors.

The ache intensified as I followed the Pirates through their drive to the championship that same year. In 1960, the Bucs were a team of destiny. They battled for a pennant while I fought to stay warm in the frozen Northern League.

I dreamed of someday playing in the majors. But even more than that, I dreamed of playing for a team like the 1960 Pirates. That team had it all—power, style and charisma. Playing in the bigs and winning a World Championship was always my dream.

Shortly after the conclusion of the season, I packed my belongings into Clear's car and left Grand Forks forever. Since we lived in the same area, Clear had suggested that we share the ride home, instead of each of us going alone.

As we drove through the prairies of North Dakota and into the mountains of Montana before stopping in Idaho Falls, Idaho, where Clear had previously managed, the Pirates were consistently slaying opponents. They won 17 of 23 games in the last month of their season, many decided in the late innings or during the team's final at-bat. They clinched the National League pennant late that same month.

I ached to be part of such a team, a team that boasted of such greats as Roberto Clemente, Bob Skinner, Bob Friend, Vernon Law, Don Hoak, Dick Groat, Dick Stuart, Harvey Haddix and Bill Mazeroski, a team of fire that constantly fought back to capture victories but rarely relinquished a lead. I followed the Bucs through their World Series battle with the New York Yankees. Though they had led the National League in hitting and runs scored, the Pirates were outmatched offensively against the Yanks, but they weren't outplayed. Though the New Yorkers doubled the Pirates' scoring total for the World Series, the Team of Destiny rose from defeat in the final game of the Series to capture the crown on second-baseman Bill Mazeroski's lead-off homer in the ninth.

The 1960 team established a winning tradition for the Smoky City that would carry the pride and enthusiasm of its people forward. Not only would the Pirates achieve further success, but the town's pro football team, the Steelers, would mirror the Bucs' totals. I dreamed of becoming a part of such a tradition,

Although I dreamed of becoming part of such a tradition, I never regretted playing in the Northern League. The league possessed a variety of future major-leaguers besides myself. Joe Torre, future batting champ and major-league manager, led the Northern League with a .344 average. Future Yankee second-baseman Horace Clarke hit .307 for the Fargo-Moorhead team. Crafty shortstop Dal Maxvill, from Winnipeg, Canada, who played on a few St. Louis Cardinal World Series teams, was also in the Northern League in 1960. I never regretted playing in the league, I only regretted not winning there.

The following off-season was an extremely special one for me. But not solely because I was fortunate enough to land a job in the Chevy plant, and not solely because I was back home with Mom, Percy, Sandrus, Lois and the Ivy League. I took all that good fortune for granted. It was the meeting of two very special people that made this off-season so outstanding.

The first was Joe Morgan, a shortstop I met playing semi-pro baseball. He was small and stocky but exceptionally quick. Joe was two and a half years younger than I and he reminded me a great deal of myself. He loved baseball as most men love a woman. He'd been bitten by the baseball bug.

Joe was always full of questions. He was constantly asking me about the minor leagues, the players and the cities we played in. I soon became Joe's close friend and adviser. I hoped that I would be able to have a positive effect on his future.

I also met Rudy May, who later pitched in the majors for California, Baltimore, Montreal, the Chicago White Sox and the New York Yankees, and Leroy Reems, who played in a few games with Philadelphia. We all played in the same semi-pro league. But I was most impressed by Joe's gutsy style of play. I saw in Joe what Coach Reed had seen in me. I decided to take steps to help him live his dream.

I began by contacting Bob Fontaine, a good friend and local scout for the Pirates. I asked Bob to attend one of our games to watch Joe play. He agreed. Fontaine was instantly impressed with Joe, and that's when I turned negotiator. I posted $2000 as Joe's minimum signing bonus. At that price, Fontaine wasn't interested. But I knew how much Joe was worth and I wouldn't lower my price. Unfortunately, since Joe hadn't been scouted by other teams, he was relatively unknown. I had no bargaining power.

I did all this negotiating on my own. Joe was totally unaware. Thus while I was still bargaining, Joe signed a letter of intent to attend Oakland City College. He played a couple of years there before graduating to California State University at Haywood, California. Joe never found out about my negotiating until it was too late. I was afraid he would sign for less than he was worth if he knew. That's why I did the negotiating in secret.

After a few successful seasons in college and only three years in the minor leagues, Joe was made the Houston Colts' regular second-baseman. He was named the National League's Rookie of the Year in 1965. He remained in Houston until late in 1971, when he was traded to the Cincinnati Reds, where he first acquired his fame.

Partly because of Joe, the Reds were the winningest team in the majors during the seventies. Though he was only 5'7" and 155 pounds, Joe had surprising strength. Combined, his power, speed and defensive ability made him one of the finest all-around players in the game at that time. If he didn't hit a homer, he'd steal his way around the bases. And if he was unproductive at the plate, he'd beat you with a great defensive play.

Joe was also a natural leader. He was competitive but not forceful. He bred camaraderie. He was the main cog in the Big Red Machine, which made three World Series appearances in the seventies. On two of those three trips, in 1975 and 1976, the Reds were crowned World Champions. Joe was chosen as the National League's Most Valuable Player both seasons. Fontaine later told me that not signing Joe was the biggest mistake of his career.

The Pirates and Reds were the fiercest of rivals in the seventies. In two of the Reds' three trips to the Series, they defeated the Pirates for the National League Pennant. Both clubs were awesome hitting teams with effective pitching staffs. The Bucs and the Reds constantly battled each other for the top spot in the league.

Joe and I exemplified the competitiveness of both our teams. Though we were close friends, we waged a war against each other on the diamond. In one of our battles, I devised a tactic to stop Joe on the base paths. For it was said that if you could keep Joe intact on the bases, you could stop the Reds.

I was playing first base at the time. In one game, Joe had just singled and was standing on the first-base bag. As the pitcher looked to the catcher for a sign, Joe leaped off the base, taking his usual large lead. As he ventured farther from the bag, I stepped slowly back into the baseline, blocking any return he might attempt to make to first base. He was trapped, a sitting duck for a pick-off move.

Sensing the danger, Joe immediately called time out and began pleading his case to the first-base umpire. The Cincinnati crowd of over forty thousand fans caught onto Joe's dilemma and began echoing his sentiments. My friend, though small in size, was large in his anger. He went face to face with the umpire.

The crowd noise grew louder. It was obvious that the crowd loved the show of fury by their fiery second-baseman. Unable to stand idly by, I began taunting Joe. He turned and came at me. The crowd noise was deafening. They were expecting a fight, as was the ump, who quickly separated us.

As both of us backed away, the umpire returned to his position and the noise died down. Both of us broke down laughing. We had only been showboating, just like the old days in East Oakland. We'd gotten the forty thousand fans buzzing and that's all that mattered. The conflict between Joe and me was eventually brought before the Commissioner of Baseball, Bowie Kuhn, who ruled that I had to keep out of Joe's way on the basepaths.

But once the game was over, the battle was forgotten and Joe and I usually met for dinner. Our routine never failed. We always battled on the diamond but dined together afterward. Playing Joe and the Reds always brought out the best in me.

My second meeting that off-season was even more unexpected. My father, William Stargell, who was living in Los Angeles at the time, telephoned my mother. He wanted to see me. My mother didn't stand in our way.

I was eager but nervous to meet my father. I didn't know what to expect. What I discovered was a kind, loving, sincere person, who actually cared for me. All that I had ever known about him before had been derived from my mother's description of him.

He and I talked for a long time. I began to understand his reasons for running away. Negroes at that time were forced to fend for themselves or perish. I believed each and every word he said. I learned a lot about life and about myself from that conversation.

I never held a grudge against my father. I was just happy to finally meet him. At that time in my life, I began to realize how a variety of factors make each person's life different. My father had his reason for leaving. It wouldn't be fair to compare his life with mine. It would be like comparing baseball and football. I simply accepted my father as he was. I didn't offer judgment on what he had done, and I eventually grew to love him for what he was.

As time passed, my father and I grew closer and closer. We began spending a considerable amount of time together. Often, I'd drive up to L.A. to spend the weekend with him. After I reached the majors, I'd contact him on every West Coast trip. I became extremely proud of our relationship.

I crumbled like a leaf when I received the call on December 14, 1982, informing me that my father had died. I was in New York working for the Eastman School of Music. I couldn't control my tears. The boy in me surfaced immediately. The time was always worse when I was alone. Being with other people helped me to forget my sorrow.

I'd grown to love my father. It didn't matter that he hadn't surfaced until I was nineteen years old. I had always saved a spot in my heart for him, hoping that someday he'd find me. His absence didn't matter. But what did matter was that I had lost a father, a very close friend. It was a long time before I fully recovered from my father's death. Now, I'm just thankful for the time we were given to spend together.

By my twentieth birthday, I'd grown significantly larger since my lanky days in high school. My luck had changed, too. I was placed in a top-notch minor-league club, a replica of the 1960 World Champion Pirates. Like the Team of Destiny, my Asheville, North Carolina, team had it all—pitching, power, speed, defense and a crafty manager, Ray Hathaway.

The city of Asheville also had plenty of conveniences that neither Roswell nor Grand Forks had possessed. Asheville was a real city. It wasn't a country town in a southern setting. It had culture. And in a lot of ways, it reminded me of California. Asheville had class.

Asheville was located on a plateau surrounded by the Blue Ridge, Pisgah and Newfound Mountains, and the French Broad River. It was the cultural and economic center for eighteen counties and featured several tourist and health resorts.

The beauty and culture of Asheville inspired several writers and artists to take up residence there. Thomas Wolfe—the author of *You Can't Go Home Again*, *Of Time and the River* and *Look Homeward, Angel*—was the best-known writer to surface from the Asheville area. The city also boasted of several other talents, such as Edwin Bjorkman, author; Ruth and Latrobe Carrol, illustrators; Olive Dongan, poet and author; Helen Topping Miller, novelist; William Sydney, short story writer; and Lula Vollmer, author.

Though Asheville was segregated, its 12,000 Negroes offered me more than enough social life. Social life was extremely welcome, since I had been starved for such activity in my previous two seasons in the minors.

I usually frequented the Negroes' two main business districts in Asheville. The area around Eagle and Valley Streets was one, and the other was located on Southview Avenue. It was nice to be able to walk through the front door of a restaurant again.

The city, the setting and the situation all inspired me to my finest year in the minors. In Asheville, I showcased the ability that Coach Reed and Bob Zuk had seen in me, and for the first time I loved playing professional baseball.

Being a member of a dream team helped. For the second consecutive season, I was stationed in center field. But in Asheville, I was surrounded by a strong supporting cast.

Rex Johnston, who had his second consecutive outstanding season, flanked me at one outfield position. His .283 batting average ranked tenth in the league, slightly behind me. He also hit 18 homers and drove in 66 runs.

Jesus McFarlane, a native of Oriente, Cuba, who liked Asheville so much that he eventually made his home there, was our catcher. Like most Latins during that time, Jesus was a free swinger—any pitch, whether a ball or a strike, was fair game. He hit .301 at Asheville, sixth in the league, and added 21 homers, 74 RBIs and 27 stolen bases, a surprisingly high number of thefts for a catcher.

Jesus became the first in a long line of Latin catchers to come out of the Pirate farm system. He eventually made two quick stops with the Pirates in 1962 and 1964, before ending his career by playing in Detroit, then for California.

Gary Rushing was our first-baseman. He was also our best hitter and RBI-man. At Asheville, he led the South Atlantic League with

25 homers, 99 RBIs and 108 runs scored, and finished second with a .311 batting average. Gary was one of six Asheville players to hit ten or more homers in 1961.

Duncan Campbell was our third-baseman. He anchored the left side of our infield with 16 homers, 75 RBIs and a .298 batting average. Duncan was joined in the infield by second-baseman Leonard Alley.

Leonard was an outstanding lead-off hitter. He led the league with 548 at-bats. He also added 14 homers, 61 RBIs and a .263 batting average.

But my biggest ally was shortstop Reggie Hamilton. Though he wasn't a powerful hitter, Reggie was extremely fast. His excellent coverage of shallow center field made my job much easier by cutting in half the area I was expected to cover. I enjoyed playing behind Reggie. He spoiled me.

But baseball isn't immune to politics. Halfway through the season, with Asheville significantly ahead in the standings, Hamilton was replaced by bonus baby Bob Bailey at shortstop. Straight out of high school, Bailey didn't seem mature enough to play in the South Atlantic League. But the Pirates had paid Bailey a $150,000 signing bonus, one of the most publicized signups in baseball history. Bailey's signing bonus may have won him the starting shortstop job.

The Asheville fans welcomed Bailey, who was big, strong and handsome. But he wasn't worth the $150,000 the Pirates had paid him.

As my teammates and I watched Bailey play, we wondered why he was given $150,000 while most of us received approximately one seventy-fifth of that amount. We never resented Bob as a person. He was a nice guy. But he hit only .220 at Asheville, which did make us resent the money he made, the publicity he received and the doors that opened so easily for him.

What disturbed me most about Bob was his fielding. At best, he was half the shortstop that Reggie was. He didn't have much range, he had little speed and his arm was no better than average at best. I'd been spoiled by Reggie. But my teammates and I survived the dissension over the replacement of Reggie. I began chasing my own shallow fly balls again and we won the league championship with a sparkling 87–50 record, 13 games ahead of our nearest challenger.

As a team, we led the league with a .269 batting average, 155 homers (62 ahead of our nearest competitor) and 774 runs scored.

At Asheville, I had the most productive season of my three years in the minor leagues. My .289 batting average ranked ninth in the league. I also hit 22 homers and drove in 89 runs. Surprisingly, I struck out only 83 times.

But the biggest difference between Asheville and my previous other minor-league teams was our abundance of good pitching. Never had any other minor-league club that I played with been able to consistently hold down the run total of our opposition. The Asheville pitching staff was led by James Hardison, who had a 16–2 record, Larry Foss, 10–3, and Tommie Sisk, 12–3.

Both Foss and Sisk eventually pitched in the majors. Foss saw limited action with Pittsburgh in both '61 and '62. Sisk's first season as a Pirate was '62. From 1963 to 1968, Sisk was a permanent fixture on the Pittsburgh roster. Sisk's finest season as a Bucco was 1967, when he compiled a 13–13 record. He later pitched for San Diego before finishing his career with the Chicago White Sox in 1970.

Because of the fine season the team had, I could overlook the politics of playing Bailey over Reggie. The city of Asheville and the team had been exactly what I had needed. Until this point, I'd struggled. But in 1961 I could see the light at the end of the tunnel. I knew that my time was coming soon.

Why? Because Pirate general manager Joe Brown told me so. I'd made a name for myself in Asheville. The fans called me "On The Hill Will" because the majority of my 22 homers in '61 were planted on the hill beyond the right-field fence in Asheville. My power had made me a celebrity in Asheville. I'd also established myself as a major-league prospect. That's why Joe Brown appeared in Asheville one day to meet with me.

Joe wanted to congratulate me personally on my fine season. He also told me that I was now considered a prospect to make the major-league club. A prospect is a term used by big-league officials to describe players who are given consideration as potential major-leaguers. Not all minor-leaguers are prospects. I wasn't one until after my season in Asheville.

Prospects are not chosen because of their statistics. They are picked according to their levels of physical and mental maturity. Several players in the Pirate farm system had better stats than me but were never considered prospects. In Brown's eyes, I had what it would take to become a major-leaguer.

For the first time in my career, I was told exactly what I wanted to hear. Joe Brown said that my destiny was in my hands. My dream was there if I wanted it. Brown told me that he expected me to make the big club.

I was free, free from the pressure of being what someone else wanted me to become. Brown liked me for the player I was. My future lay in my own hands, no one else's.

After my meeting with Joe Brown, I began to reflect on my three seasons in the minors. Though I didn't always understand at the time, each incident in my career happened for a reason.

The case in Plainview, Texas, immediately entered my mind. At the time, I felt that it was the worst possible thing that could happen to me. But in retrospect, it had actually been the best. It added conviction and determination to my life. Without it, I may not have advanced as far. The incident had strengthened my spirit. I was ready for whatever lay ahead and I wasn't afraid of anyone or to do anything. I had effectively transformed the Plainview incident from a minus to a plus.

Like most of the organization's budding big-leaguers, I was invited to the Pirates' Instructional League camp in Arizona. The league is specifically designed for prospects. Nonprospects need not apply. The purpose of the camp is to assist prospects individually in areas in which they may need some fine tuning.

A few major-league coaches and most minor-league managers are present, in addition to the general manager, major-league manager and the club's most trusted scouts. A player's progress is usually gauged by comparing his present ability with his ability from the previous spring. His weak areas of play are highlighted, and a specific program is designed to fit his individual needs.

Like all my fellow prospects, I had attentively followed the progress of the major-league club. But what happened to the Pirates in 1961 wasn't pretty. The spirit of the '60 club, the Team of Destiny, had been broken. The Pirates had tumbled to a lowly sixth place finish in the eight-team league.

The Buccos, who had thrived on emotion in 1960, died because of a lack of it in '61. The spark, the spirit, the charisma were gone. The 1960 team had not been a freak, it had been a miracle, a miracle the city of Pittsburgh wouldn't feel again until almost a decade later.

Most of the Pirates' World Series heroes had faltered. Series hero Bill Mazeroski hit only .265. Pirate pitchers Bob Friend, who held a 14–19 record in 1961, Elroy Face, 6–12, and Vernon Law,

3–4, all faltered. The only bright spots on the '61 Bucs were right-fielder Roberto Clemente, who led the league with a .351 batting average; first-baseman Dick Stuart, who hit 35 homers and drove in 117 runs, and third-baseman Dick Hoak, who batted .298.

No one was capable of bolstering the team's sagging morale. The killer instinct had been zapped from their swords. But Joe Brown kept the 1960 World Championship team intact in hopes that they would somehow rekindle their fire.

After my stint in the instructional league, I returned to East Oakland. I constantly received encouragement from Joe Brown, a great motivator. In his weekly letters, he reminded me of the opportunities that lay ahead and promised me a spot on the Pirate roster if I turned in a sterling performance in spring training.

I really didn't need the extra encouragement. I was already biting at the bit. I ran and took batting practice daily. As I worked out, I thought back to my youth. Only a few years before, I had stood in the street hitting stones through windows, dreaming of becoming a major-leaguer. I could now taste that dream. It was within my grasp. The added encouragement caused me to run farther and swing harder. Brown's letters of encouragement became fuel for my fire. I would be ready.

I anxiously reported to the Pirates' spring training camp in Fort Myers, Florida. Nothing and no one could stop me from playing my best, not even racism. Florida basically followed the racist ideals of Alabama, Georgia and Mississippi. But an entire company of Klansmen couldn't have caused me to drop my bat and run. I just played the role. I never revolted. I saved my energy for the ball field. I didn't waste it on such meaningless activity as complaining or revolting about racism. To me that would have been counterproductive.

I ate in the kitchens of restaurants. I used the Negro bathrooms and drank water from the filthy Negro drinking fountains. I sat at the back of the bus. I played the role.

But that never bothered me. I saw the racial route as just another obstacle to be stepped over. I never complained. I wasn't going to blow my chance because I didn't like sitting at the back of a bus or drinking out of a separate drinking fountain.

I battled racism in my own manner. I never allowed it to defeat me. In that respect, I believe I won.

That spring, the white players on the team were housed at the Bradford Hotel, known as the finest hotel in Fort Myers. Each day after practice or one of our games, the team bus would stop at the Bradford. My Negro teammates and I would wait inside the bus until all the white players had gotten off. From there, the bus would proceed to our separate living quarters.

Several of my black teammates complained about the segregation. They complained about the poor housing, the separate restaurants, the segregated bathrooms. As the spring wore on, their complaints grew louder. But I never complained even once. I wasn't about to let something as ridiculous as racism stand in the way of my dream. I made the best of each situation.

I learned to enjoy the accommodations. The other black players and I had a nice place at Mr. Earl's house on Evan Street in Fort Myers. The situation was fine with me. I had my mind on baseball.

There was really no reason to complain anyway. Our house was a much more homelike setting than the Bradford could ever be. We were served home-cooked meals each evening and we never had a curfew. We were away in the black section of Fort Myers, and no team official cared enough to drive all the way to our house for a bed check. We were free from the pressures that the white players were exposed to. But I was the only one who didn't complain. My black teammates didn't see the situation as I did. They always felt that they were being given the short end of the stick. But their complaining only helped to further frustrate their situations. I feel sorry for the negative people of the world.

I did my best to win a job with the Pirates that spring. I chased down every ball hit in my direction and returned it to the infield with a strong, accurate throw. At the plate, I was at my best. I hit ten homers and drove in almost thirty runs during the short Grapefruit League season. I felt that my bat and glove had definitely been up to the challenge.

But then came the footsteps, those of equipment manager John "Hully" Hallahan. Hully was responsible for fetching players into Pirate manager Danny Murtaugh's office. Hallahan's steps stopped behind Elmo Plaskett and me. We were the two lone remaining youngsters on the Pirate roster. I knew what the summons was for, as did everyone else in the clubhouse. Though it wasn't a surprise, it was a disappointment. I'd played my heart out.

Murtaugh handed me a set of keys to a rent-a-car parked outside. I'd been reassigned to the Pirates' minor-league farm in Daytona Beach. Elmo had been sent down, too. There were tears in

84

ONONDAGA COMMUNITY COLLEGE
LIBRARY BLDG.
SYRACUSE, NEW YORK 13215

our eyes. We'd come so close that we actually could taste the major leagues, but we couldn't touch them.

Before I left for Daytona Beach, I walked over to the Bucs' playing field one final time. The Pirates were playing the Milwaukee Braves. Hank Aaron, whom I had admired since my childhood, played the outfield for the Braves. I watched Hank effortlessly hit two massive 450-foot home runs that afternoon. Watching Hank play helped ease my pain. He was such a great hitter. I knew that I still had a long way to go. I wasn't a major-leaguer yet and I certainly wasn't on the same level as Hank Aaron. Maybe I did belong in the minors.

My next stop was at the AAA level in Columbus, Ohio. Because I'd come so close to making the Pirate team, I viewed my reassignment to Columbus as a demotion at first. But in retrospect, the move was an essential step in my career. It was the final event in a series of circumstances that carefully nudged me in the proper direction, carefully refining me as a player both physically and psychologically.

When I arrived in Columbus, I discovered a big, beautiful, non-racist city. Until this time, Asheville had easily been my favorite minor-league city but it was no comparison to Columbus. Negroes, whites, Latins and several other races meshed together on the streets and in the business world of Columbus on a daily basis. Though I'd never complained about racism to anyone, I breathed a sigh of relief when it finally disappeared from my life.

Columbus was a holding bin for future major-leaguers. It gave me time to adjust to the unique surroundings of a major-leaguer. Almost all my teammates were prospects, and the Pirates treated us like precious gems. No more long rides. We flew to all our destinations. Our coaches weren't terribly outmanned. There were more instructors. We were given individualized attention.

The league was filled with great cities—Atlanta, Syracuse, Richmond, Toronto, Rochester, Jacksonville and Buffalo. Each city held its own special mystique. But Columbus was easily my favorite. It had all that I had dreamed a baseball town would have. Columbus had beauty, style and class. Our team and the league were also filled with ex-major-leaguers, whom I zapped as much knowledge from as possible. Columbus had restored my faith in professional baseball.

The atmosphere surrounding Columbus helped me to forget my reassignment. I transferred all my sorrow into enthusiasm. I had four hits in my first five at-bats with Columbus. I was ready to play and I knew that the major leagues were only a successful season away. Every swing I took, every fly ball I tracked down, I thought of the major leagues. I would not be denied.

Elmo was reassigned to Asheville. Though he was obviously depressed about not making the club, he had the finest season of his minor-league career in Asheville. He led the league with a .349 batting average while also hitting 29 homers and driving in 96 runs. He obviously had turned his sorrow into enthusiasm, too.

The 1962 Columbus Jet team was a talented group of players but only an average team. Though the squad was stocked with several players who would soon be in the major leagues, we finished in a disappointing fifth place, with an 80–74 record, 14 games behind league-leading Jacksonville.

Bonus baby Bob Bailey, who'd survived a disappointing season at Asheville, was chosen as the International League's Player of the Year. He led our team with a .299 batting average, 28 homers and 108 RBIs. The bonus baby had been worth his weight in gold with us.

Columbus also boasted of several other future big-leaguers: Gene Alley, who had also spent time with Asheville that season; Gene Baker; Ron Brand, "Old Blood and Guts," who'd been converted to a catcher and could still be heard bragging about how he'd out-homered me at Roswell; Donn Clendenon, who later became the Pirates' regular first-baseman; Rex Johnston, whose batting average slipped slightly to .273; Jesus McFarlane, who later played with the Pirates that season; Tommie Sisk; Bob Priddy, who had a 10–6 record at Columbus; and power pitcher Bob Veale. Also eight Jet players would play in the majors before the end of the '62 season. Three more would make their debut in '63, and Johnston would finally wear a big-league uniform in 1964. An extremely high number of Columbus players progressed to the majors, a result of good schooling by the Pirate farm system and a few transitional seasons for the Bucs.

Bailey, Veale and I were the big headlines for the Jets. Though having a fine year, Bailey was often preceded by the greatness of his contract. Veale, a 6'6", 212-pound lefthanded pitcher, and I gained our fame through our raw power, Veale from the mound and I from the plate.

Anytime a pitcher averages anywhere near one strike-out per

inning pitched, he's considered a hard thrower. But Veale carried the meaning a step further by fanning 208 batters in 201 innings pitched. He never let up. He threw everything hard. Batters were always leery of becoming a target of one of Veale's errant fastballs, one reason for his success. He either wore out batters or frightened them away.

On August 10, 1962, the intimidating lefthander posted the most electrifying strikeout performance in the history of the International League when he struck out twenty-two batters in nine innings. That means that Veale struck out twenty-two of a possible twenty-seven outs. But oddly enough, he failed to win the game.

Veale had blanked the Buffalo Bisons through seven innings and had fanned the side on six different occasions. But the big lefthander was victimized by a four-run seventh inning and a game-tying homer in the ninth. He was removed from the game with the score deadlocked 5-5. He listened from the clubhouse as Columbus eventually won the game in twelve innings by a 6-5 score.

I matched Veale's prowess on the mound with my power at the plate. I hit 27 homers and drove in 82 runs for the Jets in 1962. My reputation for the long ball had followed me into the International League. Several of my shots are remembered in awe by Columbus fans.

My consistent display of power was my key to the major leagues. Where others has ostracized themselves because of fear, I remained consistent. I retained my faith in myself no matter what city, league or conditions I played in. Other players may have had better seasons but they weren't as consistent as I. And the key to my consistency was my conviction to the game. Thank you Plainview, Texas.

Shortly after a game late in the season, I was sitting in front of my locker half undressed. Out of the corner of my eye, I spotted our manager, Larry Sheppard, headed my way. What had I done now?

He stopped at my locker. He gave me one of those stern looks that usually preceded a reprimand. I braced for the worst.

"They want you in Pittsburgh," he told me.

"I would always reserve
a special place in my heart for
Pittsburgh."

4 AFTER ALL THE LONG BUS RIDES and shaky airplane flights, I thought the drive to Pittsburgh would
be a long journey but it wasn't. It was the quickest and
happiest trip of my life.

Bob Veale, who had also been recalled by the Pirates, and I had
quickly loaded our belongings into his newly purchased used Studebaker which cost $250 and headed for the Smoky City. The trip was
our dream come true.

We rolled swiftly through the farmlands of Ohio and into the
rolling hills of western Pennsylvania. Soon we found ourselves at
Pittsburgh's western gate, the Fort Pitt Tunnels, the last link of
roadway before entering the city.

Veale pushed his massive foot farther down on the Studebaker's
gas pedal. We sped into the dirty, dingy bowels of the tunnels,
commonly referred to as the "Tubes" by native Pittsburghers. On
the hill above the tunnels was located the most luxurious living
accommodations that the city had to offer, Mt. Washington, an area
lined with fashionable restaurants, attractive apartments and classic
houses.

But a few hundred feet below lie the Tubes, the cause of several
daily traffic jams and a common eyesore. Bob and I didn't care, for
they led to our dream. To us they were beautiful.

The city was only a small spot of light when we first entered the Tubes but it steadily grew larger as we sped along the cobblestone roadway. Suddenly, the Studebaker sprang out of the tunnels, and there was Pittsburgh in all its splendor spread out before us. With its bright lights glimmering in the dark of the night, the city seemed to be reaching out to greet us.

Little did I know that this sight would warm my heart a thousand times in years to come. Whether I was arriving home from a long trip with the team or only a short jaunt into the South Hills district of Pittsburgh, the scene always represented home to me. It eased the pain and loneliness of long road trips and losing streaks and exaggerated the joy I felt when we won.

To me, no sight would ever be more beautiful. I grew to love the warmth and atmosphere of the city. I would always reserve a special place in my heart for Pittsburgh. I feel the same warmth today as I did back then. The magic of the city and its people has never left me.

Bob steered the Studebaker onto the Fort Pitt Bridge, a structure suspended above the lifelines of Pittsburgh, the Allegheny, Monongahela and Ohio Rivers. All three came together in Pittsburgh. The Allegheny, which flowed from the north, and the Monongahela, which has its roots in the east, joined together below the bridge to form the Ohio. Pittsburgh is a river city built much along the same designs as Cincinnati and St. Louis.

Bob steered the car onto the exit ramp that led to the city's freeway, commonly referred to as a parkway. Our eyes were glued to the beauty of the city, located to our left.

The parkway ran parallel to the Monongahela. Steel mills, the source of Pittsburgh's wealthy economy, lined the river. The orange light of their furnaces reflected off the river's gentle glow. It was a wondrous sight to see.

Bob veered onto the Oakland exit ramp. The Oakland area of the city was the home of the Pirates and Forbes Field. The exit ramp merged directly onto Forbes Avenue, Oakland's main drag, a four-lane roadway, lined with large houses, two-story office buildings and tiny stores. Only one building stood out above the rest—the Cathedral of Learning, the University of Pittsburgh's Old Main. The Cathedral was easily the tallest building in the region. It was situated in the center of Oakland, visually represented the area and could be seen from almost any eastern borough of the city. The Cathedral was the University of Pittsburgh's national symbol.

It towered above the Studebaker. I had to bend down level with the car's dashboard to see the top of the Cathedral's steeple through the windshield.

At a forty-five-degree angle across the street and up Forbes Avenue a bit from the Cathedral stood Forbes Field. Surrounded by several blue-collar bars and fast-food restaurants, which filled with fans on game days, Forbes Field was the major drawing card for the area. Oakland had also bred a large percentage of the Pirate office personnel, most of who had been reared within earshot of a Forbes Field audience. The roar of the crowd on a bright Sunday afternoon or on a warm summer evening was commonplace to them. A fan attending a ball game at Forbes Field was treated to the beauty of an entire neighborhood geared toward baseball. Several of the office personnel had once been members of the local student body, which frequented the cheap seats in the outfield. To them, there had been no better place to spend an afternoon or evening than in Forbes Field's bleacher seats watching a ball game.

Oakland revolved around Forbes Field. Nothing in the city could match the atmosphere created by the field's ivy-coated outfield walls, the smell of the ball park's hot dogs and the chatter of Pirate fans in the street.

The Field had been constructed in 1909 for baseball—and baseball only. The seats were close to the playing field and angled toward the action. A fan felt a part of the game and thus associated closely with the action on the field and the players. He could see the smiles and feel the pain of each player who took the field. Forbes Field made the baseball fan more than just a spectator. It made the fan a part of the game.

Football failed there; the Pittsburgh Steelers played at Forbes Field, but the stadium hadn't been built for their use. Its seating was designed for viewing the World Series, not the Super Bowl. The Steelers were given very little consideration by either the fans or the city. They averaged only twenty thousand fans a game, a low total by today's standards, and were forced to play under inadequate conditions. For example, the pitcher's mound was rarely removed for a Steeler game, forcing the gridiron stars to play around it.

Such tales are a part of the rich Forbes Field heritage I had heard so much about. The Pirates won their very first World Series against the Detroit Tigers in 1909, the first year of Forbes. The most famous baseball player of all time, Babe Ruth, played his final game there on May 25, 1935. The Bambino, then a Boston Brave, hit three homers in his grand finale. The last home run of his career was a massive seventh-inning shot off Guy Bush. The Babe's final homer was the first ball to ever clear the right-field stands of Forbes.

The Field had also housed such greats as the Waner brothers, Paul and Lloyd; Burley Grimes; Fred Clarke; Honus Wagner; Pie Traynor and the memorable Pirate World Championship teams of 1925 and 1960. It had also been a house to such cellar dwellers as the Rickey-dinks, teams short on size and talent who were titled after their general manager, Branch Rickey. Each season, the dinks continually lost over 100 games of their 154-game schedule. Powerful Ralph Kiner had been the only draw at the time. It's said that fans hurried out of the gates after Kiner's final swing each game. Few if any fans ever stayed to the end of a Pirate game unless Kiner was the last hitter.

The Greenberg Gardens, an area marked by a shortened left-field fence, was added to Forbes Field in 1947 to take advantage of the righthanded power of Hank Greenberg. The Gardens were constructed to increase the Pirates' attendance. The Bucs thought fans would flock to see both Greenberg and Kiner play, but Greenberg proved considerably less of a player than the Pirates had hoped for. The Gardens were torn down in 1953.

The richest part of Forbes Field's heritage, the left-field fence where Bill Mazeroski had hit his Series-winning homer in 1960 still remained. The city still buzzed from the Pirates' dramatic World Series win. The former world champs had lost their magic, but you never would have known it by the look in my eyes when I took the field on my first afternoon in Pittsburgh. The tradition and magic of the Pirates was still very much alive in me.

I hardly slept the night before. I scurried to the park hours early for practice the next day. I couldn't wait to begin the next phase of my life. It didn't bother me that the Pirates were locked in fourth place in the National League and were quickly approaching elimination in the pennant race. It didn't matter that I was given a small, temporary locker in the Pirate clubhouse. I was just happy to be there. I was finally living my dream.

I hurried into the Pirate uniform reserved for me. The sleeveless jersey was outlined in thin gold and black lines. The black sleeves of my warmup shirt matched perfectly with my top. I was as proud as a little-leaguer preparing for my first game. Once dressed, I hurried down the narrow, poorly lighted runway that led to the Pirate dugout and my first look at Forbes Field.

I tested the turf with my spikes and spun around to look into the empty seats surrounding the field. I turned to look at the right-field roof where Babe had hit his final shot. I continued to scan the field. I didn't miss a thing. Batting practice was going on. Players agitated each other around the makeshift batting cage. A pitcher repetitiously threw pitches to the plate. Players scurried in and then out of the cage after their allotted number of swings, never breaking the pitcher's rhythm.

I ran to the outfield to shag balls. Shagging balls is the lowest form of a pre-game workout but I didn't care. I did so willingly. I'd rather shag balls in Pittsburgh than play in any minor-league park in the world. My eyes still wandered around the stadium. I couldn't believe that I was finally wearing a Pirate uniform and playing in Pittsburgh.

Pirate outfielder Bob Skinner, who in the late seventies became the Pirates' batting instructor, later told me that I was different from any other player he'd ever seen in his life. "I could see how much you loved playing the game," he said. "I could see it in your eyes. And twenty years later in your final season, at the age of forty-one, that look was still there."

As I shagged balls I began to appreciate the series of events that had led me to the majors. The long bus rides, the racial insults, the poor pay had all played roles in my success. I had learned a lot about life. I'd learned the essentials. I'd been dropped to the lowest strata of life where it was easiest to see what lay ahead. I was given an open perspective on life. I had been prepared, conditioned to survive. I realized again how important my struggle had been. In fact, the struggle was the gateway of my success. My struggle bred humility, conviction, integrity and guts. I believe that the Lord places each of us in trying situations for a reason. We are being tested. Life is one big test.

I believe that each person is tested by struggle in their lives. It's how a person reacts to adversity that transforms them into what they are to become. Some persons fall prey to adversity. Some merely survive and some lift themselves to a higher level and over-come it. That's what I did. To survive my trials, I had to become stronger than I'd ever been before. I really had no other alternative. I couldn't live without baseball.

While shagging balls in Forbes Field for the first time, I appreciated the sweetness of my success more fully than ever before. Surviving all the adversity had magnified my accomplishments. It tasted sweeter than one hundred pounds of sugar. The pain, the fear, the tears had all been worth it.

I shagged hundreds of balls at dozens of practices before I was finally given the opportunity to show my wares. I wasn't a star with the Pirates. It didn't matter how many home runs I'd hit at Columbus or Asheville. Major-leaguers don't care. In fact, they're often hard on rookies because they're afraid of losing their jobs. Pitchers are embarrassed by any rookie who takes him deep for a home run. I know my fellow teammates knew that I had talent. But like all the rookies elevated to the majors at the end of a season, they hoped I was only there for a look-see.

But I had different ideas. I was there to stay. I practiced hard and listened to every piece of advice I was offered. I tried to absorb each bit of useful information. I asked questions of veteran players and coaches. I made some mistakes but I learned from them, too. The entire experience was invigorating. I was mad when each game came to an end, and I couldn't wait for the next day and another game to begin.

Unlike Bailey, who had also been recalled but was immediately placed in the starting lineup, I had to wait quite some time and spend quite a few practices shagging balls before I was given my first opportunity to play. Though I'd progressed rapidly my first few days in the majors, I was taken to school on my first at-bat.

Our team was only a few games from elimination when Pirate manager Danny Murtaugh summoned me to pinch-hit in a contest against the San Francisco Giants. The Giants' pitcher was Stu Miller, known as the original head jerker because he specialized in a slow delivery and almost idle velocity on his pitches. His change-up was his best pitch. It was almost always certain death to a fastball hitter like me. Slow pitches tied me in knots.

Pirate first-baseman Dick Stuart, who'd just stepped from the dugout, spoke to me as I walked from the on-deck circle to the batter's box. "When you KO, rookie, don't feel bad." Stuart and I both knew the veteran pitcher would be coming at me. It would have been embarrassing for a veteran pitcher such as Miller to give up a hit to a rookie on his very first appearance at the plate. It may have even been worse for a pitcher in the class of Miller, who finished the season with a lowly 5–8 record.

I strolled to the plate extremely anxious but not intimidated. Miller made small change of me in a hurry. In no time, I was on my way back to the dugout. I'd struck out for the first time in my major-league career, number one in a long line of strikeouts. But I didn't hang my head low for I'd learned something. I'd seen a major-league change-up and felt the intensity of Miller's competitiveness. I thought about the entire experience as I sat back down on the bench.

I would strike out 1935 more times in my career, more than any player in the history of the game except Reggie Jackson. But I was never depressed after striking out. I was doing my job. It wasn't my fault that the pitcher sometimes didn't throw the ball in the right place.

I eventually became extremely proud of my strikeouts, for each one represented another learning experience. I believe that the more one fails, the more one is given the opportunity to improve and learn what success really means. Like it says in the song "The Rose," made famous by Bette Midler, "It's the heart afraid of breaking that never takes a chance." The key to my success is as simple as that. Each time I walked away from home plate after striking out, I had learned something, about my swing, not seeing the ball, the weather, the pitcher, whatever. My success is a culmination of the knowledge I extracted from my failures.

But to be able to learn from and survive a failure, one must be flexible enough to bend but never break. During a bad streak, I bent like a palm tree in a hurricane but I never allowed myself to break. The knowledge I gathered from my failures always nullified my fear. And the less frightened I was, the more I began to succeed.

During my career, I found my two biggest foes to be pride and judgment. Pride causes a person to gloat over temporary success while at the same time inhibiting a person's ability to accept minor setbacks and learn from his mistakes. Pride is a dangerous ingredient for anyone who has sights set on a dream. It inhibits flexibility and stops you from acquiring the knowledge you need to succeed. It keeps you from learning from life's best teacher, adversity.

Judgment is equally dangerous. Each person has different abilities and goals, and it's ridiculous to compare your life or your situation to anyone else's. Judgment traps you within the limitations of your comparisons. It inhibits freedom. I never worried about a competitor's results. I only worried about my own. I didn't allow another person's adverse results to strike fear into my own plans. I realized that each person's life is different. And just because someone failed before me, doesn't mean that I'm going to follow the same route. But if I did, I'd learn from my mistake and be a better person the next time around. Avoiding both pride and judgment allows me to learn more about my life, my friends and my associates each day.

My first major-league strikeout was only the first of several experiences I learned from before registering my first big-league hit. September 21 was the date. We were facing the Cincinnati Reds at Forbes Field. We'd been mathematically eliminated from the pennant race the night before via a 4–0 Los Angeles victory over Milwaukee, but we had clinched a fourth-place finish just the same.

Bob Veale was our starting pitcher. Bailey started at third base and batted seventh. I played right field and batted fourth, or cleanup. The Reds took an early 1–0 lead. We tied the score one inning later when Bob Skinner doubled to left field and scored on my deep blast past Red center-fielder Vada Pinson. Skinner scored easily as I scurried around the bases. As I headed for third, Frank Oceak, the Pirate third-base coach, waved me home. I was nailed at the plate, an easy out. Oceak had given me an opportunity to try to score on an inside-the-park home run on my first major-league hit.

Veale pitched seven innings and allowed only four hits. But the no-control fast-baller walked five hitters.

We eventually won the game in the bottom of the ninth on Bailey's two-run double. The bonus baby's name was painted across Pittsburgh's sports pages: ROOKIE'S DOUBLE IN NINTH CLINCHER. The story of my first major-league hit was buried near the end of the story. I wound up hitting .290 for Pittsburgh that season. Bailey hit .167 but received all the publicity. At times, even the veterans on the club resented the large chunk of money and huge amount of publicity the rookie was given.

Bailey, Veale and I were only three of several rookies given an opportunity to make the major-league club. Joe Brown was in the midst of rebuilding the Buccos. He had cited 1962 as the former World Champs' last chance to recapture their spark. Until this time, Brown had left the '60 team basically intact. But the spark had disappeared from the club, and as a result the Team of Destiny's magic had passed. All that remained were twenty-five talented ball players not good enough to win a pennant.

The '62 Pirates disappointingly finished in fourth place with an exceptional 93–68 record. Rising superstar Roberto Clemente led the team with a .312 average, 10 homers and 74 runs batted in. He was followed closely behind by Skinner, .302, 20 homers and 75 RBIs; 1960 National League Most Valuable Player Dick Groat, .294 and 61 RBIs; catcher Smokey Burgess, .328, with 13 homers and 61 RBIs; and 1960 World Series hero Bill Mazeroski, .271, with 14 homers and 81 RBIs. On paper the former Team of Destiny had all the ingredients of a great club, but they were no match for either the San Francisco Giants or the Los Angeles Dodgers.

The Giants were paced by center-fielder Willie Mays, the say-hey kid, who led the league with 49 homers. San Francisco also sported top-notch hitters in Orlando Cepeda, Harvey Kuenn, who later in life as a manager led the Milwaukee Brewers to the 1982 World Series, Felipe Alou and Jim Davenport. Juan Marichal, who had an 18–11 record, and John Sanford, 24–7, were the Giants' best pitchers.

The Dodgers, who sported the likes of Frank Howard, batting champ Tommy Davis, Willie Davis, Maury Wills and Junior Gilliam, were equally impressive. The Los Angeles pitching staff was paced by Sandy Koufax, who led the league in earned run average, Don Drysdale, 25–9, who led the league in both victories and strikeouts, and reliever Ron Perranoski.

Cincinnati, which finished slightly ahead of us with a 98–64 record, was paced by outfielder Frank Robinson, who led the National League in slugging percentage, runs scored and doubles, and Vada Pinson. Bob Purley, who led the N.L. in winning percentage, was the Red's top hurler.

The Giants and Dodgers eventually finished with identical records. A three-game play-off was scheduled. The Giants defeated their former crosstown rivals and advanced to the World Series to play the powerful New York Yankees. The Yanks, led by pitcher Ralph Terry, who'd given up the Series winning homer to Mazeroski in '60, defeated the Giants by a 1–0 score in the seventh game of the Series to capture the crown.

Though we finished fourth, I felt as if I had been playing in the World Series myself. I was living my dream with the Pirates and I made the best of each opportunity. I led all recalled players with my .290 average. I also knew the players on the team reasonably well, since I'd played with them during the spring.

But I didn't realize how close I was to becoming a full-time major-leaguer until Pirate clubhouse manager John Hallahan offered me a single-digit number for my jersey. Like all the rookies, I'd worn a number in the high fifties the previous spring. Such uniform numbers are given to players who have very little chance of making the club.

I chose number eight for no special reason. It just looked nice when I wrote it. Later in my career, I allowed my number to represent me wherever I'd go. In fact, I became so well known by the numeral that I often decorated the cover of my Christmas cards each winter with it. My friends always knew who sent the card. Number eight became not only a representation of me on a roster but also a representation of me as a person. Number eight became my insignia, my symbol.

After the season ended, I once again reported to the Pirates' Instructional League camp in Chandler, Arizona, where my Aunt Ocie and cousin David Patterson live even now. It was good that I loved the game so much, for it had become a year-round occupation.

Shortly after the institutional league, I headed home to Lois, who I'd married at the beginning of the season, and our daughter Wendy, who would be the first in a long line of Stargells. We moved into an apartment building in East Oakland, the area in which both my parents and in-laws lived.

At the age of twenty-one, I was entering the most exciting time of my life. I was consumed by childish enthusiasm. I was also a husband and a father, and I loved Lois, but being married dramatically changed my lifestyle. I didn't have the free time I once had. Basketball had been one of my favorite pastimes during the off-season. It was the first to go. The Ivy League and my weekly dancing sessions were next. I began spending almost all my time at home. I accepted the responsibility of being a good husband and a good father and transformed myself accordingly.

Unfortunately, I hadn't been home for the birth of Wendy, but such is the lot of the ball player. Unlike people in commanding positions elsewhere, professional baseball managers, usually former players themselves, don't allow any of their players to leave the team to help their wives through delivery. Such a request is regularly denied in the world of pro sports, where each game is viewed as special and birth is considered routine.

While I was busy playing husband and father in East Oakland, Joe Brown was busy cleaning house in Pittsburgh. On December 14, he traded Dick Groat, solid shortstop and catalyst of the 1960 team, to the St. Louis Cardinals for former Pirate shortstop Dick Schofield. Don Hoak, the Buc's stellar third-baseman, was the next to go. He was dealt to Philadelphia. One of the most powerful Pirates in history, Dick Stuart, was then traded to Boston.

With the three deals, Brown had opened spots in the lineup for three young stars—Schofield at shortstop; Bailey at third base; and Clendenon at first base. But there still wasn't any room in the outfield for me, where the Pirates had Clemente, Virdon and Skinner. Just the same, I reported to the 1963 spring training camp confident of making the club.

I wasn't exactly greeted with open arms. Joe Brown took one look at me and threw a fit. He was furious about the added poundage I had acquired in the off-season. The extra weight signified laziness to Brown, but actually I'd gained the weight because of devotion to Lois and Wendy. I had even given up exercising to be with them. But there was no reasoning with Joe.

This spring training was the first chapter in a long saga of my continuing weight problems. Though I was far from obese or even fat, Brown yearned for the lanky outfielder I had once been. No matter how long or how hard I exercised and dieted, I found it impossible to shed all the extra poundage.

Joe was so dissatisfied with my results that he began complaining to the media, most of whom were sports writers. Soon my situation was unfairly covered throughout sports sections everywhere. In a varying assortment of terms, I was called fat and lazy, neither of which I had ever been before in my life. Joe was no longer kind and complimentary. He became stern and forceful. It was obvious how dissatisfied he was with me.

But aside from my weight problem, spring training was basically routine. The white players stayed at the Bradford Hotel while the other blacks and I were housed in a home in the black section of Fort Myers. I adjusted to the situation quite well. But then if given a choice, I would have chosen to remain where I was rather than to be boxed up in the Bradford anyway, though not all my teammates shared my sentiments. In fact, as before, most voiced their opinions quite adamantly about the segregated conditions. Clemente, easily the Buc's finest positional player, and Al McBean, one of the club's best relievers, spoke out louder than anyone concerning the situation.

But I overlooked the pleas of my teammates and made the best of the situation. I didn't have any grounds on which to gripe anyway. I was a rookie and didn't have the same leverage as a veteran player. I was just fighting for a spot on the roster. That's why I never formed a solid rebuttal to Joe's attacks either. At the time, it was better for me to be silent and obedient than to be loud and in the minors.

During my stay that spring, I became exceptionally close friends with several of my black teammates. I especially respected and admired Clemente, who later became one of my best friends. Roberto was superhuman on the ball field. He played right field with the grace and style of a ballet dancer. His agility and strength enabled him to perform plays some fans thought to be impossible. But he was also an intensely fierce warrior who played every game as if it were his last.

I'm an observing type of person, and there was no one I loved to watch more than Roberto. I learned a lot about him. I watched his reactions to a variety of everyday game situations. A silent, strong type, Clemente vicariously taught me a lot about life and baseball. I hear talking all the time, but words do not always translate to action. That's why I feel observation is often the best way to learn about someone. I'm more interested in what a person does than what he says, and Roberto did a lot. Plus you can't learn anything when you're talking. You have to listen and observe to learn.

But when Roberto did speak, I was always around to catch an earful. He spoke to me about personal pride and being a ball player. There was nothing that made Roberto prouder than being a major-leaguer. One could see it in the way he dressed and carried himself. He played the part to an extreme, but in doing so, he taught me about destiny and told me how fortunate I was to be in the big leagues. "There are only a few hundred major-leaguers in the whole world," he'd tell me, "and you should be proud to be one of them." After speaking with him, I felt blessed.

I was always an attentive student who never missed class, and Roberto and 1960 World Series hero Bill Mazeroski were my most influential teachers. Where Roberto taught me to be proud of my profession, Maz taught me the value of patience and consistency. Though reaching the majors was the most difficult task I had ever accomplished, staying in the majors was even tougher. The key to a long career is consistency, and the key to consistency is patience. That's what Maz gave to me.

The sturdy second-baseman never came unraveled. There was always a smile on his face. He never got too high after a victory or too low after a loss. Whether the team was winning or losing, Maz never changed. He never allowed outside factors to influence what was happening inside him. That's why he was so consistent, because he was so patient with life, the game and himself. He left the worrying to the opposition.

Because of Maz, I became a more consistent player. I became more flexible and learned to roll with the punches better. The situation, the cities, the opposition and the scores may have changed regularly but I always remained the same. I owe the twenty years I survived in baseball not only to what I learned from Maz but also to what I was taught by Bill Virdon and Bob Skinner. The three were very influential in the early years of my career. All three taught me the value of patience.

No major-leaguer, no matter how talented, remains in the bigs for very long without patience. The constant ups and downs of an inconsistent player zap too much energy and attention over the course of a season for him to produce regularly. Baseball is played as much in the mind as it is on the field. Once the mind is thrown slightly out of whack, the person's effectiveness follows closely behind.

The same situation exists in the business world and in life in general. The person who overreacts to each situation of the day spends more time reacting to situations than handling them. Everything in life must be placed in perspective. Once people become a product of a constantly swaying disposition, their effectiveness is altered significantly and their production drops. Usually, those people will soon be out of a job. Worrying does no good anyway. Things happen too quick to worry. It's better just to react.

By the time the Pirates headed north from spring training, I had changed significantly. I was better schooled, more patient and more experienced. The steady influence of Maz, Skins, Virdon and Roberto was molding me into a major-leaguer. I properly channeled all my energy to the playing field.

The Pirate outfield of '62 remained intact at the beginning of 1963. Clemente was in right field, Skinner in left and Virdon in center. I had been designated as a reserve outfielder/pinch-hitter. But I didn't scoff at the limited role. I was just happy to be on the team.

I believe Murtaugh was the perfect manager for me at the time. He was schooled in the gentle art of managing and he was especially patient with rookies such as me. He never pushed me too hard and he was always around to offer encouragement or advice. He had confidence. I never worried about failing. I was relaxed. He kept the conditions simple. He always had a rocking chair in his office and sometimes even in the dugout. At times during the less exciting parts of a game, it was said that he'd often nod off to sleep. But he instantly awoke each time a situation called for his expertise. He had plans designed for every situation in advance.

Murtaugh had plans for me, too. He wanted to bring me along slowly. The pressure of the major leagues is often rough for rookies to handle. He wanted me to adjust to the surroundings slowly. That's why I was placed in a reserve role. When he felt that I was ready, he'd start me. Danny planned everything months in advance and he rarely broke away from his original ideas.

The semi-transformed Pirate team captured eleven of its first sixteen games. At the end of April, we were only one game behind league-leading St. Louis. But because of a variety of factors—a leaky defense, lack of hitting, injuries and a shortage of leadership—we dropped swiftly through the standings in both May and June.

Though we rebounded effectively in both July and August, our 7–22 record in September doomed the team to an eighth-place finish in the new, expanded ten-team league. In fact, the only teams we finished above were the expansionists, the Houston Colts and the New York Mets. We couldn't beat the good teams. We dropped thirteen of eighteen games to the league's top four clubs—Los Angeles, St. Louis, San Francisco and Philadelphia. The Dodgers eventually won the World Series in a four-game sweep of the New York Yankees.

The major difference between the '63 team and the '62 team, which had won ninety-three games, was the loss of both Groat and Hoak. Groat led St. Louis in '63 with a .318 average, while Schofield batted only .246 for us. Also, Schofield was one-half the fielder Groat was.

With the loss of Hoak, the Pirates lost not only a talented player but also a capable leader. Bailey struggled at third the entire season and finished batting only .228.

On the bright side, Roberto hit .320 and had another fine all-around season. Rookies Gene Alley and Ron Brand made their debuts in the majors, pitchers Bob Friend, Al McBean and Bob Veale all turned in productive seasons and I became a regular fixture in the lineup.

About mid-season, Murtaugh felt that my time had arrived. An outfield position had opened up after Skinner was traded to the Cincinnati Reds for Jerry Lynch. Though Murtaugh initially started Lynch in left field, it wasn't long before I was given my chance. And after I was given the opportunity, it wasn't long before I became a fixture in the Pirate outfield. Lynch appeared in sixty-four games as a Pirate outfielder. I played in sixty-five. My finest day of the season came in our June 17 game against Milwaukee, when I hit two homers and drove in six runs. My performance left fans asking, "Willie who?"

I began to build a name for myself from this point forward. Though I was mistakenly called Wiliver by everyone in my family and all my boyhood friends, I became known as "Willie" in the majors. My given name, "Wilver," just sounded too formal and was too hard to pronounce. Only one baseball announcer continually referred to me as Wilver—Vin Scully of the Dodgers. Scully was easily the best play-by-play man in the game. No name was ever too difficult for him to pronounce. He was always my mother's favorite announcer simply because he referred to me as Wilver. But to everyone else throughout the baseball world, I was Willie.

Though I hit only .243, with 11 homers and 47 RBIs in '63, I was awarded with a contract to play for the Aguilas' winter-league team in the Dominican Republic. Latin American winter-league teams usually offer luxurious contracts for only a small amount of a major-leaguer's time. I was fortunate that I had become well known enough to be offered one. To me, and other young players such as myself, the winter leagues were training grounds, a time to experiment with new batting stances and to try other positions. I gladly accepted the Aguilas' offer, and shortly after the conclusion of the season, rushed off to the Dominican.

But receiving a chance to play with the Bucs and being offered a winter-league contract weren't the only highlights of my year. I also fathered another child. We named her Precious. My paternal responsibilities mounted. I was struggling financially. First-year major-leaguers aren't given large salaries, and even with the addition of the winter-league contract, I still came up far short.

Fans today associate lofty salaries with major-leaguers. But one must remember that million-dollar-a-year contracts didn't come into existence until the late seventies. Before free agency, major-leaguers were victims of a major-league monopoly. Players were at the mercy of their team's annual salary offer. And since no other club was permitted to negotiate with them, they either accepted the offer or were forced to leave baseball. Even the top players were often denied salary requests.

A good example of this happened with Ralph Kiner in the early fifties. Kiner had just completed another successful season for the Pirates by leading the league in home runs. Unfortunately, the Pirates had finished in last place that season. Since he had such a fine season, Kiner expected a lofty raise but surprisingly wasn't offered any extra money for the next season at all. Reportedly Branch Rickey, who was the Pirate general manager at the time, told Kiner, "We finished in last place with you, we can finish in last place without you." Any further pleas made by Kiner were denied, and his salary was cut twenty percent.

Fortunately, I wasn't dealing with Rickey, and Joe Brown was extremely sympathetic to my needs. He often issued personal loans through the club to help me over the rough times. I then paid the loans back in stages during the following season.

I trekked off to the Dominican, a husband and a father who was trying his best to forge his way through the early years of a major-league career. Though my paternal and financial worries hung above my head at all times, I found contentment and relaxation at the ball park each day. I loved baseball. I forgot all my troubles when I took the field. I also loved playing in the Dominican. The winter league offered stiff competition, only a notch below the major-league level.

The winter league was also a confidence builder. I was once again a star. I knocked the rough edges from my game by playing every day. I led the league in homers with eight. I played with and against a variety of major-leaguers. As always, I learned a lot from each player and situation I faced. There couldn't have been a better spring training tune-up for me than the winter leagues.

I arrived at Fort Myers confident, proud and more experienced. I was more ready for '64 than I had been for any season in my life. Even before the season began, I was penciled in as the starting left-fielder.

As usual, I had a productive Grapefruit League season. Not much had changed that year—except that Brown completed his overhaul of the '60 team by trading Harvey Haddix, winner of game seven of the Series and the author of a twelve-inning no-hit game in 1959, to the Baltimore Orioles for minor-league shortstop Dick Yencha. Otherwise, camp remained basically the same. Fort Myers was still segregated. The whites stayed at the Bradford while the black players were housed in the black section of town on Evans Street. My attitude hadn't changed either. I still didn't allow racism to bother me. I had my sights set beyond segregation and on glory.

We surprised everybody by notching winning records in each of the season's first four months. In fact, at the all-star break we were in fourth place and within striking distance of the leaders. Our 40–35 at the halfway mark was a result of Roberto's lofty production, Veale's strikeouts, Maz's consistency, McBean's stellar relief pitching and my home runs.

Four Buccos, including myself, were named to the 1964 National League All-Star squad. Surprisingly, I finished second in the balloting for the left-field job, behind Billy Williams of the Chicago Cubs, an up-and-coming superstar who was a few years older than I. Thus, Walter Alston, manager of the 1963 National League Champion Dodgers, chose me as an extra man.

Roberto was the lone Pirate starter on the team, which boasted of such greats as Orlando Cepeda and Willie Mays of San Francisco, Joe Torre of Milwaukee, and Sandy Koufax of the Dodgers. Maz and catcher Smokey Burgess, a survivor of the '60 squad who had hit .280 in 1963, were the other Bucs named to the squad.

But Roberto and I were the only two Pirates to see action. Roberto, who started in right field and was inserted in the lead-off spot in the lineup, scored one run and had one hit in three at-bats. The National League defeated the American League in dramatic fashion that year. Trailing 4–3 going into the bottom of the ninth, the Nationals rallied for four runs, three of which came on a Johnny Callison homer, to defeat the Junior Circuit by a 7–4 score.

But my pinch-hit appearance in the third inning was much less dramatic. Because of the quantity of quality pitching that each squad possesses, the starting pitcher for each team is usually removed after only three innings to give another talented hurler an opportunity to showcase his wares. Don Drysdale, a nineteen-game winner for the Dodgers the year before, was the National's starting pitcher. I pinch-hit for him in the bottom of the third inning. With Ron Hunt of the Mets on first base and none out, I hit an easy one-bopper to pitcher Dean Chance of the Minnesota Twins, who threw gently to first-baseman Bob Allison, also of the Twins, to record the out.

Though the quality of our play tailed off slightly after the all-star break, we were in third place on August 17 with a 63–53 record, one and one-half games behind the Cardinals. That's when our milk went sour. We lost ten of our next eleven games, then dropped twelve of our last sixteen. The result was an 80–82 record and a sixth-place tie with the previous World Champion Dodgers.

St. Louis, led by All-Star and former Bucco Dick Groat, rallied past both Cincinnati and Philadelphia to capture the pennant. The Cardinals' momentum carried them into the World Series and to a hard-fought Series victory over the powerful Yankees. Skinner, used mostly as a pinch-hitter, was one of Groat's teammates, as was second-baseman Dal Maxvill, whom I'd played against at Grand Forks.

But the season hadn't been so sweet for us. Only 759,496 fans came to see us play at Forbes Field, the lowest attendance total since 1955, when the Bucs lost 94 out of 154 games and drew only 469,-397.

Sure, there were bright spots. Roberto hit .339 and won his second batting title. Bob Veale won eighteen of thirty decisions, sported a 2.73 ERA and captured the National League strikeout crown. McBean led the league in saves with eighteen and became recognized as one of the game's top relievers. Second-year catcher Jim Pagliaroni hit .295 and had a fine season, as did Bailey, who hit .281, and Maz, who hit 10 homers and drove in 64 runs.

I also had a fine year, considering the injuries I overcame. I outlasted a knee injury, an injured thumb and a tooth extraction. Though I only played in 117 games, 201 at-bats less than Roberto, I still led the Pirates with 21 homers and finished second on the club with 78 RBIs. I also became only the fourteenth player in Pirate history to hit for the cycle—a single, a double, a triple and a home run all in one game.

But individual laurels don't count in the win column. I was

never as concerned about entering the record book as I was about our team's record. Our club was finely tuned in a few areas but ran like a wreck as a whole. Thus, my season wasn't as successful as my individual stats may have stated.

Fans don't consistently attend baseball games to watch individuals. They come to see teams. Occasionally, a large crowd will turn out to watch a classic pitching match-up or the last hurrah of some home-run hitter. But such instances are usually few and far between. Again, consistency and the productivity of the team is the name of the game.

Though we had a handful of individual stars, the fans didn't turn out at Forbes Field because of our poor showing as a team. We were a terribly inconsistent squad. We drew even fewer fans than we did en route to our eighth-place finish in '63. Pittsburgh fans are smart fans who spend their money wisely. We were a group of good players but a poor team.

The low part of the year came when Danny Murtaugh resigned as our manager. He cited his health as the reason for his resignation. It was a well-known fact that Danny had had some high blood pressure and heart problems through the years. But you would never know it to be around him. Because he was always the cool, calm, collected one, the steady force, never drastic or irrational, I felt confident and at ease playing for Danny. I trusted his judgment of both me and the team. Danny had made my transition to the majors an easy one. I hated to see him go.

I'm sure Danny suffered through a bad off-season. He loved the game. I can imagine how difficult it was for him to leave it behind. But like Danny, I also had a bad off-season. To begin with, I underwent surgery to repair my damaged knee, the same one I'd injured playing football at Encinal with Harp.

Things got even worse after that. I flew home to Oakland shortly after surgery to Lois, who had filed for a divorce. The marriage hadn't worked for either party. It wasn't what we thought it would be. Lois had wanted a normal husband and father for our children, someone who would always be around. Though I loved Lois and the girls, I was still a kid chasing a dream. I wanted baseball. I had been married to Lois, but I had also been married to my career. I would have had to change to make Lois happy, and that was something I wasn't programmed to do.

After our day in court, we parted peacefully, though I was worse off financially than ever. Because of the hurt I felt as the result of our failure at marriage, I devoted myself even more fully to the game. It helped hide my guilt and pain. Baseball filled my every waking moment. It was the only way I could give my broken heart time to heal. I didn't spend too much time crying or grieving. I transplanted my anxiety into energy on the ball field. I made my hurt work for me.

As a result, I arrived at the 1965 spring training camp more relaxed and at peace with myself than I'd ever been. Though I still mourned the loss of Lois, the weight of a lot of responsibility, that I probably wasn't mature enough to handle, had been lifted from my shoulders. My only responsibility in 1965 was to baseball.

With Danny reassigned to a job in the Pirate front office, several changes took place. The most significant of all was the hiring of Harry "The Hat" Walker, known as "the teacher" in baseball circles, as our new manager. Unlike Danny, Walker was a strict disciplinarian who relied more on percentages than on personality.

Walker was known for his expertise as a hitting instructor. The son of a former major-league pitcher, Ewart "Dixie" Walker, the nephew of former major-league outfielder Ernest Walker, and the younger brother of the National League's batting champ in 1944, Dixie Walker, "the Hat" came from a long line of big-leaguers.

Though his career as a player in the majors was basically uneventful, Walker did win the National League batting crown in 1947 with a .363 average. "The Hat," who was known as a genius on the technical side of hitting, later wrote a book on hitting fundamentals.

As a manager, he had very little major-league experience. Though he managed for nine seasons in the minors, where he was known as an outstanding manager, his only major-league experience came in 1955, when he took over for Eddie Stanky, of the Cardinals, who'd been fired in May of that year.

It was obvious where Walker's strong suit lay, and even though we hit .264 as a team the previous season, which was good enough for third in the league, we knew he was bound to instill some of his own beliefs in us. In my case, he decided to platoon me in left field. According to his scouting reports and what he had already seen of me, he didn't believe that I could hit lefthanded pitching.

I strongly disagreed with my new manager. I thought of myself as a very good hitter against any type of pitching and I was somewhat insulted by his request. I didn't want to share my position with anyone. I felt that the reason I was less effective against lefthanders was that I was unfamiliar with them. I was new in the league and hadn't totally familiarized myself with each hurler's repertoire of pitches.

But as usual, I never allowed my pain or anger to surface. There wasn't any use in complaining about something I couldn't control. I decided to work within the system to make the system work for me. I thought about all the positive factors in my life that helped to cool me down. I had one full year as a starter under my belt. I felt comfortable in the National League. I felt accepted on the team. I'd been an All-Star. It's difficult to accept a lower opinion of yourself than you know you deserve. But I decided not to allow my disagreement with Walker to lessen my production at the plate.

Walker inherited a strange breed of players from Danny. The 1965 Pirates were a conglomeration of several races, colors, religions and socioeconomic backgrounds. Each Pirate was his own unique character. As a result, the team had a crazy character all its own.

With Walker at the helm, the Pirates began the season playing like a bunch of individualists. The club dropped their first six games of the season and had a lousy 9–24 record through mid-May. They played like sheep without a leader, exactly the reason for their last-place ranking. Our two leaders, our steadying forces, weren't in full form at the beginning of the season, and neither were we.

Roberto, who'd contracted malaria in the off-season, reported to spring training 20 pounds underweight. In his absence, I became the team's regular right-fielder. Still recovering from the malaria, he began the season very slowly, hitting only .257 for the first four weeks of the season. Roberto was an extremely proud athlete who instantly became frustrated with himself when he wasn't playing up to his own ability. In early May, Roberto became so disappointed with his own performance that he demanded to be traded. That's called displaced aggression. Roberto was venting his anger in the wrong direction: his demands were the result of frustration with himself, not with the team. As a result, his demands fell upon deaf ears. Joe Brown wasn't about to trade the finest right-fielder in baseball.

Maz also wasn't in the lineup when the season began. In fact, because of his right foot, which he had fractured in a spring training exhibition game, he didn't make his first appearance of the season until May 7, and that was as a pinch-hitter. Maz returned to the starting lineup on May 19.

Maz's return, combined with Roberto's resurgence, ignited the Pirates on a twelve-game winning streak. The duo's value as leaders was obvious to everyone associated with the team. Without their steadying influence, we would have been battling to climb out of the cellar all season long. But instead, the team caught fire and we won 81 of our next 130 games, a sparkling 81–49 record.

The return of Roberto and Maz also helped me tremendously. I just felt so much more mature and confident with them around. Wherever they would lead, I'd always follow. And they always seemed to lead us to victory.

I celebrated in June by posting the finest month of my young career. I hit 10 homers and drove in 35 runs for the month. I was hitting balls out of ball parks like there was no tomorrow. On June 8, I hit a breath-taking homer over the left-field scoreboard at Forbes Field. No lefthander in the sixty-one-year history of Forbes Field had ever accomplished the feat before.

Later that month on June 24, I hit three homers in Dodger Stadium and barely missed a fourth. My consistent display of power was beginning to build a reputation for me around the league. I was named co-winner of the National League's Player of the Month Award with teammate Vernon Law—or the Deacon, as we called him—a thirty-five-year-old pitcher who ran off eight consecutive wins after Maz's return. Later that season, Law would reel off nine straight wins. As a result of our fine play, we won nineteen of our thirty games in June and moved back into the pennant race.

But to be successful, one must take chances. In 1965, I was a confident hitter at the plate. I wasn't afraid to take a chance. I struck out 127 times in 533 at-bats, a ratio of one strikeout for every four at-bats. I was ranked among the league leaders in strikeouts at the conclusion of the season. But I saw that as a good sign. Strikeouts and production had formed a positive correlation throughout my career. The more chances I took, the more times I succeeded. Strikeouts are only part of the game, an occupational risk.

Only one Pirate, first-baseman Donn Clendenon, who fanned 128 times in 1965, struck out more than I. And only two players in the National League, the Philadelphia Phillies' Richie Allen, who struck out 150 times, and former Pirate Dick Stuart, also a Philly, who fanned 136 times, struck out more than Clendenon. But look at their stats. Allen hit .302, with 20 homers and 85 RBIs in '65. Stuart hit 28 homers and drove in 95 runs. Strikeouts are only the negative results of chances taken. I was proud to be considered a power hitter on the level of Clendenon, Allen and Stuart.

Oddly, I tied with Harp for fourth in the league in strikeouts. He was out of his class. As a Cincinnati Red in '65, he displayed rare power by hitting 18 homers, a personal high for his four years in the majors. But Harp, who was a lead-off hitter, had 113 more at-bats than me. I led the league in the ratio of chances taken. I was proud of that fact. It was my place in the lineup to take chances. That was my job. But in Harp's case, his lofty number of strikeouts severely tainted the productive image of his season.

I set goals for myself each spring training by which I could measure the effectiveness of my efforts at the conclusion of the season. I'd write my goals, which I always thought to be within my reach, on the circular form lining on the inside of my batting helmet. Each time I stepped to the plate, I was reminded of what kind of season I was expecting from myself, much the same effect as a string tied around a finger would cause. My goals helped me to retain my sharp, competitive, someone-is-always-after-your-job edge throughout the entire season.

I practiced the procedure for two seasons before my goals were discovered by a fellow teammate, who passed the predictions on to a reporter. My seasonal goals made sports-page news. The following season, reporters clamored for my predictions. But I'm an extremely private person. And after a few seasons of my predictions being exploited, I stopped practicing the procedure. To them it was only a few numbers in a newspaper, but to me it was the basis for my entire season.

My 1965 goals read: 30 home runs, 100 RBIs, a .300 batting average. Even though I was snakebit by injuries that season, I still managed to hit .272 with 27 homers and 107 RBIs, in the range of my pre-season predictions.

Though I considered Walker pushy at times and he and I even feuded occasionally, I must admit that he had relit the Bucs' competitive flame. We finished in third place that season, with a 90–72 record. As a result, we were once again respected in Pittsburgh. In 1965, games at Forbes Field drew 150,000 more fans than they had in '64.

But '65 had only been basic training for the Bucs, who in 1966 approached perfection as a team. We were the second team out of the gate in April, with a 10–5 record, which left us only one game behind the league-leading Giants. By the beginning of May, we were in first place. From that point forward we were a fixture in the pennant race.

We were in first place as late as the first week of September. But our breaking point had come a week before, on September 1. We were four games in front at the time and were playing the second-place Dodgers. We and the Dodgers were tied 1–1 after the regulation nine innings. We were hot on hitting but unfortunately low on pitching and eventually lost to the Dodgers in ten innings. Our overworked relief corps was beginning to tire. Our lead was sliced in half. Not long afterwards, we were in second place. We fell out of the pennant race for good on September 21 after a game versus the Giants. We had just defeated San Francisco three straight games and were on the threshold of completing a four-game sweep when our relievers gave up three runs in the bottom of the ninth. The Giants won the game and we fell one and a half games behind with only twelve to go.

We went on to lose seven of our last eleven games, including our final three. The '66 club was a direct reflection of Walker. We were known as the heaviest-hitting team in the league. But unfortunately, that's all we were capable of doing.

As had become routine, Roberto was our best hitter, even though he'd exchanged some points off his batting average for a few extra homers and RBIs. The All-Star outfielder finished with a .317 batting average, 29 homers and 119 RBIs.

But the Pirates' biggest surprises of '66 were outfielders Matty Alou and Manny Mota. Although Alou, who had been acquired from the Giants before the season, was only a mediocre hitter before he joined the Bucs, under Walker's guidance he became a hitter extraordinaire. Walker taught the young outfielder to hit to the opposite field and to scrape for base hits. Choked up on the handle of the bat approximately six inches, Alou had the best bat control in the majors. He could slap a ball to any field with ease. Alou batted .342 in '66 and captured the National League batting title. He credited Walker with his improvement as a hitter.

Mota, who was also acquired from San Francisco, was our backup center-fielder and one of our reserve outfielders. But "The Hat" must have known something about Mota that no one had ever noticed before. Under the guidance of Walker, Mota hit .332. Though he didn't have enough at-bats to qualify for the batting race, he was an essential cog in our hitting machine.

Walker's influence also emerged in the efforts of Clendenon and Alley, both of whom hit .299. Maz also contributed. His 82 RBIs were a career high. And as usual, he was chosen as the National League's Gold Glove winner at second base.

I hate to admit that Walker's influence may have helped me in '66 but it didn't hurt. I was platooned against lefthanded pitching. I didn't like that. In fact, I was insulted when he suggested the idea, but I was forced to live with it, so I kept quiet and played by the rules. Surprisingly, I had the finest season of my career in '66: a .315 average, 33 homers, 102 RBIs. My 33 home runs established a new Pirate record for round-trips by a lefthanded hitter. My .315 average also ranked sixth in the league.

But Walker's presence did nothing for our pitching, which eventually proved the downfall of our season. Veale was the ace of our staff, with sixteen wins. Rookies Steve Blass and Woodie Fryman recorded twelve wins apiece, while veteran Vernon Law added a dozen. Our bullpen corps was the workhouse division of the league, a result of our starters' inability to complete games. Young Pete Mikkelson was our top reliever. He appeared in seventy-one games in '66, a new club record.

At the conclusion of the season, Mikkelson and his cohorts were exhausted, a significant reason for our season-ending slump. The strong-armed relievers simply could no longer pick up the slack left behind by our starters, and our powerful bats couldn't produce runs fast enough to keep pace with our porous pitching.

I injured my knee on September 26 versus Philadelphia and I was out of the lineup for the remaining five games of the season. We won only two of those five games.

But it wasn't my fault that the team had folded. Our pitching hadn't been good enough. The Pirate organization overlooked the importance of pitching and concentrated solely on hitting. The front office believed that to win a team must score in abundance. Our pitching staff wasn't given enough consideration, a situation that would haunt the team for years to come.

"I chose to give away free chicken to any customer who had an order placed when I hit a home run. 'Chicken on the Hill with Will,' we called it."

---

5 PITTSBURGH IS A CITY PROUD of its heritage. It is a town anxious for champions, especially World Series champions.

During the mid-sixties, the Pirates were considered to be the only team in town. At that time, the soon-to-be-prestigious Pittsburgh Steelers were the brunt of many a joke. They were never expected to win, and when they did win, it was called a miracle.

But the people of Pittsburgh always expected the Pirates to be winners. The World Champs of 1960 had spoiled Pittsburghers. The fans didn't understand why the Bucs couldn't win the pennant every year. They had become frustrated with the Pirates' poor showings since 1960. Pittsburghers consider themselves winners and don't care to be associated with losers. They especially voiced their dissatisfaction at the turnstile, where the Pirates averaged only 14,000 fans a game.

But because of the Bucs' strong showing in 1966, Pittsburgh fans once again jumped on the Pirates' bandwagon. During the winter months following the '66 season, the Pirates were the talk of the town, on the brink of a championship, a good bet to capture the pennant and conquer the Series, just as they did in 1960.

The city was readying itself for a championship long before the season even started. The media fanned the fire with predictions, cartoons, columns, pre–World Series stories. The citizens of Pittsburgh could taste another pennant. "Who could stop such an awesome hitting attack?" thought Pirate fans. "There weren't any better hitters than Clemente, Clendenon, Alou, Mota, Mazeroski, Alley and Stargell." The Pittsburgh fans were correct. We were the finest hitting team in the majors.

But what had cost us the pennant in '66 was our lack of pitching. Joe Brown, a perfectionist, immediately answered the fans' pleas for a few fresh arms by acquiring Juan Pizzaro from the Chicago White Sox and Dennis Ribant from the New York Mets. Pizzaro was expected to steady our quivering bullpen, while Ribant, who was 11–9 with a lowly Mets team the year before, was expected to bolster our starting staff. The pair were far from Cy Young Award candidates, but with our massive hitting attack, mediocre pitchers stood a chance to become twenty-game winners. The fans felt Brown had glued together another World Championship. They were happy with the acquisition of Pizzaro and Ribant.

Then in a blockbuster of a deal later that off-season, Brown traded Bailey and Gene Michaels to Los Angeles for record-setting base-stealer and Dodger team captain Maury Wills. In the Pittsburgh newspapers, Brown was credited with just clinching the pennant for the Buccos, twenty-four shopping days before Christmas and four months before the start of the '67 season.

Wills, who played shortstop as a Dodger, was transformed into a third-baseman as a Bucco. His biggest assets were his base-stealing ability (he'd set a major-league record with 104 thefts in 1962) and his leadership qualities. Wills had been a member of four World Series teams as a Dodger. He was expected to add a lot of leadership to the team. The people of Pittsburgh once again walked proud, spoke loud and cheered wholeheartedly. They couldn't wait for another Pirate season to begin. They expected great things of the hometown team, as did the players.

My teammates and I once again began believing in ourselves. We heard what the fans were saying and read the predictions in the newspapers. We were convinced, too. As usually happens during the off-season, players help promote the team for the upcoming season. They speak at banquets, visit hospitals, answer questions—whatever. Often the hype players muster is frivolous. Fans don't always believe all the hype. But in the winter of 1966–67, Pittsburghers listened to every word.

"We should win the pennant this year and next year," boasted Clendenon late in January of '67. "We'll probably have it clinched by the early part of September."

But Donn wasn't the only Pirate to be speaking so boldly. All of us were confident of our chances and weren't afraid to tell anyone. Our success was also predicted on a national basis. The DelMar Sports book, out of Las Vegas, picked us as 8–5 favorites to win the pennant. In pre-season interviews, even opposing managers chose the Pirates over their own teams. Our club was picked by almost every baseball authority in the country to win the National League pennant in 1967.

Money from eager fans buying tickets flowed into and out of the Pirate ticket office at a record pace. Everyone wanted to see the Pirates play. The team that had drawn 1,196,618 fans to Forbes Field in 1966 sold 300,000 advance tickets during the off-season— a large number, considering that the Pirates had only drawn slightly over twice that many fans in both 1963 and 1964.

Joe Brown didn't spare a cent in rewarding his top players for their efforts either. The flow of incoming money made meeting his salary budget much easier. He made Roberto the highest-paid player in Pirate history, with a $100,000-a-year contract. Wills was given $70,000 and I was offered $30,000, a nice salary considering I was only a fifth-year player.

Though certainly not because of my salary, I may have been the least satisfied Pirate. I had hit .315 the previous season and I was still unhappy with my production. I wasn't proud of what I'd accomplished. I felt Walker had protected my batting average by platooning me against lefthanded pitching. Because I considered myself a good hitter and a complete player, I felt dishonest playing only against righthanders. No player likes to be held back by his so-called limitations. I dreamed of being an all-around player, like Roberto. I knew I was a better player than Walker gave me credit for being. I didn't need to be protected. But there wasn't much I could do. I had very little leverage in the situation. I decided to make the best of whatever happened.

I didn't run and hide when both Brown and Walker jumped on me about my weight that spring training either. I weighed in at 225 pounds, far heavier than either had expected me to be. Though I carried the weight well, Brown and Walker had fleeting visions of me becoming an all-hit, no-do-anything-else-well player. Both were perfectionists, and neither would stand for such an insult. They viewed my added weight as a sign of laziness. They wouldn't accept any of my alibis.

The truth was that I'd gotten remarried in the off-season to Dolores Parker. I'd met Dolores at an Ebony fashion show in Pittsburgh the year before. She was one of the show's models. I was immediately attracted to her. I liked her down-home attitude. We were both plain and simple people.

I courted Dolores for approximately one year. I stayed in Pittsburgh the following off-season. I'd fallen in love with the city and its people. I no longer called California my home. Pittsburgh was now first in my heart, as was Dolores, a native Pittsburgher. We were married in the winter of '66.

After I married Dolores, I discovered many things about her that I had never known. The most significant fact was that she was an excellent cook, the reason for my added weight that spring.

But that wasn't good enough for Brown, who subtracted $1500 from my salary that year for reporting to spring training overweight. I was the first player in the game ever fined for being overweight. Still frustrated with my weight, Brown ordered the team physician, Joseph Finegold, to design a specific weight-reducing diet for me. I was placed on a no-potatoes, no-dessert diet. Brown expected me to lose 15 pounds by the end of spring training.

The media blew my weight problem out of proportion, always in search of a way to sell newspapers. Joe's dissatisfaction with me became the number-one story on radio sports shows and in daily sports sections. I was not so humorously referred to as not-so-wee Willie. I was incorrectly described as an overweight ball player feeding off a fat salary. I didn't agree with their accusations. Most of all, I was hurt by what they said of me. I was proud to be a ball player. Their jokes scratched my heart instead of tickling my sense of humor. I never formed a rebuttal. I didn't want to give them any more ammunition than they already had.

But soon the hurt wore off and I could joke with the reporters about my weight. A good offense is always the best defense. That was also about the same time that Finegold took me off the no-potatoes, no-dessert diet and prescribed a grapefruit diet and exercise instead.

In Brown's eyes, no exercise could be enough exercise for me. Each day he expected me to work until I dropped from exhaustion. In fact, I even exercised while my teammates played. Joe was too much of a perfectionist to be satisfied with anything less than a slim, trim Willie Stargell.

I was the only Pirate player wearing longjohns in the 80-degree Florida heat. Brown usually saw to it that I was left out of each day's lineup so I'd have time to exercise. I exercised in foul territory during exhibition games. I did sit-ups before, during and after each game. I was always the last player to leave the field each evening. I was also responsible for doing a series of post-game exercises which usually kept me at the ball field much later than my teammates. Brown was obsessed with thinning my waistline.

As a result, I played sparingly in our exhibition games. Yet, I still predicted that the '67 season would be the finest season of my career; .320 batting average, 40 homers and 120 RBIs. I only believe in going forward, never backward. Though I spent most of my time exercising, I still performed well when given the opportunity to play. Overall, I hit .359, 12-for-27 versus righthanded pitching (.519) but 0-for-12 against lefties (.000). Though thirty-nine at-bats do not make a career or even a season, my .000 average versus lefthanders substantiated Walker's theory, at least in his mind. I was once again platooned in left field.

Though I was in great physical shape to start the season, my lack of practice against live pitching surfaced immediately. My timing was off, my confidence was down and soon my pride was hurt. I was struggling through the worst slump of my career. I couldn't do anything right. Though the media had softened their attack on my weight situation, my lack of productivity was discussed daily.

Though I was batting only .193 through May, my performance didn't seem to affect the team's record. The Bucs boasted of a 23–18 mark through the second month of the season. But such good fortune was short-lived—the Buccos soon dipped to my level.

In June, the bottom fell out for the Pirates. The team won far fewer than half its games that month. The Bucs were a tense club. All their bragging and pre-season predicting was now slapping them in the face. Though we kidded about disappointing our fans, deep down inside we felt terrible.

Our disastrous road trip at the end of June was the clincher. When we boarded the return flight for Pittsburgh, we were in sixth place. We wondered what surprise our fans would have for us. Jokingly, I suggested that we all walk in groups of four or more. Pete Mikkelson said that we should land our plane one hundred miles outside of Pittsburgh and sneak in. Pitcher Tommie Sisk warned us about shopping. "I'm not going to walk in any stores. I'm going to make my wife do all the shopping."

But our slump was no joking matter for Walker, who received the majority of the blame for our poor showing. The media felt that he wasn't a take-charge manager. They sensed a large amount of desertion of the club, which they said inhibited our play. But Joe Brown let us know who was at fault in a closed-door meeting on June 30 and he wasn't pointing any fingers at Walker. His finger was pointed at us. During the meeting, in a pledge of support for his manager, Brown promised not to fire Walker. But as often happens in baseball circles, decisions last only as long as one's patience. Walker was fired on July 19.

Murtaugh was hired to replace Walker. Though I didn't hold anything against Harry, the sight of Murtaugh was a breath of fresh air for me. I needed Danny's presence to rekindle my confidence. Danny's easygoing, confident style affected me immediately. I diagnosed the cause of my slump almost instantly. I had been holding my hands too high up on the bat handle. I learned to relax more and wait on the pitch.

It also helped when Murtaugh tabbed me as his regular left-fielder. Because of the extra boost of confidence, my play improved instantly. The fans soon began to sympathize with what I had gone through that spring. Their cheers of "not-so-wee Willie" changed to a "let Willie alone" theme. They were definitely back on my side. Even Hall of Famer and former Pirate Pie Traynor spoke out in my behalf. He was quoted by the Pittsburgh media as saying that if the Pirates left me alone and quit worrying so much about my weight, I'd become the greatest home-run hitter in Pirate history. Pie was a wise old son of a gun.

We finished the season in sixth place with an 81–81 record, far below our fans' expectations. I hit .271, with 20 homers and 73 RBIs, far below my expectations.

Several reasons were offered by various authorities for our disappointing season. Joe Brown blamed us, the players. Roberto, a fierce competitor who was possibly the most disappointed of all my teammates, blamed a few players for not giving a hundred percent.

Even the Pirates' travel plans caught some heat from the players and press, who were forced to work after enduring consistently late evenings.

But to me, the Pirate team of '67 suffered from a variety of symptoms. My poor showing didn't help matters much and neither did Clendenon's. Then there was our pitching, both starting and relief, that never materialized. There wasn't much continuity either. We possessed a lot of talent as individuals, but as a team we were at best an average squad. We never consistently brought all the right ingredients together.

My sense of humor was about all that survived the '67 season. In the wake of all the negative publicity the team received about dissension and fighting among teammates, I began referring to myself as the "fat, fighting outfielder."

But my humor did not capture the heart of Brown, who never softened his stand about my weight. He only altered his approach. Instead of placing me on a strength-draining, crash diet during the off-season, he decided to send me to Alex Martella, a local authority on fitness at the Pittsburgh Athletic Club. I was allowed to keep what weight I had, but I would have to be solid. "Conditioning will bring him to his correct weight," Martella was quoted as saying by a local newspaper.

I began working with Martella shortly after the end of the season. I worked ninety minutes daily on a variety of exercises, skipping rope, working over a punching bag, tossing a medicine ball.

While I was busy training for the season, Brown was readying the Buccos for 1968. The team was starving for two components, a spunky manager, who knew the Pirate players and specialized in pitching, and a veteran righthanded pitcher who could team with Veale to give the team a powerful one-two, rightie-leftie duo.

Unfortunately, Murtaugh took himself out of the picture before any decisions were made. Though I was hoping he'd change his mind, Danny was hired only as an interim manager. He refused the job because of his poor health. By the time Danny had been appointed to finish the season for Walker, we were completely out of the pennant race. His role at that time was to evaluate the playing personnel and report back to Brown, who used whatever information Danny provided to help him make a variety of decisions regarding the team.

Brown solved one of our problems by hiring Larry Sheppard,

who'd been my manager at Columbus, as our new skipper. Supposedly Shepp fit all the qualifications. He was known as a take-charge manager. He was also an authority on pitching. But after eighteen years in the minors, Shepp was somewhat inexperienced in dealing with major-league situations. At times, he allowed his youthful enthusiasm to run away with him.

"I expect the Bucs to win the pennant and I'll be very disappointed if they don't," he was quoted as saying shortly after being hired. I could see the same mistakes as in '67 rising again.

But the press immediately developed a liking for Shepp, who'd waited almost two decades to make the major leagues. The media blamed Walker for our poor showing. They drew comparisons between Walker and Sheppard and described the new Bucco manager as all that the former manager had failed to be. They described Shepp as a sincere, strict disciplinarian and a no-nonsense manager. There would not be any dissension on his club. As the press pumped all of Sheppard's virtuous qualities, Pittsburgh's confidence in us steadily grew. Fans began to believe that our failure in '67 had been a hoax.

Brown acquired our second-most-needed component on December 16 in the presence of Jim Bunning, a 184-game winner in the majors. To acquire the thirty-six-year-old veteran righthander, Brown had to send two of the Pirates' finest young players—pitcher Woodie Fryman and infielder Don Money—to the Philadelphia Phillies, along with two other lesser-known minor-leaguers. The Pirate management always believes in playing for the present, even when it may sacrifice its future. Bunning was the best righthanded starter we could have acquired.

With Bunning, Brown felt confident that we'd win the pennant, and the media echoed his sentiments. Sixty-seven was written off as a fluke. Though more cautiously than the year before, the Pirates were favored to capture the National League pennant.

Besides my daily workouts with Martella, I worked at making Pittsburgh my home. At that time, I had four children: Precious, Wendy, Dawn and my newly born son, Wilver, Jr., who I proudly insist struck an incredible resemblance to his father. Dolores and I set up house in the city's old but rustic east side and I began to civically circulate throughout the community.

The first area I touched was Pittsburgh's Hill District. A few decades before, the Hill had been one of the city's most attractive

This is my step-grandmother Ocie Stargell standing in the yard I used to play in as a young child in Earlsboro.

This is me. Grandpa called me Little Dumpy.

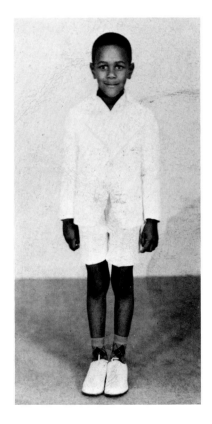

I was always a happy child who never minded posing in front of a camera.

At age nine I was as skinny as a rail. No wonder my mother force-fed me on the train ride back to Alameda from Orlando.

Upper left: The night of my graduation from Encinal High in 1958.

Above: A family gathering on Labor Day 1963 at our house in Oakland. Percy is sitting on the ground in the lower right-hand corner, Aunt Lucy is standing in the upper left-hand corner and Lois is the young lady kneeling in front of her.

Left: My father, William Stargell.

Lower left: Here are the projects in Alameda where I was raised. Sandrus, age three, is standing in the foreground. We lived in the apartment in the lower rear corner.

Below: Percy, Sandrus, age twelve, and my mom.

GRADUATION PHOTOS

Above, left to right: Robert Davis—"Girls are no problem to me, I can take them or let them be." Tommy Harper—"This guy is really on the beam. He's wanted on any team." Curtell Motton—"He will go places because he has the ability to lead others." Wilver Stargell—"Let me sing until I 'flat' myself to death."

Left: George Reed, my rookie high school baseball coach, who taught me a lot about being a veteran.

ENCINAL: we almost won it in '58. *Top row, from left:* E. Throckmorton (manager), G. Fenstermaker, M. Smith, W. Stargell, T. Harper, R. Davis, J. Lewis, T. White, D. Oakes (manager), B. Neuman (manager). *Bottom row:* J. Bownds, M. Millet, M. Jaramillo, D. Pinion, C. Motton, F. Elmore.

Top left: Vernon Law, the Deacon, and an inspiration to any man who ever played beside him.

Above, left: Spring training, 1962. I would meet my dream later that year when the Pirates would recall me from Columbus.

Above: Bill Virdon, whom I looked to for inspiration as a young player, makes a leaping catch behind Roberto. *(United Press International)*

Left: Sangy, Maury Wills and I at a spring training barbecue in 1968 *(right to left).*

Upper left: Dolores and I at spring training in the late sixties.

Upper right: Danny Murtaugh in a familiar pose in his rocking chair after a game at Three Rivers.

Left: Harry ''The Hat'' Walker argues with a home-plate umpire. *(Malcolm W. Emmons)*

Above: Larry Sheppard watches his troops practice on the field while Sangy passes by in the background.

Above: Dolores, me, Mom and Sandrus in front of Mom and Percy's house in East Oakland (right to left).

Upper right: My high school teammate Curt Motton as a Baltimore Oriole.

Right: Blazing Bob Veale in the early seventies, approximately ten years after he and I were recalled from Columbus.

Below: Just me giving away some more free chicken to my customers in the Hill District. *(Dan E. Stauffer)*

My old friend Roberto greets me at home plate after one of my 475 career homers.

I redeem myself by scoring the winning run in the 1971 World Series. Elrod Hendricks is the Baltimore catcher.

One of Roberto's sons kisses a poster of his deceased father.

The entire city of Pittsburgh mourned Roberto's death, as this display board on Mt. Washington shows.

areas. But in the late sixties it had become a low-income housing area and represented crime and filth to the citizens of Pittsburgh, much like the projects I grew up in. That's why I was so attracted to working with the Hill people, it reminded me of home. I felt I owed something to the individuals who had helped me along the way. What better way to repay them than to carry on their tradition of caring and kindness?

While working in the Hill District, I envisioned myself as a child growing up in the projects. I thought of some of my childhood buddies who hadn't been as fortunate as I. Many still roamed the streets in search of a dream. I worked with the children of the Hill in memory of my friends who hadn't made it.

At this time, I set a precedent for myself of always being associated with the underdog. It wasn't that I favored the poor over the rich, the retarded over the intellectual or blacks over whites. It's just that I circulated to where the most help was needed. I didn't consider myself special for what I did. I considered everyone I worked with as special—hard-working, normal people trapped within the limitations of society. I wanted to help free these people from what held them captive. I received as much satisfaction from associating with the poverty-stricken people of the Hill as from any group of people I would ever associate with in my life. While Shepp, Joe and the Bucs talked of a championship, I talked of life to kids who perhaps had never really known one.

Helping someone is what life is all about. It's not receiving that matters but giving. I was fired up for the '68 season. I had made some significant strides in my life and the lives of several others around me. I was happy with my new wife and family. I had nothing to worry about but baseball.

I was hungry and ached for a pennant that spring. I felt that we had a good chance in '68. Since we had come so close in '66, my memories only made me ache even more. I had tasted the sweet meat of a pennant race.

I also felt good about myself physically. I'd worked hard under Martella and done all that Joe had instructed me to do. I no longer worried about my weight. I was willing to do whatever was needed to bring a pennant home to Pittsburgh. I thought only of baseball. My prediction for 1968: a .330 batting average, with 50 homers and 140 RBIs.

But even with all I was thankful for and all that I had to look forward to, I was tight—not mentally but physically. After watching me take my first few swings of the spring, Shepp instructed me to work on exercises that would tone down my chest muscles. It was obvious that Martella's program had tightened and slowed me up.

I immediately began doing exercises to partly undo what I had spent all winter building. But 1968 was not a routine season anyway. Strange occurrences were expected, as evidenced by Brown's hiring of a psychiatrist to conduct motivational tests on me and my team-mates. The season progressively worsened from this point forward.

After we had compiled a 15–11 exhibition season record, our season came to an immediate halt with the assassination of Martin Luther King, Jr. Black major-leaguers, including myself, refused to play until after King's funeral. We canceled our final two exhibition games of the spring and postponed our first two regular season games.

I, like many millions of others, had learned a lot from King. He was a deeply religious leader, who allowed God to work through his life for the betterment of people. He led out of love and conviction for the Lord and not out of hatred for the white man. He loved and prayed for his enemies. To him the key to revolution was love, not hate.

King showed me what can be done with love. I adopted several of his theories for use in my own life. I try to inject love into every situation I run across. I also have learned that in times of need, love is the key, not hate or violence. Love soothes wounds, while hatred and violence deepen them.

King's giving of his life for the cause proved to me that the movement he started must continue at all costs. From King, I'd learned to deal with all the challenges in my life. He showed me that life is a test, a test before the Lord. Our score at the end of the test determines whether we pass the course and go on living or perish from his sight. I, like King, have always followed my calling and tried to pursue all activities in the name of love.

Baseball is a microcosm of our nation as a whole. It reflects every sway in this country's economy and morale. It rolls with every punch and adjusts itself to every situation. Baseball molds itself around life. The mold may change, but baseball always changes with it. Baseball survived World War I, the Great Depression, World War II, the Korean War. It has also survived strikes, scandals, bankruptcies and breakups. Baseball also survived the death of Martin Luther King,

122

Jr. Though his death left a gap in my heart, I instantly filled the void with knowledge from what he had taught me.

Soon the major-league diamonds throughout the country were once again decorated with players and the stands were filled with fans. Everything was back to normal. Roberto was chosen as the favorite to win the league's Most Valuable Player Award. Shepp was picked by many writers as the favorite to be named the National League's Manager of the Year, and the team was picked to finish first.

Shepp decided to make me his cleanup hitter. Much to my satisfaction, he pledged to start me every day against all types of pitches. He hoped his added confidence in my ability would push me to even greater heights as a player. But Shepp, somewhat unsure about himself, was quick to change his mind. Plagued by my muscle-bound torso, I slumped at the beginning of the season. He hedged on his commitment to me by appointing Clendenon as his cleanup hitter versus lefthanded pitching. His confidence was gradually swaying away from me.

"I think it's preventing him from getting around on pitches," the rookie manager told newsmen about my muscle-bound condition. "He's been taking exercises to loosen up, but the tightness is still there."

Also during this time, Roberto, who'd severely injured his right shoulder in an off-season mishap at his home in Puerto Rico, was suffering through the slowest start of his career. The former batting champ was hitting only .208 on May 13. Add to this the fact that our bullpen had blown several leads in the ninth inning and you'll understand the reason for Shepp's closed-door meeting on May 20. At the time we owned a 15–19 record and were only one slot away from the league's basement.

Fortunately for Shepp's blood pressure, the wind at Chicago's Wrigley Field was blowing out the next day. Wrigley is one of the few parks in the major leagues that is a total slave to the elements. With the help of the Wrigley wind, I hit three homers, drove in seven runs and stopped our five-game losing streak all the next day.

My outing started the team on a three-game winning streak and started me on a torrid trek through the National League. On June 3, I jumped my batting average to over .300 with 6 hits, including 2 homers and 6 RBIs, in a doubleheader versus Los Angeles. My efforts made me the league's leader in both home runs and RBIs.

Unfortunately, my teammates weren't able to keep pace. We remained in ninth place halfway through June, with the lowly Houston club nipping at our heels.

Finally, in late June, the Buccos caught fire and reeled off nine consecutive wins to up our record to 31–31. We moved into sixth place. Our fans and my teammates were once again high on our chances. But our success was short-lived. We lost several more games than we won in early July. On July 15 our record had slipped to 40–47, good enough for only seventh place in the league, seventeen games out of first place.

"I never saw a team so helpless. We can't do anything right. We can't hit, can't run, can't do anything," said Shepp, who was often quick to praise but also quick to discredit and who had already dropped twenty-six pounds because of worry.

During our bad stretch, I was meeting the outfield wall as much as the ball. And considering how well I was hitting, that was quite often. But I was determined to lead our team to victory. I believed in our ability. I would do anything to win. I saw crashing into walls after fly balls as a part of my job. I was learning that teams win games, not individuals.

Unfortunately, I had two painful collisions with outfield walls that significantly lessened my output for the remainder of the season. On June 23, I badly bruised the area around my mouth when I crashed into a scoreboard at Forbes Field en route to making a spectacular catch. Shortly after, I collided with another wall, was knocked unconscious and suffered severe facial lacerations. As a result, I began periodically having headaches. The headaches persisted. I tried wearing a neck brace, glasses, anything that would stop the pain. But nothing seemed to work. The neck brace didn't help and the glasses were too awkward. I decided to put up with the pain and to hold off trying any other remedies until the off-season.

By this time, Shepp had begun to panic. He forgot about my success in late May and early June, never considered my injuries and lost faith in my ability as a player. My production suffered from my injuries. But Shepp didn't understand and once again made me into a platoon player.

Frustrated and terribly confused, Shepp tried another closed-door meeting in mid-July. But nothing seemed to work. We'd already fallen too far too fast. We were miles away from the pennant race. We became the butt of our fans' jokes. One article in a Pittsburgh newspaper stated that we were guaranteed at least a sixth-place finish our next season. Of course, the same article also explained that the league was expanding to two six-team divisions the next year.

The most complimentary part of the '68 season was that the media and fans began to recognize me as a team leader. I was glad that my outgoing display of enthusiasm had done something for me, though I never tried to be a leader. That was never my objective. I only tried to be the best that I could possibly be. And that meant being whatever the team needed. But maybe that is the definition of a leader. I was just glad that my teammates responded so positively to me.

In a Bill Christine column in the Pittsburgh *Press* in July of '68, I was cited as the emotional leader of the Bucs. In the piece, Christine recognized Maz as the team captain, Roberto as the player representative and me as the club's emotional leader.

My ache to lead the team to the pennant was the reason for my enthusiasm. My collisions with the walls had been a tangible reflection of my efforts. But my frustration with failure, combined with my ever-present ache for victory, caused me to declare that I no longer cared to play the outfield. I wanted to give up challenging the walls. I didn't want to wear glasses the rest of my life. The collisions had just been too painful and too realistic. They had jolted some sense into my brain.

Though because of various injuries I only hit .237 in '68, I still led the club with 24 homers. Brown didn't want to trade me so it seemed only natural that he would try to find another position for me. First base was the only logical choice. But my switch wasn't the only change Joe was considering.

Joe was terribly dissatisfied with his team's play the last two seasons and sensed that a lot of changes needed to be made in a variety of areas. The Pirate farm system was overflowing with fine, young talent, and Brown knew he'd lose a few players in the expansion draft. "I'm sure there'll be many changes next year," he said.

Joe was right, several changes were made, but not only with the Bucs. The next year, 1969, was a turning point for the nation, the first year of the love generation. Their theme: I'd Rather Be Red Than Dead. Students led antiwar rallies and sit-ins on college campuses all across the nation while their parents retaliated with their theme: America, Love It or Leave It. Their parents were partial to patriotism and the American way. They proudly displayed small American flag decals in the rear windows of their automobiles. The flags supposedly represented support for the United States effort in the Vietnam War, exactly what their children, who wore the flags on the backside of their faded blue jeans, were protesting against.

Also on the liberal side, miniskirts became prevalent among the nation's youth, as did love beads, casual, colorful clothing and NBC's *Laugh-In* show. All were parts of the nation's metamorphosis.

As I said before, I see baseball as an extension of life in the United States, and major-leaguers weren't exempt from the changes taking place in the nation. The younger major-leaguers began wearing love beads and flashy clothing, while their older teammates still sported crew cuts. The younger wives also joined in the movement and were photographed by local newspaper photographers dressed in their miniskirts.

Brown was correct in his prediction—1969 was a year of metamorphosis for both baseball and the nation. The grand old game was changing right along with the nation. In an answer to fans' complaints that baseball was becoming a sport dominated by pitchers, the pitchers' mound was lowered, offering pitchers less of an advantage over hitters.

Baseball also began experimenting with ideas to increase the attendance at games. One idea being considered was the designated hitter, a player who was only in the lineup to take a pitcher's turns at bat. I didn't like the rule, and as I grew older I never considered becoming a DH to prolong my career. I wouldn't have felt like the complete player I wanted to be remembered as being. The idea of becoming a DH never entered my mind. Though the American League eventually adopted the DH in an attempt to bolster sagging ticket sales, I'm glad the National League never stooped quite as low to bring fans into the park.

In the flow of baseball's changes, Bowie Kuhn, a tall, confident, forty-two-year-old Manhattan lawyer, became Commissioner of Baseball. Kuhn's job was to transform the major leagues into profitable businesses. He immediately accepted responsibility for increasing the attendance around the majors. From this point forward, the attendance figure at games became as important as the final score. The transformation began slowly, but eventually the entire philosophy of baseball changed. It was no longer just a pastime. It became business.

Amongst Kuhn's inheritances was a legal battle with Players' Representative Marvin Miller, who was leading a fight to up the amount of capital placed in the players' pension fund each year. The players threatened to strike over the issue.

As you can see, the owners weren't the only ones who began viewing the game differently. The players, led by Miller, also began looking for a larger cut of the action. Kuhn tried to become a liaison between the two parties. But as he later found out, there is no one man anywhere in the world who alone can handle two parties as wealthy and influential as the owners and the players.

Along with baseball's new wave of ideas came divisional baseball. In '69, both leagues expanded by two teams, making twenty-four major-league franchises. The twelve teams in each league were then divided into two six-team divisions, with members of each division chosen on the basis of locality. We were placed in the Eastern Division with New York, Philadelphia, St. Louis, Chicago and the Montreal Expos.

Divisional play would create stiffer inter-team rivalries, added exposure and more revenue through expanded national television coverage. The more teams, the more divisions; the more divisions, the more play-off games; the more play-off games, the more games on national television; the more TV coverage, the more cash placed in the owners' pockets. The reason for expansion and divisional play was the ever-increasing costs of running a ball club.

Along with the expansion came the expansion draft. New teams need players. Major-league clubs were permitted to protect only a certain number of players on their forty-man roster; the rest were eligible to be drafted. Those players drafted would instantly become either Expos, San Diego Padres, Kansas City Royals or Seattle Pilots.

We lost four players in the draft: Mota, Wills and Clendenon were all claimed by the Expos, while McBean became a Padre. The loss of Clendenon appeared to open up a slot for me at first base. But Brown had other ideas. He never intended to play me anywhere else than in the outfield. He was considering two minor-league sensations, Bob Robertson and Al Oliver, for the first-base job. Brown also expected three other minor-leagues—third-baseman Rich Hebner, catcher Manny Sanguillen and shortstop Fred Patek—to make the club. Brown was planning a youth movement. Shepp agreed with the Pirate GM's move and stated that Hebner and Robertson would definitely be in his starting lineup.

But when spring training did open, about the only players who reported on time were rookies. Miller had called for all the veterans to strike over the pension issue. Camp opened without us. But I couldn't keep myself out of camp very long. I was itching to get started. I was the first big-name Pirate to sign a contract and report. I had too many obligations to myself, my family and my game to wait any longer.

Beginning in 1969, the Pirates had a new training site: Bradenton, Florida. Joe Brown had constructed our own training complex, Pirate City. Players would no longer be housed at the Bradford.

Pirate City resembled a roadside Holiday Inn with four baseball fields and a clubhouse in the rear. The complex boasted of several conveniences such as a cafeteria and office space for Pirate front office personnel. But its construction was purely a financial move by Brown, who was trying to offset the rising costs of the players' meal money. With the installation built, the Pirates were obligated to pay the players only $2 a week, the difference between their meal money and what it cost the club to house them at Pirate City.

By February 25, the players were given a sizable increase in their annual pension allotment, and the majority of my teammates reported directly to Bradenton. I weighed in at 225 pounds. Roberto reported with a sore arm. Shepp, a bit shell-shocked after his rookie year, was less boastful than in his previous season.

"The only thing I'm going to say about this club is that we'll be interesting," he said.

We were interesting. Roberto, still frustrated by the results of the team's showing in '68, chose to lash out at the sports writers. The right-fielder had been under a flow of constant criticism for quite some time. The press had accused him of not being a team player.

"The only people who criticize me are writers. You say I'm not a team player."

And he was probably correct in his thinking. No one on the team disliked Roberto. We all respected him both as a player and a person. The fans may have booed him at times, but usually they were only reacting to what a newspaperman had written about him.

The reporters didn't understand why Roberto lashed out at them. They thought that they were doing their jobs. But they never took any time to understand Roberto. Few people other than his teammates ever made such an effort.

The reaction of the Pittsburgh reporters was typical of the

media attitude toward Latin ball players, who enter a strange country with strange customs and a strange language and they basically don't know anyone. All they know is how to play baseball. Latin players are proud players and they become hurt when they are constantly made fun of. They don't understand why Americans laugh at them. Would we laugh at ourselves if we were in the same position in their country? Certainly not! But we're permitted to laugh at them when they go against one of our customs or misunderstand one of our gestures.

Roberto's frustration was a result of unfair criticism by the media. He died with each one of our losses. He was a leader, a perfect team player. No one wanted to win more than Roberto. His individual stats never mattered to him. What mattered was the success of the team. But just because Roberto played well while his teammates performed poorly, the writers wrote that he was only playing for individual glory. Yes, Roberto was proud of his accomplishments as a player but he thought first of the team.

Yes, '69 was an unusual year and we began it in an unusual fashion. To begin with, the statue of legendary third-baseman Honus Wagner, outside of Forbes Field, was defaced by Yippies the evening before our home opener. Next, Roberto, the most productive Pirate since 1960, was booed in his first trip to home plate, a result of his battle with the media. Third, we had become a relatively young club, whereas we had once been notable for our crafty veterans. The average age of a Pirate was twenty-five.

But even with all the confusion, we started off the season quite well. We were locked in second place for most of the early going, until May 18, when our record was chopped to below the .500 mark. Our pitching staff totally collapsed from that point forward. At the end of June, we were swept four straight games by the Cubs. By early July, we were unofficially eliminated from the pennant race. By July 8, slightly before the All-Star break, Shepp's status as our manager was considered shaky.

The oddest fact concerning the first half of the '69 season was that I was leading the league with an average above .340 at the All-Star break. A team player all the way, I felt terribly out of place. I was almost ashamed of my batting average. It wasn't my job to hit for average. It was my job to hit the long ball and drive in runs. My batting average made me feel as if I wasn't doing my job. But then, '69 was a very strange year.

Though I was leading the league in hitting, I wasn't chosen for the All-Star team. That didn't bother me; plenty of players were having great years. One player, the Detroit Tigers' Denny McLain, was chosen as one of the starting pitchers for the All-Star game, a dream come true for most hurlers, but he refused to go because he had a dentist appointment scheduled for the same time. About the only event that caused the citizens of this nation to momentarily halt their feuding was the landing of *Apollo* II. But once the *Apollo* II splashed down, it was back to the battle.

Our poor play in '69 affected everyone. We knew that we were a better team than we'd shown. On July 13 Shepp, who had already lost twenty-six pounds to worry, was taken to the hospital with chest pains. Pirate coach Bill Virdon was named as acting manager. Shepp was discharged three days later. His chest pains had been diagnosed as an insufficient flow of blood to his heart. It was obvious that he was on his way out as our manager.

Our poor showing also affected me, though my pain wasn't as obvious. I hid it behind my big, broad smile and a constant flow of jokes. But it was there. The ache to be on a championship team never left. I just didn't let anyone know.

I tried to be a more likable person in all respects. The best defense is often a good offense. I declared all Sundays as Ladies' Days in Pittsburgh. I refused to sign autographs for anyone but the ladies on Sundays. If the boys couldn't get me to sign between Monday and Saturday, then they wouldn't be able to get my autograph at all. The media picked up on my idea and everyone got a kick out of reading about it. With all my jokes, pranks and smiles, I was only trying to make myself forget the ache I felt inside, but it never went away. I hurt worse than anyone. I couldn't stand losing, especially when I knew we were a better team than we had shown. I was a winner.

I hit .307, with 29 homers and 92 RBIs in '69, but I would rather have batted .000 and finished in first place. About the only highlight of our season was when Bob Moose, a young pitcher in only his second full year in the majors, pitched a no-hitter versus the Mets on September 21. The low part of the season came when Shepp was axed with only five games left in the season. Alex Grammas, one of our coaches, was named as our interim manager. And in a surprise move, Danny Murtaugh was rehired shortly after the conclusion of the season.

On the national front, St. Louis outfielder Curt Flood refused to accept being traded to Philadelphia. Flood's veto nixed a seven-player deal between the two clubs. Such behavior had been unheard of before in major-league circles. A large court battle between Marvin Miller and the owners soon followed.

A true representation of how strange a year 1969 was could be found in the winner of the World Series that season. After a rash of mysterious plays and unheard-of reversals, New York's amazing Mets defeated heavy favorites, the Baltimore Orioles, to capture the crown. I remember the '69 Mets better than any team I ever played against, not because of their tremendous talent but because of their magic. Man for man, we were twice the team they were. But they had the magic. They won games they should have lost, and in the oddest of fashions.

They beat us with miracle plays. Balls that should have been home runs would bounce off the top of outfield fences and into the glove of an unsuspecting Met outfielder, whose miraculous throw would nab the tying run at home plate. We were snakebit by the Mets, but then so were all the other teams. We just kept asking ourselves, How can we lose to this team? But we did, and the Mets were crowned World Champs in 1969, a very strange year.

The team Brown planted in 1969 bloomed in '70. Our luck as a team changed. Good things happened for us in 1970. For me personally, my youngest child Kelli was born during the off-season. Next, Danny Murtaugh was back as our manager. And third, Three Rivers Stadium, the new home of the Pirates, was due for completion during the season.

I forgot all about 1969 and set my sights on '70. Though I still ached inside, I wanted to win the pennant. I hoped this would be our year. We were loaded with talent. We had plenty of hitters. We had Al Oliver, who hit .285, with 17 homers and 70 RBIs for us in '69, and Bob Robertson, who hit 34 homers at Columbus, battling for the first-base job. Manny Sanguillen—Sangy—who hit .303 in '69, was our catcher. Richie Hebner, .301 the previous season, was our third-baseman; dependable Gene Alley was our shortstop; Maz was at second; Alou, .331 in '69, was in center; Roberto was in right field and I was in left.

From a player's standpoint, I felt that there was no way we could be beaten. But most sports writers disagreed with me. Most picked us to finish fourth in the National League East, behind Chicago, New York and St. Louis. The Dodgers and the Baltimore Orioles were favorites to make the World Series.

But I rarely listened to sports writers anyway, because most had never even played baseball themselves. Sports writers are writers first and authorities later. Few have ever felt the depression of a losing streak, the blisters on a hitter's hands or the pressure of a pennant race. Sports writers compose vicariously. They are educated spectators. They base their predictions on statistics, though only a fourth of what happens in a game shows up in a box score. Sports writers bet on the favorites. That's why we were picked to finish fourth. No sports writer in his right mind would risk his reputation by choosing the third-place Pirates of '69 to finish in first place a year later.

There were too many intangibles that the writers hadn't taken into account in making their predictions. One of the intangibles was Danny Murtaugh. He was just what we needed. He was confident and strong. He knew the game like no one else in baseball. We could look to Danny for guidance. He never crumbled. He was our Rock of Gibraltar, a true leader.

Danny inherited a talented but diverse crew of players. No two Pirates were the same. We had whites, blacks and Latins from all socioeconomic backgrounds. Each Bucco had to be handled separately. Each of us had our own style.

There was Sangy—he was a humorous, lovable Panamanian, who was a free swinger at the plate. Sangy would swing at any ball he could reach with his bat. There was Roberto, strong, straight-laced, a leader by example. There were Hebner and Robertson, two wild and crazy white guys. There was Al Oliver, strong, black, talented and quiet. There was Dock Ellis, loud, some thought obnoxious, radical, talented but deep inside a pussycat. The list goes on and on. No two Buccos were the same. We resembled a meeting of the United Nations.

To squeeze every ounce of potential out of me and my teammates, Danny had to treat each one of us individually. Danny began by simply letting us play. He didn't boggle our minds with too many rules and policies. He allowed us to be ourselves both on and off the field. We no longer felt like robots, we felt like people.

Danny was also patient with each one of us. He trusted each of us and very rarely swayed from his game plan. I started off the season with an 0–23 slump, but Danny's confidence in me never swayed. He just kept penciling me in the lineup each day. In fact, I was going so bad that I even considered holding a promotion to give away free chicken in my All-Pro restaurant when I got my first hit of the season.

I had opened the restaurant in the Hill District before the beginning of the season. It seemed like a perfect location for a chicken restaurant. There wasn't one for two miles in any direction. I felt the restaurant would survive on the convenience factor alone. But before the season, I decided to help promote sales.

I chose to give away free chicken to any customer who had an order placed when I hit a home run. "Chicken on the Hill with Will," we called it. The idea spread like wildfire. Soon my restaurant was packed with customers during Pirate games.

Bob Prince, the Gunner, a very close friend of mine and the radio and television voice of the Pirates, often took the gimmick to extremes. "Spread some chicken on the Hill, Will," Bob would often yell as I approached the plate. Bob, who thrived on emotion and hype, once became so involved in one of our games that he promised to pay for all the chicken purchased at my restaurant that evening if I delivered with a homer in my next at-bat.

Of course I hit a homer, and the people of the Hill, most of whom were either poverty-stricken or on relief, went wild. Every piece of chicken in the restaurant was devoured. Police and guard dogs had to be called out to restrain the crowds. I lightened Bob's wallet of about $800 worth of wings, legs and breasts.

Danny was never as emotional as Bob, and his quiet confidence in us paid off immediately. We won eleven of nineteen games in April and were in second place at the end of the month. My hitting had improved slightly, but my brilliance ran mostly in spurts. For example, though at the time I was struggling for a base hit, I hit two homers onto the right-field roof of Forbes Field in the final week of April.

But the main topic of conversation in Pittsburgh was not our fast start or my memorable blasts onto the roof of Forbes Field but the construction of our new stadium. Construction updates and feature stories detailing the advantages of the modern, multi-purpose stadium appeared in local newspapers daily. Though our record slumped slightly in May and the early part of June, our production picked up significantly as we neared the completion of our stadium.

My teammates and I were no better than the average fan when it came to the new stadium. Every major-leaguer loves to play in front of big crowds and in beautiful stadiums. Major-leaguers are proud of the stadiums in which they play. Three Rivers was being described as one of the most beautiful stadiums ever built. We couldn't wait to move in.

The stadium wouldn't be just a nice place for us to play. It would be an opportunity to vacate the history of Forbes Field and start a new tradition of our own. We wanted a new image. Three Rivers would give us a new start, a second wind. We were on the brink of stardom and we wanted to reach it in Three Rivers. We wanted the stadium's first year to be our best season.

Like the fans, we closely followed the progress of the stadium's construction. We were happy to hear that it was moving along smoothly. But like everyone else, we feared that the completion date would be moved back because of bad weather, labor disputes and strikes.

As we entered the second week of June, we began to pick up our pace. On June 12, my roommate, Dock Ellis, pitched a 2–0 no-hitter over the Padres in the first game of a doubleheader. Dock's no-hitter marked the second consecutive season that a Pirate hurler had accomplished such a feat.

Though we had extremely different personality traits, Dock and I were extremely close friends at the time. He was the Muhammad Ali of the major leagues. He loved to taunt his opponents. The press thought Dock was a rebel, but deep inside he was one of the nicest, most sincere people I had ever met. He only showed that side of himself when he was away from the public eye.

When the spotlight hit him, he'd change completely. He was a Malcolm X type leader, while I believed more in the teachings of Martin Luther King, Jr. Dock tried to do as much as he could to help the black people of this country whenever he could. That's the reason he carried his façade to such extremes. He tried to lead the blacks of this country by example.

On the field, Dock was a fierce competitor who loved to win. I did some of my best hitting with Dock on the mound. In fact, I scored both runs in his no-hitter, with my eleventh and twelfth homers of the season. Though we were different in many ways, we always supported each other well, both on and off the field.

We closed out Forbes Field in late June by winning our last

seven games at the old park. The field was eulogized by dozens of city and baseball officials before the game. Thousands of souvenir-seeking fans dismantled much of the park after our 4–1 win over the Cubs. But my biggest memory of the afternoon was not found in an old seat or a piece of the scorecard. What I remember most about that day is that our win moved us into a first-place tie with the Mets. That's what mattered most to me.

We were now officially in the pennant race. Our young team reacted well to the added pressure. We won nine of our next thirteen games, all on the road, and moved into sole possession of first place on July 11. At the All-Star break a day later, we sported a 50–39 record and were in first place, one and one-half games ahead of the Mets.

Our next game was scheduled for July 16 versus the leaders of the Western Division, the Cincinnati Reds. We were scheduled to play our first game in Three Rivers that day, the answer to several dreams come true. First, my ache to be in a pennant race had left me. Our confrontation with the Reds would be a classic—the two best teams in the league meeting for the opening of one of the world's most beautiful stadiums. Chills ran up and down my spine each time I thought of it. The game would ignite one of the most fiercely played rivalries in the seventies. We and the Reds would become archenemies from this point forward.

I didn't care that I wasn't chosen to play in the All-Star game that year, and to most fans Roberto didn't seem to care that he *was* chosen. As part of his plan to raise attendance figures in major-league parks throughout the country, Baseball Commissioner Bowie Kuhn had decided to involve the fans more in the sport. Thus, he turned the voting for the All-Star game over to them. Roberto was chosen as a backup outfielder, the only Bucco on the squad. But since he'd been suffering from chronic neck problems during the first half of the season, he initially decided to bypass his appointment to the All-Star squad. The fans were insulted. But after a few weeks of negative publicity, Roberto changed his mind and decided to accept the invitation, another case of misunderstanding by both media and fans.

Roberto hadn't turned down the invitation to insult anyone. He was simply a team player solely devoted to helping the Pirates win the pennant. He felt that he would be better suited to help the team if he used the All-Star break to undergo treatment. But his gesture was incorrectly perceived by the fans. That's why he eventually reversed his decision and decided to play. He didn't want to hurt anyone's feelings.

Roberto's pinch-hit sacrifice fly in the ninth inning of the All-Star game scored Joe Morgan from third base and knotted the score at 4–4. The Nationals eventually won the game in the twelfth inning, when the Reds' Pete Rose bowled over Indians catcher Ray Fosse with the winning run.

While Roberto was struggling with the media and listening to the boos of the All-Star game fans, I was dreaming of playing in Three Rivers. I was like a kid on Christmas Eve who couldn't wait to open his presents. I dreamed of the big crowds, artificial turf, our new tradition and my increased home-run production. Forbes Field had been one of the most spacious parks in baseball, especially in right field, my power alley.

Three Rivers would be symmetrical. It would be 340 feet down the foul lines, 385 feet in the power alleys and 410 feet to straightaway center field. Dolores, who had carefully charted my progress the year before, predicted that I would have hit an additional 22 homers if I had been playing in Three Rivers instead of Forbes Field.

I also had plenty of other reasons for wanting to move into Three Rivers. To match our new home, we were going to be given brand new uniforms. The uniforms were not scheduled to be unveiled until the sixteenth. We were planning on surprising our fans.

The new uniforms were every bit as modern as our new stadium. They had a unique double-knit construction, with form-fitting jerseys and tailored pants. Unlike the loose-fitting wool uniforms we wore at Forbes Field, the new uniforms were light and durable. The word "Pirates" was printed in Gothic letters across the front of our jerseys, while a matching "P" decorated the front of our new gold caps. I shook with excitement when I thought about wearing the new uni.

Our new clubhouse was also a sight to behold. At Forbes Field we'd been shoehorned into a tiny clubhouse, but the Three Rivers clubhouse resembled that of a country club. There was room enough to ride a bicycle around the room, and it had wall-to-wall indoor-/outdoor carpeting. Moving to Three Rivers was like moving from an apartment into a house. The atmosphere of a team's clubhouse is often overrated. But to major-leaguers, the clubhouse is their office, since they often spend up to eight hours a day there.

But even with our new stadium, new uniforms, new clubhouse and close to 50,000 fans to cheer us on, we couldn't beat the powerful Reds in Three River's opener. In a relief role, Clay Carroll of the Reds defeated Dock by a 3–2 score. Though we only got five hits in the entire game, one of them was the 490-foot blast I hit to right field in the sixth inning that tied the score at 2–2.

I received $1000 for hitting the homer, or $975 net after paying for the chicken I spread around the Hill, from Fred Babcock of the Babcock Lumber Company, who told Danny before the game that they would award a grand to the first Pirate to hit a homer at Three Rivers. Tony Perez of the Reds, who hit a two-run homer in the fifth, marking the first round-tripper hit in the new stadium, mildly contested not receiving a grand himself.

The opening of Three Rivers also showcased another important event in Pittsburgh baseball history: the breaking of the sex barrier in the Pirate pressbox. Beth Dunlap of the Pittsburgh *Press,* who was scheduled to cover the opener, was the first woman writer to enter the pressbox at a Pirate game—and, may I add, not inconspicuously. Beth Dunlap's appearance opened the door for a new era of sports reporting in Pittsburgh.

Moving into Three Rivers solidified us as a team. We'd been freed of all the traditions of Forbes Field. We were writing our own record book. We all loved playing there. We felt so free. After slumping in the first half of the season, I hit a potent .290 in the second half. On August 1, I exploded for five extra base hits, three doubles and two homers, to lead us to a 20–10 win over the Braves in Atlanta. On August 10, I hit my first homer into the upper deck at Three Rivers. The switch to Three Rivers was definitely good for me and great for the team.

From July 16 to the conclusion of the season, we fell out of sole possession of first place for only four days. We fell into second place, behind the Mets, on July 31 and August 1 before regaining sole control of the top spot on August 2.

Then in early September, as the pennant race intensified, we dropped three consecutive games on September 7, 8 and 9 and fell into a first-place tie with the Mets, while the Cubs nipped at our heels only one game behind. But we regained our momentum by winning twelve of our next seventeen games and clinched the National League Eastern Division pennant on September 21 with a 2–1 victory over the Mets.

Winning the pennant had been a total team effort. Danny had effectively used each player on the club. We were fortunate to have such able replacements as infielders Dave Cash and Jose Pagan and outfielder John Jeter. Their presence helped to absorb the pressure placed on the team by a rash of injuries. Roberto constantly suffered from a sore neck. Maz was still recovering from the leg he had injured in '69, Gene Alley was bothered by a thumb injury and I suffered most of the season from a bruised heel. Our bench never let us down.

As always, our forte was our hitting. Though Roberto played in only 108 games, he still led the team with a .352 batting average. Bob Robertson, who hit 27 homers and drove in 82 runs, gave us power from the right side of the plate. Oliver hit 12 homers and drove in 83 runs. Sangy finished second in the league with a .325 batting average and I led the team with 31 homers and 85 RBIs.

On the pitching side, we sported five starters with at least ten wins each—Steve Blass, who suffered a broken arm only halfway through the season, Dock, Moose, Veale and Luke Walker, who led the team with a 15–6 record. Our bullpen was paced by Dave Giusti, whom we'd acquired from St. Louis in the off-season. Dave finished the year with a 9–3 record and a 3.02 ERA.

But it was Danny who molded all our components together into a championship team. Unlike his two previous predecessors, he allowed us to play our own brand of baseball. He didn't try to make us into something that we weren't. Danny was also our confidence-builder. We were a young team, and his wisdom pulled us through the pennant race. Danny rightly deserved it when he was chosen as the National League's Manager of the Year.

But our season wasn't over yet. We still had to face the Western Division Champions, the Reds, in a best-of-five game face-off for the right to go to the World Series. Our clubs were very basic and very similar. We both relied on our hitters to win. While we were led by Roberto, Robertson, Sangy, Oliver, Alou and me, the Big Red Machine sported Tony Perez, Pete Rose, Lee May, Johnny Bench and Bobby Tolan. In addition to their hitters, the Reds also boasted of a handful of steady starting pitchers and a group of tough relievers.

The only advantage that the Reds had over us was their experience and the fact that the final three games of the play-off were scheduled to be played in Cincinnati. Most baseball authorities felt that we had to win the first two games to stand any chance of winning the series. But Danny was untouched by the pressure. "The bases are still ninety feet apart at their park, too, aren't they?"

Oddly enough, we and the Reds battled to a 0–0 tie through nine innings of the first game. Dock had held the powerful Reds to only six hits. But leading off the tenth inning, the Red's pinch-hitter Ty Cline tripled to right field. Pete Rose, the next batter, ended the scoreless tie by bouncing a single to right, which sent Cline in for the score. Two hitters later, both Rose and Bench, who had walked, scored on Lee May's double. The Cincinnati relief corps held us scoreless in the tenth, and the Reds took a 1–0 lead in the series.

The second game went much like the first. Luke Walker pitched brilliantly for us but we didn't give him any offensive support. A combination of three different Cincinnati pitchers held us to five hits, while former Pirate farmhand Bobby Tolan accounted for all three Cincinnati runs. I went 0-for-4 in the game, including flying out in the sixth inning with two on and two out, one of our rare scoring opportunities. We lost by a 3–1 score.

We entered Cincinnati's Riverfront Stadium for Game Three with our backs to the wall. Again our pitching held the Big Red Machine down. We were tied 2–2 through seven innings. In the eighth, Cline, pinch-hitting again, walked and advanced to second on Rose's single to left. Tolan then drilled a no-balls, two-strike pitch to me in left for a single. Seeing Cline rounding third base, I hurried my throw. The ball landed two feet wide of home plate. Cline scored easily. The Reds were on their way to the World Series and we were on our way home.

I was named as the Pirates' most valuable player in the series. I was given a brand new automobile. But I would have traded that car in a minute for another chance to drive the Buccos to the World Series.

We were disappointed with our showing against Cincinnati but not with our season. Hidden beneath our bowed heads and gloomy faces was a quiet optimism that we would be back the next year. We learned a lot that season. We would be a better team in 1971. My only worry was whether Danny would be back with us. Because of his health, he hadn't yet accepted Brown's offer to manage the Pirates again in '71. For everyone's sake, I prayed that he would.

The following off-season was extremely unusual for me. Instead of relaxing in Pittsburgh, I vacationed in Vietnam. A few weeks after the season and what felt like a hundred injections of vaccine later, on November 21, Bob Prince (the Gunner), Pirate reliever Mudcat Grant, the Braves' Phil Niekro and Ed Watt, and Merv Rettenmund of the Orioles and I were off to Vietnam on a USO hospital tour. We spent five weeks in Asia.

We were devastated by what we saw. On one of our first helicopter flights, we almost crashed because of the monsoons. The rain was so thick that our pilot couldn't see the ground. The Gunner and I formed a very tight partnership on the trip. We both kissed the ground when the helicopter landed safely.

Though I'd heard how bad the conditions in Vietnam were, I'd never experienced anything so shocking. On our initial hospital visit, the first patient I saw was a soldier burned from head to toe. I'd never seen anything so severe. I felt so sorry for him yet I was so shocked that I began to get sick. I ran out of the tent and threw up. Then I began to cry. Bob followed me outside. Though I wasn't a drinking man, the Gunner lifted me off the ground and pulled me into the nearest bar. We quickly proceeded to down a fifth of whiskey to calm our nerves.

As we continued our tour, I became more accustomed to such scenes, yet I struggled to place all that I was feeling into perspective. After visiting all those soldiers and listening to the constant roar of artillery mortars and guns in the background, I changed my definition of a hero. To these soldiers I was visiting, I was a hero because I could hit a little white ball a long way. Most had dreamed of becoming baseball players just as I had. Vicariously, I related to them extremely well.

But after seeing them, I couldn't possibly consider myself a hero. The biggest risk I took in my profession was striking out, but these boys were playing with their lives. They gave their limbs, their eyes, their ears, their sanity and their lives to win. And as a whole, they weren't given any credit. They had no cheerleaders, no fan support, and their faces never appeared in *Sports Illustrated.* But they had guts and conviction and they were fighting for us.

Visiting them helped me to realize who the true heroes really are in this world. It's not the home-run hitter or the quarterback who can throw a football eighty yards. A hero is a person who gives his life to save ours. All the participants in all the wars were heroes. Heroes are also the doctors, surgeons, scientists and biologists who give their entire lives to curing a disease or keeping us alive.

I'm flattered each time a fan asks me for my autograph, but I don't really feel that I deserve all the applause. I always remember one soldier who especially caught my attention. He had lost all his limbs, a quadruple amputee. The Gunner and I were shocked when we first spotted him. But then we looked at his face. Expecting a look of grave desperation, we were even more shocked to see a big smile on the soldier's face. He was just happy to be alive. He is my hero still today. I think of him often and vividly remember that smile on his face. It was hard for me to accept that I was this man's hero when all I had done for a living is hit little white balls.

My experience in Vietnam, combined with a circumstance concerning one of my kids, led me to want to contribute in a different way. During the '70 season, my daughter Wendy began having fainting spells. When the spells continued, we took her to our family doctor, who after a series of tests told us that Wendy had traits of sickle-cell anemia, the great slayer of Negroes in America. Sickle cell indirectly weakens its victims in a variety of ways. No one has ever died from sickle cell, only from the other diseases it causes or from the death of an organ that it affects.

Naturally, I was extremely worried about Wendy, even after the doctor told us that he could control her condition with medication. But her condition, in combination with what I'd seen in Vietnam, caused me to want to do something to help. I wanted to fit my own definition of a hero.

After doing some research, I discovered that sickle cell was one of the most widely spread but least researched diseases in the country. I wanted to help find a cure but I had almost no knowledge of the subject—I wasn't a doctor or a scientist. So I decided to use my influence as a national sports figure to help raise money for the cure of the disease. I spoke with Hank Aaron in Atlanta, who sponsored an annual bowling tournament each off-season to raise money for the Atlanta Sickle Cell Foundation. I decided to do the same thing in Pittsburgh.

I sponsored the tournament for over ten consecutive years. Each year, more and more celebrities agreed to attend, and I raised more and more money for the Willie Stargell Foundation, which I founded to collect money for sickle-cell research. I enjoyed the tournaments and became extremely happy with our turnout. We raised a substantial amount of money for sickle-cell research each winter, and each year I gave approximately $10,000 out of my own pocket to sponsor the tournament.

But in the early 1980s, I was late on getting the taxes done and we had to close the doors until we got what was needed together. After I understood what I had been doing wrong, the Lord showed me a side of myself I had not seen before. I was limiting my influence too much. By causing me to close the foundation, He was actually nudging me to achieve greater heights, to start a national campaign. I eventually was named to serve on the National Advisory Board in Washington, D.C., by the president of the United States. There is justice in each situation we encounter, but it's up to us to use the Lord's will to benefit our lives. With my work with sickle cell, I am helping to save lives, and I feel like a hero and not just like a guy who hits little white balls a long ways.

Like the experience with the closing of my foundation, I allowed our play-off demolition at the hands of the Reds to work for me. I entered spring training of 1971 with a slightly altered perspective on the game. I also think all of my teammates had changed slightly during the off-season. We weren't kids any more. We had had the entire off-season to think over our defeat at the hands of the Reds. We now knew what we had to do. We had been to the mountain and this time we didn't want to come down.

Silently, we went about our work. No one said anything about our chances. But then we didn't have to. We knew we had the talent. But it was still up to us to win. The magic, that rare competitive instinct that infects an entire team, was there. We were confident of our chances, we were ready for whatever the season would bring.

Even Danny shunned his worries over his poor health and returned. He felt the magic, he knew we had the team, though he wasn't quite as vocal as Joe Brown.

"This is the best-rounded, most talented club I've had since I've been in Pittsburgh," barked Brown.

"I just hope this club is as good as Joe thinks it is," followed Danny.

Our fans sensed our potential and were behind us one hundred percent. Led by the Gunner, they carried a war cry of "Beat 'Em Bucs." Everyone favored us, even the Las Vegas bookies rated us as 9–5 favorites to again capture the National League East. But we never boasted. We saved all our energy for our job on the field. I myself was more ready for the '71 season than in any of my previous years in the majors. During the off-season, I had learned a lot about life. I'd matured like a fine wine.

We started off the season by winning eighteen of our twenty-five spring training games. I led a pack of .300 hitters, with a .375 batting average. A few changes had been made. Jackie Hernandez, who was acquired from Kansas City during the off-season, would be our starting shortstop on Opening Day. Gene Alley broke his left hand in spring training, and Hernandez was acquired as his replacement. And we'd traded Alou to the Cardinals in January for Vic Davalillo, a pinch-hitter/backup outfielder.

We opened the season at Three Rivers on April 6, the first time in sixty-two years that a Pirate opener hadn't been held at Forbes Field. We won the opener by a 4–2 score and went on to capture our next two games.

I was happier playing at this time than any other time in my life. Winning attitudes breed confidence, and confidence breeds happiness and success. I no longer felt the pain in my knees, the crick in my pelvis or the fear of colliding with an outfield wall. I was playing the game two feet above the ground.

I was also hitting home runs at a record pace. I hit nine in our first fifteen games and eleven for the entire month of April. At first the media overlooked my rapid pace. I didn't mind, though, because then I wasn't under the constant pressure of their questioning. I was well ahead of Babe Ruth's 60-home-run pace set in 1927 and I far exceeded Roger Maris's record-setting 61-homer pace set in 1961. I also hit three homers twice in one game in April. But still my home-run total wasn't what mattered to me. What I always cared about was the team's record.

After I hit my record-breaking eleventh homer on April 29, the media gathered five feet deep around my locker. We had lost the game by a 2–1 score to the Dodgers, but I had established a new mark for the most homers ever hit in April. I was far from elated. How does it feel to break the record? Can you keep up the pace? Do you know that Ruth didn't hit his eleventh until his thirty-fourth game of the season and that Maris didn't connect on his eleventh until forty games into the season? Do you know that at this pace you'll have ninety-four homers at the end of the year?

I'm sure that I was anticlimactic! I told them I was swinging for the team and not myself, not what they wanted to hear but the truth just the same. In baseball, or any other team sport, team victories are where the glory lies.

Even though I played down my achievements, I was still chosen as the National League's Player of the Month. I was named on fifty-eight of the sixty ballots. I was flattered by the rave response but I still would have traded the award for a win or two more in April. We entered May with a 12–10 record and third place in the division.

But as I learned, talented athletes don't win pennants alone. They need a winning attitude to guide them along. That was the difference on the 1971 Pirate team. We had a calm, confident attitude that only true champions possess. That was the difference between the '71 team and all the other talented Pirate teams I had been a member of.

We specialized in hitting the ball. We had tremendous faith in our ability to score runs. Though our pitching was far from being the best in the league, our pitchers knew that if they held an opponent below eight runs they had an excellent chance to win the game. They never worried if they gave up a lot of runs early. They knew that we'd get the runs back for them and in 99 percent of the cases we did.

But what is the basis for a winning attitude? How does one stimulate one's teammates to play their best? The key is confidence —without it, a team plays like a flock of blind sheep. Our pennant-winning season the year before had helped build our confidence for us. We now knew we could win; we'd proved that the season before. There were no rookies left on the club. We all played like veterans.

Even being swept by the Reds in the play-offs built character. Sure, we were embarrassed initially, but after that wore off each one of us learned from the experience and modified our attitude to cope with the failure. We used the defeat to our benefit. We had felt the pressure and lived the experience. We knew what it was to lose, which showed us what it took to win. Lesser individuals may have fallen prey to the defeat, but not the Buccos. We were back as a stronger, more cohesive, more intelligent squad in '71.

Along with the ever-confident Murtaugh, Roberto and Maz were strong contributors to the club's attitude. Both had felt the pressure of a pennant race several times before. Both led by example. Roberto kept our fighting spirit finely tuned. He was a fierce competitor who wasn't afraid to kick you in the behind if your performance slipped. He was also the finest all-around player in the major leagues at the time. Just to watch him play inspired us to give it that extra ten percent. Each one of us wanted to be like Roberto. He taught us to take pride in ourselves, our team and our profession.

Maz was nearing the end of his career in '71. He'd entered spring training as an underdog to young Dave Cash at second base. But he played his heart out that spring and won a spot in the opening-day lineup. Maz taught us to be consistent and to worry more about loving the game than losing a game. He showed us that love is the key to success. Maz loved playing baseball. Nothing made him happier than playing baseball. We borrowed a bit of that magic for our own lives in '71.

Besides contributing with my bat, I also took it upon myself to keep everyone loose. A lot of us were pranksters, so my job wasn't terribly difficult. But the players who most needed my attention were not the veterans but the rookies, who were often excluded from clubhouse pranks and camaraderie. I took it upon myself to make them feel a part of the team.

It's difficult for a young player to adjust to the major leagues. Most are intimidated by the entire idea. All that I tried to do was make them feel part of the team. Everybody needs a pat on the back occasionally, even veterans, and when they needed it, I gave it to them.

I learned that lesson quickly in my career. In the first few years I was with the Pirates, I hit bottom one day and wished someone would have been there to help pick me up. I'd struck out seven consecutive times in a doubleheader. On my eighth at-bat, I popped out to the catcher. The crowd gave me a standing ovation. I hurt so bad that I cried. Each time I saw one of our guys hanging their head, I thought of that experience and rushed over to give them that much-needed pat on the back.

Not all established major-leaguers realize that the difference between themselves and a young player may be only a few years and a touch of experience. Veterans are often afraid of losing their job to a rookie. They forget about what's best for the team and think only of themselves. Most forget that a team is only as good as its weakest member. I took it upon myself to help strengthen our weakest members, and all it usually took was a simple pat on the back when they were down.

I feel that my consideration towards Hebner, Oliver, Robertson, Sangy, Blass, Dock and Moose helped them to mature quicker and more efficiently as major-leaguers. All they needed was to feel a part of the team, to feel needed. The smoother the transition, the more effective the player produces in the long run.

We had the correct attitude in '71. We had all the needed ingredients—confidence, pride, love for our profession, leadership, cohesiveness, experience and maturity. Each organization needs every one of these ingredients to develop the correct attitude. If even only one of these factors is missing, it will show up in the box scores. But if all are present, the potential of the organization's workers is limitless. They will depend on one another, work with one another and succeed together. They will become a self-sufficient working force and will rely only on one another to survive.

That was our team. We bound together tightly in a pinch and would come out smelling like a rose. Even when Danny was taken to the hospital before our game with Cincinnati on May 20 with chest pains, we didn't collapse. We just bound tighter together. We learned to depend on one another more. We had just moved into first place at the time, and Bill Virdon took over for Danny in his absence.

Even with Danny gone we played well. Though we dropped out of first place, that look of determination never left our eyes. On May 30, I hit a homer into the upper deck at Three Rivers. It was the second homer that I had hit there. On May 30, May 31 and June 1, Moose, Blass and Dock hurled consecutive shutouts over the Cubs in a Memorial Day homestand.

On June 6, Danny was released from the hospital. Fortunately, the doctors found him in good health. Four days later, Blass beat the Cards in St. Louis and we moved into first place again. From that point on, we played like champions. We won twenty-two of our next thirty games and were in first place at the All-Star break by nine games, with a 57–31 record.

I had set a major-league record with my 28 homers through the end of June. I was in the correct flow. I led the league with 30 homers and 87 RBIs at the All-Star break. I finished third in the voting for National League All-Star outfielder. This was the first season since 1966 that I'd been chosen as an All-Star. I was excited, but I was more excited about our team's record. Dock, Roberto and Sangy were also named to the team that year.

But slightly before mid-season, when I had tried to field a ball, my left shoe had got caught in between the dirt surrounding first base and the outfield turf. I had badly twisted my knee. At the time, my other knee was also causing me problems. Because of my inability to pivot with my left leg at the plate, my rate of production dropped significantly. Danny was well aware of the pain I was feeling. He and a few others even suggested that I undergo immediate surgery to repair the left knee. But I declined. There was no way I was going to miss the '71 season. I knew that something very special was waiting for us just around the corner.

We slumped slightly in the beginning of August, winning only eight of our first twenty-three games. Our lead slipped to four and a half games. I went over 100 RBIs during that period. The experts calculated that I needed at least one homer in every three games to break the single-season National League mark of 56 set by Hack Wilson.

Because of my aching knees, I never regained my first-half form, but my teammates did well just the same. After our slight slump, we won twenty-two of our next thirty-three and clinched the N.L. East pennant on September 22 with a 5–1 win over the Cards. The Buccos were once again called the Pride of Pittsburgh. Maz said that it felt just like it did in 1960.

Our next foe was the San Francisco Giants and Candlestick Park. The Giants had narrowly captured the pennant by one game over the Dodgers. They were led by forty-year-old center-fielder Willie Mays, pitcher Juan Marichal and first-baseman Willie McCovey.

The Giants were a good team, but our biggest enemy was said to be Candlestick Park. Candlestick, slightly down the beach from where I grew up as a kid, is a park haunted by the elements. Though the bright California sun warms millions of Californians inland, Candlestick was built on the ocean shore, where it's always cold and windy. Gloves and jackets are worn year 'round at Candlestick. The experts related our lack of success against the Giants in San Francisco to Candlestick. Though we'd lost our last five games there and ten of our last twelve, we were still rated as six-to-five favorites to win the best-of-five series. But our first two games were in Candlestick. The experts were saying, as they had said about us when we played Cincinnati, that the Giants had to take the first two games on their home turf to stand any chance of winning the series.

The Giants made it six straight over us in Candlestick, with a 5–4 win in the first game of the series. Some of my teammates were beginning to feel snakebitten, but not Roberto, who vowed that we would win the next game.

Bob Robertson, in the best game of his young career, hit three homers and drove in five runs to break the so-called jinx. Dock was the winning pitcher. I was 0-for-9 so far in the series and hadn't even driven the ball out of the infield.

Back at Three Rivers for the third game, it was Robertson and his roomie, Hebner, who hit solo home runs to lead us to a 2–1 win over the Giants. Bob Johnson was the winner. Marichal, easily the Giants' best pitcher, was the loser. I went 0-for-3 in the game.

In Game Four, the Giants took early leads in both the first and second innings but we came back to better their totals each time. Hebner and Oliver hit home runs, while Roberto delivered a big hit to lead us to a 9–5 win. Rookie Bruce Kison won the game in relief. We were on our way to the Series!

All my life I had dreamed of this moment. I had seen and read about the Series many times before. Maz, Roberto and a few other players had told me about how thrilling it was to play in a World Series. I had talked about it a lot and now I was finally going to play in one. I didn't want this moment to end. I had finally caught up with my dream.

I felt like a kid again. I was so nervous, that I felt as though I had forgotten all that I had learned. I was happy and excited. I didn't know what to expect. All types of thoughts ran through my mind. We had never played the American League Champion Baltimore Orioles before. All that I knew about them I had heard from someone else. I knew they were a great team and the defending World Champions. They sported four twenty-game winners on their staff.

I remember a lot of players' telling me that playing in the Series is anticlimactic. They say that everything you hear about the Series builds on an exaggerated image of what it is really like to play in one.

But I recalled most what Ernie Banks, of the Cubs, had once said to me. He told me that he'd go 0-for-50 just to get into a World Series. I thought about that as we got ready to play the Orioles. I only got about four or five hours sleep each night. I couldn't wait to wake up and get out to the ball park the next day for the game. That's what I had been living for.

No one could have exaggerated the happiness I felt when I was introduced along with my teammates before Game One in Baltimore. My body quivered with chills of joy.

We jumped on top in Game One with three runs in the top of the second. But Baltimore retaliated with one run in the second, three in the third and one in the fifth, to defeat us by a 5–3 score. We were slightly embarrassed by our performance. We had been terribly outplayed by the American League Champs. Their pitcher, Dave McNally, had held us to only three hits, while our pitchers gave up ten. Very rarely were we ever out-hit.

Game Two in Baltimore was even worse. The Orioles pounded our pitchers for eleven runs in the first six innings while holding us scoreless until the eighth. Were it not for Hebner's three-run homer that inning, we would have been shut out. Instead, we lost by an 11–3 score.

But we didn't head back to Pittsburgh for the next three games with our tail between our legs, even though the so-called experts in the press were calling for a four-game sweep by the Orioles. They made fun of us. They described us as elephants going home to die. They said our situation was not only desperate but terminal. They also said that the Series had lost most of its zest and sparkle because the Orioles were obviously a far better team than we were.

But most of these so-called experts, who had never pulled on a jockstrap in their lives, totally underestimated the character of the Pirate team. We were still calm and confident. Maz best exemplified our patience. He related our situation to the Bucs' showing in the '60 Series, when they had been beaten by scores of 10–0, 12–0 and 16–3 and still came back to win the championship. Maz spoke for all of us when he told the media that it was much easier to rebound from losing by a lot of runs rather than just one.

Danny also held a clubhouse meeting. He told us to forget about the money, the glory and all the extras and play for our pride. He told us to show them what a Pirate team could do. His words landed hard.

By this time, I was 1-for-20 in post-season play, 0-for-14 in the play-offs and 1-for-6 in the Series. I had also slumped in the second half of the regular season. I was booed when I was introduced in Pittsburgh for Game Three.

No one likes to be booed. Everybody likes to be appreciated. I began to wonder why people do boo others. I'd even asked people if they would like it if I came down to where they were employed and booed them while they were trying to do their job.

But I didn't allow the boos to bother me. I realize that they are a part of playing baseball for a living. I knew that our fans in Pittsburgh were good fans, who showed their appreciation when you did your job well and booed you when you didn't. I also knew that they didn't understand the entire situation with my knees. But Danny did and kept taking a chance by inserting me in the lineup each day. That's all that mattered. No matter how lame, I knew I would somehow contribute to our winning the Series.

In Game Three, we showed our real colors to the Orioles. Blass three-hit the Birds in a masterful decision over twenty-game winner Mike Cuellar. Robertson supplied all the runs we needed with a three-run homer, on a missed bunt sign, in the seventh inning. Roberto and third-baseman Jose Pagan drove in our other runs in the first and sixth innings. We won convincingly by a 5–1 score. I went 0-for-1 but walked three times and scored a run.

The Orioles jumped out to a three-run lead in the top of the first inning of the fourth game. Starter Luke Walker was relieved in the top of the first by the twenty-one-year-old Kison, who only the previous year had been skipping college classes to watch the Series on television. The rookie held the Orioles to one hit over the next six and a third innings while we regained the lead. I had my finest game of the Series. I went 2-for-5, including a double, an RBI and a run scored. We won by a 4–3 score.

Game Five was over quickly when we scored two runs off McNally in the second. Nellie Briles, our starter, held the Orioles to only two hits the entire game and moved us ahead in the Series with the 4–0 win. Robertson hit another homer and I went 1-for-4.

Even though we'd just swept the Orioles three straight games and led by a three-games-to-two advantage, most so-called experts still sided with the American League champs to win the Series. The final two games of the Series were scheduled to be played in Baltimore.

We took an early 2–0 lead in Game Six and were leading by a 2–1 score only seven outs away from a world championship. But our lax play allowed the Orioles to tie the score in the seventh. Then in the tenth, with one out, the Orioles scored the winning run to even the Series at three games apiece. I went 0-for-4 in the 3–2 loss.

Game Seven was all I could ask for. I didn't feel any pressure, only excitement. I didn't consider it pressure when the game was on the line. In fact, such situations always brought the best out of me. I couldn't wait for the game to begin. I wanted to win this game for the team. It was reported that Danny might retire after this season. I wanted him to go out a winner.

For the first time this season, Danny took me out of the cleanup spot in the lineup. I didn't blame him. I hadn't hit the ball well for over a month. He moved me to the sixth spot in the batting order and elevated red-hot Robertson up to the cleanup position.

The game was a rematch of Game Three, pitting Blass against Mike Cuellar. We scored first on a solo homer by Roberto in the fourth. But Cuellar gave up only one hit after that over the next three innings. Blass had held the Orioles scoreless to this point.

Then in the eighth, I led off with a sharp single to center. A few pitches later, with Pagan batting, Danny called for the hit-and-run. Jose lined a ball to deep center field. I raced for third but stopped to watch the play. When I saw the ball drop in front of the fence, I raced for home while Jose pulled into second. The Orioles scored their lone run in the bottom of the same inning. At 4:10 P.M. on a Sunday afternoon in Baltimore, we were crowned World Champions via our 2–1 win, and I had scored the Series' winning run, a dream come true.

> *"We were more than team-mates—we were friends, and that's what mattered most. . . . That's what made being a Bucco so much fun."*

6 OUR WORLD SERIES WIN did a lot for each one of us. It wasn't the money that really mattered, or the beautiful World Series rings. What mattered was that we had captured something that could never be taken away from us. Our names couldn't be rubbed out of the record books. Our victory had been immortalized.

The crazy, competitive Bucs of 1971 became household names in Pittsburgh. Gene (Gino) Clines, Dave "A.C." Cash (we called him that because he was so cool), "Scoop" Oliver, Hebner, Dock, Robertson, Pagan, Vic Davalillo, reserve catcher Milt May, Sangy, the nutty trio of Blass, Giusti and Moose, "Buster" Kison, Walker, Johnson, Hernandez, Briles, Maz, Veale and Roberto, who finally received some well-deserved acclaim.

He was a shoo-in as the World Series' Most Valuable Player. Roberto, always a pressure player, hit safely in all seven World Series games, twelve hits in twenty-nine at-bats, .414, including 2 homers and 4 RBIs. He'd also hit safely in all seven games of the '60 World Series.

But what worked to Roberto's benefit the most was that all the Series games had been nationally televised. He received some rave reviews. In fact, the fourth game of the Series was the first night game ever played in World Series history. Roberto wowed the national television audience with three hits in four at-bats. I believe that God had chosen the Series to showcase Roberto's talents. After watching him perform, no newsman could deny his ability, though before this point several had tried. Local sports reporters had called Roberto lazy, a hypochondriac, a selfish player, a moneymonger.

He had been terribly misunderstood by the fans. The reason for the misunderstanding was their lack of knowledge. Sports reporters didn't give Roberto a fair shake. They blasphemed him on a daily basis. I don't care how objective reporters are supposed to be, they're still human. And if a reporter doesn't like the person he's writing about, it shows up in his article.

For some reason, reporters didn't like Roberto. It may have been because they were jealous of his great talents or maybe he was too honest of a person. He always told a reporter exactly what he thought. If a reporter would ask him if his back was hurting and it was, Roberto would answer yes. But the next day in the newspaper, Roberto would be accused of being a hypochondriac. Reporters usually wrote that Roberto complained too much when really all he did was answer questions honestly.

We must remember that controversy sells newspapers and that a reporter's job is to write stories that will sell newspapers. Articles accusing Roberto of any of about a dozen false accusations probably sold millions of copies for local Pittsburgh papers. And once a writer finds a subject that sells, he keeps coming back to the same source.

I remember one specific incident in a series versus the Philadelphia Phillies. Roberto was prouder of his throwing arm than any of his other talents. He loved to constantly challenge base runners. His strong, accurate throws from the outfield were so consistent that they were often considered routine.

Once in a series versus the Phillies, Roberto failed to throw out any base runners, unusual for him but no indication that his tremendous ability was lacking. On the other side of the coin the Phils' right-fielder Johnny Callison, who had a good arm but nowhere near the strength of Roberto's, threw out two runners in one game. A story in one of the Pittsburgh newspapers the next day said how much better an outfielder Callison was than Roberto, based on Callison's number of assists that series.

There wasn't any comparison between the two. I'm sure Callison would even admit that. But the reporter had written the story just to infuriate Roberto, which it did. What I found to be amazing was that the reporter showed up in our clubhouse the next day to rub a little more salt in Roberto's wound.

In an effort to create salable copy, reporters often forget that athletes are human beings. They sometimes treat us like caged animals. They forget that we have the same feelings as them. They fail to realize that we feel poorly about ourselves when we make an error, strike out or lose a game. Instead, they laugh and chuckle behind our backs.

They fail to remember that we devote our entire lives to becoming good ball players. We take batting practice until our hands bleed, we throw until we find it hard to lift our arms and we run until our legs get wobbly. We take as much pride in our profession as any working stiff anywhere.

The difference is that when they misspell a word, their mistakes basically go unnoticed, but ours become front page news. We hurt just like any person. Stick a pin in us and we bleed. After we shower and leave the clubhouse following a poor game, we feel bad. We don't need any reporter telling us how poorly we played. No one knows better than a ball player when he hasn't had a good game. The way the press continually needles us about our deficiencies, I think they believe we wear blinders during a game.

Roberto's appearance in the World Series allowed the baseball fans across the nation to evaluate his abilities on their own. The fans were no longer dependent on the unobjective views of the press. As a result, reporters found it difficult to deny Roberto the credit he deserved. Were a reporter to do so, he would have looked ridiculous to his readers, most who had probably seen Roberto play in the Series. Finally, Roberto began to receive his due.

Besides being named as the Most Valuable Player in the Series, Roberto was also chosen as *Sport* magazine's Outstanding Player in the World Series and won the Babe Ruth Award as well, in addition to several other awards.

Whereas the Series had benefited Roberto, it hurt me. Though post-season play is not supposed to be considered when choosing a player for the league's MVP, I'm sure my poor showing in the play-offs and World Series cost me the award. I finished second in the voting to Joe Torre of the Cardinals. I don't want to take anything away from Joe's fine season, but I was surprised when I wasn't chosen. After all, I practically carried our team for the entire first half of the season. I led the league with 48 homers, drove in 125 runs, hit .295 and played on a pennant winner. What more could I have done?

All that I could figure was that the sports writers who had voted had unfairly taken into consideration my poor post-season showing. No matter, for I had accomplished what I had set out to do anyway. I had played on a World Championship team.

And our chances again looked good, since our club remained basically intact for the '72 season. The only major change was that Danny had stepped down, as expected. Bill Virdon, who was Danny's righthand man, was chosen as his successor.

Virdon was a slightly different manager than Danny. He was stricter, more of a disciplinarian, and he believed in curfews and outlawed wearing blue jeans on travel days. But we still were the same crazy Buccos.

We loved being around each other. We were more than team-mates—we were friends and that's what mattered most. There wasn't any jealousy. Every player pulled for his teammates no matter what his position with the team was. That's what made being a Bucco so much fun. You get ten of the best racehorses in the world, but if five go one way and five go the other way, what kind of race do you have? We were all going in the same direction. Each one of us had an accepted role. We were never envious of a teammate. We simply played our part. If someone on the team was injured and couldn't do his job, there was always someone waiting in the wings who could. Such a feeling does plenty for a team's confidence.

We liked the idea that we struck fear into the hearts of our opponents. We felt respected when we were booed in an opposing city. We saw the fans' boos as a sign of respect.

And we never allowed each other to get depressed. If we fell into a losing streak, we played even harder, laughed louder and tried to enjoy ourselves even more. A team party often served as a cure-all for a losing streak. Such an event gave us the opportunity to forget our worries and regain our confidence. We never let our-selves get down.

Not even when Roberto suffered from some chronic ailments and played very sparingly. Not even when Alley was questionable as our starting shortstop after an off-season knee operation. Not even when I began the season slowly by favoring my left knee, which had required surgery during the off-season. Not even when we won only five of fourteen games in April and fell to sixth place in May. We never let up.

Clines and Davalillo did a great job filling in for Roberto. Hernandez replaced Alley at shortstop when Gene was unable to play. And some of our younger hitters carried our offensive attack until I could get myself back into the groove.

Then, in mid-May, we went on a nine-game winning streak, seven wins of which were on the road, highlighted by four consecutive shutouts pitched by Glass, Moose, Dock and Walker. Our pitching was what put us back in the pennant race.

Finally, on June 15, we moved into first place with a 4–1 win over the Giants. I had replaced first-baseman Robertson, who was slumping at the time. From the fifteenth forward, we fell out of the top spot only once, on June 18, when we lost a 1–0 thriller to San Diego. We won the next day and jumped back into first place for the remainder of the season.

We had a six-game lead at the All-Star break and weren't even challenged the rest of the year. We clinched the pennant on September 21 with a 6–2 win over New York. We finished the year with a sparkling 96–59 record, eleven games in front of our nearest opponent.

Since there hadn't been any pennant race in our division, most of the local media coverage focused on Roberto's trek to the magical 3000-hit barrier. Roberto, who had started the season 118 hits short of the magical mark, didn't feel he could possibly accomplish the feat in '72. He'd been struck by too many injuries.

But a late-season surge brought Roberto within striking distance at the end of September. After a near miss on the 29th, which was mistakenly called an error, Roberto, suffering from a variety of painful injuries, proudly strolled to home plate the next day and drove a ball into the left centerfield gap for his 3000th career hit. He became only the eleventh player in baseball history and the first Pirate of all time to accomplish the feat.

Roberto was removed from the game a few innings later because of his nagging injuries, and he didn't appear in another regular season game that year. In a post-game celebration, Roberto dedicated the hit to the fans of Pittsburgh, the people of Puerto Rico and a friend in his native land who had pushed him to play baseball.

The divisional play-offs once again matched us against our archrivals, the Cincinnati Reds, who had also won their division by a considerable margin. We won one of two games in Pittsburgh and headed to Cincinnati for the conclusion of the best-of-five series, tied at one win apiece.

We jumped out to a two-games-to-one advantage by winning Game Three, 3–2. Sangy was the hitting star as he drove in two runs. Kison captured the win in relief.

But Cincinnati evened the score by defeating us 7–1 the next day on the strength of a two-hitter by Ross Grimsby.

We appeared to be on our way to our second straight World Series when we took a 3–2 lead into the ninth inning of Game Five with our ace reliever Giusti on the mound, but our thoughts of another World Series disappeared quickly.

The Reds' All-Star catcher Johnny Bench led off the ninth with an opposite-field home run into the right-field seats. Giusti then gave up back-to-back singles to Tony Perez and Dennis Menke.

Bob Moose was brought in to relieve Giusti, and George Foster was brought in to pinch-run for Perez at second base. Moose got the next hitter to fly out to Roberto in right. Foster challenged Roberto's arm and went to third on the play.

Moose came within one out of getting out of the inning when shortstop Darrel Chaney popped out to Alley. Moose needed to get only one more out to give us a second chance. Hal McRae, pinch-hitting for pitcher Clay Carroll, was the batter. McRae swung and missed at Moose's first pitch. The second pitch was a ball. Then with the count even at one ball, one strike, Moose threw his next pitch wide of the plate. Sangy tried to backhand the ball, but it skidded past him. Foster trotted home on the wild pitch, dancing along the baselines the last five feet. A play like that was all that could have beaten us that year. The Reds won by a 4–3 score and were on their way to the Series.

I didn't know at the time that that game would be the last time Roberto and I would ever play on the same field together. If I had known, I would have saved some appropriate words for the occasion. I may have even told my best friend that I loved him.

But I missed my chance to tell him anything when he died in a plane crash on New Year's Eve 1972. He was escorting a planeload of relief supplies to earthquake victims in Managua, Nicaragua, when his plane crashed into the ocean only a mile off the shore of San Juan.

He died a terribly misunderstood individual. But I, like all my teammates, knew what type of person he had been. We all loved and respected him. No death could be more symbolic for such a great man. Roberto died trying to help others. He was a man with a huge heart.

His death left me terribly depressed and confused. I hadn't lost anyone close to me before. I wasn't sure what to do or how to react. But what I do know is that I cried like a baby. I wasn't worried about who was going to be our starting right-fielder the next season. I was grieving for a lost friend. Our relationship went far beyond the baseball field. My love and respect for Roberto were results of our relationship as people, not just players. That's what a Bucco is—not only a teammate but a friend. We all cared for each other as people. We never allowed the frustrations of the game to stand in the way of our friendship.

Sometimes we unfairly compare our lives with those of others. We judge their dress, their attitude, their appearance. We judge too much and understand too little. Such was the case with Roberto. Only in the final year of his life did he begin to get the respect and admiration he so deserved. After his death, he was hailed as a hero.

The reporters who had blasted him for seventeen seasons now wrote eulogies about him. He was christened with the title "the Great One." A Roberto Clemente Fund was started. Though he'd been dead for months, his name still appeared in the newspaper daily. Articles and columns talked about how great a player and person he'd been, while cartoons paid tribute to him daily. He would have enjoyed seeing them all.

A huge lighted display board looms over Pittsburgh on the edge of Mt. Washington, nightly flashing its advertisements to the citizens of the city below. Shortly after Roberto's death, it carried the message "Adios Amigo." Yes, Roberto was appreciated but not until after his death.

Three months after the crash, Roberto was chosen for the Baseball Hall of Fame. Rarely is a player chosen so quickly, but Roberto was that great a ball player. The press and people of Pittsburgh may not have recognized him as the Great One while he was alive, but to fans and media on a national basis, he had always been the best. He was not elected to the Hall of Fame because of what his death meant but because of what his life had meant. No man had ever been more deserving of such an appointment.

Though he'd died months before, we still felt Roberto's presence that spring. He had influenced each of our lives. Each of us wore a small round patch with his uniform number, twenty-one, on our jerseys that season. Roberto's number was soon retired. Thus, the only places his number consistently appeared were on our jerseys and on the scoreboard at Three Rivers as a silent testimony to his greatness. Sangy, who had been one of Roberto's closest friends and was the last Bucco to see him alive, predicted that we'd win the World Series for him. I hoped we would, but I wondered if we could do it without him.

The year 1972 also marked the passing of another great Pirate. Maz retired at the conclusion of the season. He later accepted a position as a Pirate coach. The character of the team was slowly changing.

That spring, Danny, who was the Bucs' director of player acquisition and development, asked me if I would consider being the Pirate team captain, a prestigious position for a Bucco. Though Virdon was the manager, Danny was still a major influence on the team. I was shocked at first but yet flattered. I thought for a minute. What does a team captain do? That's when I came to my senses. A team captain is chosen because of what he is. Still surprised, I looked at Danny. "I'd be honored, as long as you don't expect me to change."

He nodded slightly and chuckled, "No, we won't ever ask you to change. We like you just as you are." Thus, I began my role as Pirate team captain.

As our team captain, I was mostly concerned with my teammates' mental approach to the game. We'd lost two very significant cogs in our machine and I hoped that our performance wouldn't be adversely affected. What I taught the troops was my even-keel philosophy, taught to me by Percy when I was a boy. The key is to never get too high or get too low. At either end of the spectrum, one loses a considerable amount of effectiveness. What I told the troops was this: When things are going bad, don't get too discouraged, and when things are going good, don't get too excited. Stay in the gray area in between the two extremes. That's where one's most effective energy lies. Consistency is the key to a successful season and a fulfilling life.

We survived several changes in '73. Sangy was converted to a right-fielder. Milt May was now our starting catcher. Robertson, who had an incredible spring at the plate, was back at first base, which meant that I was moved back to left field. The change was actually good for me. I wasn't as worried about my knees any more, and Roby was possibly the finest defensive first-baseman in the league. It would have been a shame to waste his talents in left field.

At that time, I wasn't a very good defensive first-baseman anyway. I'd been mostly an outfielder throughout my professional career and hadn't really been given enough time to reacquaint myself with first base. At times I felt like a pinball machine at first base, the way balls bounced off me.

I also knew that we'd be a better team with me in left field. We needed Roby's righthanded power in the lineup and his defense at first. As always I was concerned most about doing what was best for the team.

On a personal level, left field also allowed me more time to think about my hitting. I could go over the situations and the pitchers before my turns at bat, which helped me tremendously. When I was an outfielder I always approached the plate prepared for whatever situation I would face. But when I played first base I wasn't allowed any time to think about my hitting. All I could think about was my defense. I had to keep keenly alert or risk making an error and a fool out of myself.

For some reason, we just didn't play like a championship club at the beginning of '73. The spark, the efficient play, wasn't there. Maybe it was because of all the positional changes. Maybe it was because of the injuries we'd suffered. We were in last place for five consecutive days at the end of June, a position unheard of for a Pirate team. Joe Brown blamed himself and us for our poor play. He also told the media that the loss of Roberto had been a big factor.

And he may have been right. We may have been able to replace the majority of both Roberto's offensive and defensive output with other players, but we couldn't replace what he'd meant to our team. He'd been our leader. He constantly pushed us to do our best. One couldn't face Roberto after having a bad game.

I think we needed Roberto to push us. At times, we seemed to be waiting for him to get us going. Without him, there wasn't anyone around to crack the whip. Subconsciously, we waited.

I tried to lead with my bat. I was having one of my finest seasons, as were a few of our other players, such as Scoop and Hebner. But the team wasn't consistent. We never seemed to deliver with the key hits. We lacked something and were being made to look like nothings.

160

Jim Rooker, a lefthanded pitcher we'd acquired from the Kansas City Royals in the off-season, was our most pleasant surprise and our most consistent pitcher. Rook suffered most from our inability to drive home the key runs. He was what was termed a hard-luck pitcher. Though he pitched like a twenty-game winner each outing, he was lucky to win ten games in '73. Our lack of offensive support was the reason for Rook's mediocre record. But no matter how much Rook, an intimidating individual, taunted and cheered on his teammates, he never got the best out of us.

But neither could Brown or Virdon. Even though we had a losing record, we were still in the pennant race in September. An average team could have won the pennant that year or even a club that could put together a small winning streak over the last few weeks of the season. But no one in our division was good enough to even do that.

That's why Virdon was fired and Danny was rehired. The move shocked everyone, especially Virdon, who had led the Bucs to ninety-six wins the year before and to within one game of the World Series. But with Murtaugh waiting in the wings, Brown was tempted. And after Danny accepted Brown's offer, Virdon was fired. Had it been anyone else than Danny, Virdon might still have had his job.

Brown and Danny remained the best of friends. The basis of their friendship was their respect for each other's talent. Joe thought Danny was genius. He also thought Danny could give the team the extra push we so desperately needed.

We won seven of our next nine with Danny at the helm and were in first place on September 15 by a game and a half. Unfortunately, Danny couldn't hit, run, pitch or play defense for us. His presence inspired us initially, but soon we were back to our old ways. We lost five of our next six and dropped into second place. From that point forward, we won only five of our next eleven games and finished the season with an 80–82 record, good for a third place. We weren't the same Buccos as we had been in '71 and '72.

We still had plenty of fun together but we weren't the same team in the field. We weren't as hungry. We weren't as competitive as we once were.

Though I had the healthiest year of my career and played in a personal high of 148 games, I wasn't happy with my season. Even though I led the league with 44 homers and 119 RBIs, I was far from satisfied. All my individual accomplishments didn't matter, since I wasn't able to lead our team to the pennant. After three years in the top spot, it was an eerie feeling to have the season end so soon, so suddenly.

After a season like '73, all that's left are the individual glories and they don't matter much to me anyway. I'd become immune to not being named as the league's M.V.P. I turned in my third consecutive outstanding season and still wasn't good enough to win the award. Pete Rose, of the Reds, who led the league with a .338 average, was named M.V.P. I finished second in the voting. But again, I'd become accustomed to being upset in the voting and had stopped considering myself a valid candidate.

It was obvious that we were in for some changes. Joe began wheeling and dealing right after the season ended. He dealt A.C. to Philadelphia for pitcher Ken Brett. He shuttled Milt May to Houston for pitcher Jerry Reuss. He sent Nellie Briles to Kansas City for utility players Ed "Spanky" Kirkpatrick and Kurt, or Dirty Kurt as he was called, Bevacqua. Joe also added veteran second-baseman Paul Popovich and catcher Mike Ryan, who he'd gotten for Jackie Hernandez.

We were the new-look Buccos. We had youngsters everywhere. Rennie Stennett was A.C.'s replacement at second. Youngsters Frank Taveras and Mario Mendoza were scheduled to replace Alley, who retired at the end of the season; Sangy moved back behind the plate and Richie Zisk, a part-timer with us in '73, was our new starting right-fielder. But even with all these promising youngsters in the lineup, the best Pirate prospect was on the bench.

His name was Dave Parker. Six feet, five inches tall, 225 pounds and loaded with muscles, Dave resembled a black Hercules. I'd first spotted him in our spring training camp a few years before. I needed to watch him play for only a short period of time to know that he was bound for stardom.

I may have even helped him in his climb to the majors. I love to talk baseball and I especially like to talk about hitters. Whenever a reporter would ask me about a tremendous homer I'd just hit or a record I'd just broken, I'd use the opportunity to tell him about Dave. I told each reporter I knew about Dave. I felt he'd shatter all the records I'd set. He had that much potential.

He was a natural athlete. He was also one of the strongest men

I'd ever met. He could tear telephone books in half all day long. He never used a knife to cut an apple, he simply split it in two with his fingers. And he was fast. Dave could outrun anyone on our team. At 225 pounds, he led the Carolina League in stolen bases, with 38 in 1972.

Dave could have been a star in any sport. He could imitate almost any move on a basketball court, football field, boxing ring or baseball diamond after seeing it performed only once. Most players worked years to acquire their skills, but the Lord had given freely to Dave. Everything came natural to him. It almost seemed that he had done it all before.

Dave's talent needed to be refined, that's why he was on the bench. Danny was also giving him an opportunity to become acquainted with his new environment, just as he had done with me eleven years before. But Dave wasn't there just to watch. He wanted to learn. You could see the determination in his eyes. He wanted to be the best.

He wasn't afraid to ask questions. In fact, he asked often. He wanted to learn and I was happy to teach. Dave would meet me at the park early each afternoon, long before all the other players reported. We'd practice hitting. I taught Dave how to handle different pitches, what to do in different situations and how to hit to the opposite field.

In the field, we worked on his defense. He had a powerful but inaccurate arm in the outfield. I taught him how to get a better jump on the ball and how to shorten his number of strides before throwing. I showed him how to play the outfield wall and how to play defense against certain hitters. It was a pleasure working with someone who wanted to learn as much as Dave.

I talked with him about his psychological approach to the game also. Few fans realize the importance of a player's mental approach to the game. Rarely does a player survive a long time solely on his physical capabilities. Sooner or later, a player's body tires or begins to wear out. That's when the mental side of the game takes over. The correct mental attitude can prolong a career several years. It can also relieve excess strain on a player's body and add productivity to his performance.

That's what I spoke with Dave about. I told him about staying within the gray area between too up and too down. I taught him to avoid extremes and remain consistent. I showed him how to accept the good with the bad. I encouraged him to think beyond baseball and more about life.

After I began working with Dave, I had to keep an eye on myself constantly. I knew he observed my every move. Each time I struck out and strolled quietly back to the dugout, I knew he was watching. I knew that he was learning from my example. He kept me in line. I was always conscious of reacting properly in all situations. I never showed him a bad side.

Dave was the valedictorian of the Pirate dugout. I could see him rapidly maturing both as a player and a person. He didn't have to be taught something a second time. He bettered himself and his game in leaps and bounds.

Our team progressed the same way. We began the season slowly, while all our new components nudged their way gently into place. Danny was the perfect manager for our rookies. As he had with me and dozens of others, he brought the newer players along slowly, exhibiting the patience and confidence of a saint.

We started the season with a poor record after the first three months. But Joe didn't worry, for he knew Danny was at the helm. He had total confidence in his old friend.

Danny immediately hammered the problems out of our pitching staff. Young Brett was easily our best pitcher. He was nearly unbeatable in the first half of the season. Rook was pitching almost as well, though he still suffered from the hard-luck blues. An emotional pitcher, Rook eventually became so frustrated with the situation that he asked to be traded. Joe denied his request, not wanting to lose one of his best pitchers.

Like the team, I also started the season off slowly. But on June 1, I broke out of my bad spell with 3 hits, 2 homers, 6 RBIs and a double in our 14–1 win over the Reds. Though the team lost the next five games, they seemed to become a part of my hot streak. They were overcoming their lack of confidence. That was a good sign. It proved that their spirit hadn't been broken. It was only a matter of time before they would explode.

And explode we did. The date was July 14. We were playing the Reds in a doubleheader at Three Rivers. The Reds had won the first game by a 3–2 score. It was our fifth loss in a row. The team was tight, fuming. Buster Kison was pitching for us in the second game, Jack Billingham for them. By this time, young Buster had become a master of the knockdown pitch. Red shortstop Dave Concepcion was his first victim, but no tempers flared.

Then in the fifth inning, Billingham knocked Kison down. Buster charged the mound. Both benches emptied. It was a real slugfest. Both clubs were really going at it. It was just what the doctor ordered. There's nothing like a bench-cleaning brawl to help shock a team out of a slump. It would be ridiculous to try and gauge who won the fight. But we did win the game 2–1. Buster was the winner, Billingham the loser. The victory started us on an eight-game winning streak.

A young pitcher by the name of Daryl Patterson was the only real casualty. A Cincinnati pitcher by the name of Pedro Borbon bit a chunk out of young Patterson's left side. Borbon became known as the vampire from that point forward. Patterson survived but only after receiving a shot for tetanus.

But the fight did something that Brown, Danny and I had been trying to make happen the entire season. It relieved the guys' frustration, helped to bury their anger and brought them closer together as a team. From this point forward, we were pennant contenders.

We were 38–49 and in fourth place after the fight but we quickly picked up the pace. At the All-Star break we were 45–49 and still in fourth place, but we'd gained three and a half games on the leader. After the All-Star game, which was held in Pittsburgh, we went on a roll. We won twenty of our next thirty-one games and moved into first place on August 25. From there, it was nip and tuck with the Cardinals the rest of the way. My young teammates soon discovered that getting into a pennant race is not as difficult as staying there.

But they battled like champions. And aided by Danny's crafty maneuvering and the confidence he instilled in his young team, we captured the pennant on the last day of the season with a 5–4, ten-inning decision over the Cubs. You couldn't have found a happier bunch of youngsters anywhere.

But the Western Division champs, the Dodgers, a crafty group of veterans, made small change of us in the play-offs. We managed to win only the third game of what turned out to be a four-game series. Hebner and I both drove in three runs apiece, and Buster went the distance in the 7–0 win. But in the other three games we were outscored 20–3 and went home losers.

I enjoyed the '74 season as much as any of my years in the game. I liked playing beside the kids. They had spunk, life. They weren't afraid of anyone and they demanded respect from their opponents. We were a bunch of hitting fools who struck fear into the eyes of opposing pitchers. Danny liked the team too, which was the main reason he stayed on as manager. There had been rumors that he would be resigning again because of health problems.

The only part of the season I didn't enjoy was a book published about me entitled *Out of Left Field.* Bob Adelman and Susan Hall were the authors. Little, Brown and Company were the publishers. Adelman and Hall had approached me a few years before about writing the book. I entered the situation with an open heart and I got trounced on.

Adelman and Hall traveled with the club for the majority of a season, gathering interviews and researching. What they produced was not the type of book I expected; it was filled with horror stories about the players and their personal lives.

I feel fortunate that the publisher listened to my comments on the book. I never thought I would ever want to do a book again. Over the years, I turned down dozens of top-notch writers who wanted to write my life story. Each time another one asked for permission to write the piece, I refused, afraid of being used again.

Approximately eight years passed before I felt secure enough to try another book. This time I chose a trusted friend, Tom Bird, to help me write my story. The experience proved worthwhile for both of us. This book is my story, the other was not.

In '75, we were favored to win the pennant again. Brown had gently transformed the Pirates into a successful mixture of youth and experience in '74. The Mets were said to be our only competition for the title.

But we looked like noncontenders in the beginning. Though we had a potent offensive attack—with Dave in right, Scoop in center, Richie Zisk, who drove in 100 runs in '74, in left, Sangy catching, Hebner at third and me replacing Roby at first—we were having trouble scoring runs.

We were hovering around fourth place at the end of May when Danny decided to shake us up a bit. He placed speedy Frank Taveras in the lead-off spot, hoping that the young shortstop would force a few runs across the plate. Before this time, we had tried almost everything—hypnosis, visualization and transcendental meditation. Nothing had seemed to work.

Finally, I got hot and the rest of the pieces seemed to fall together. Though I was thirty-four years old at the time, I felt I was still a potent hitter. I wasn't the player I had been five years before, but what I had lost in ability I had made up for in knowledge. The press wasn't sympathetic to my slow start. As usual, they guessed wildly. But most chose the same alibi: I was getting too old, I was on my way out.

I believe that if we all adjusted our lives to fit other people's opinions of us, every person in the United States would be a schizophrenic by the age of sixteen. The only opinion that matters is your own. You can be anything you want to be if you work hard enough and don't listen to those fuzzy reports about your future.

We all knew we had the ability to win the pennant in '75—we just wondered where we had hid it. That's the reason we began searching for ways to redeem ourselves. But Danny was the one who brought us back to earth with some good, old-fashioned reality.

At the time, I also began to realize how much of an effect my presence had on the team. I didn't know if it was my bat, my personality or what. I was puzzled by the whole idea. I'd never tried to be anything other than what I was. I never tried to be a leader. I just tried to be the best person and the finest baseball player I could be. I was modest to my claim as the leader of the Bucs.

I'm a very modest person and I do agree that some men are meant to be leaders, but I never imagined myself as one of them. In fact, I never wanted to be one. But when my bat heated up in '75, the team seemed to follow closely behind. So did Dave, who was beginning to prove himself as one of the finest players in the league. Danny had brought him along slowly. He'd allowed Dave to play sparingly in the two previous seasons, just enough to get his feet wet before receiving a starting position in '75.

Dave responded like a champion. The fans began comparing him with Roberto almost immediately. Like Roberto, Dave had a powerful throwing arm. He also had strength, agility and speed. The fans had been looking for a hero to lead them from right field since Roberto died. They found the perfect leader in Dave.

Together, he, Zisk, Scoop and I provided the Buccos with more than enough power. We rolled along quite well until July 30, when

Joe Hoerner of the Phillies hit me with a pitch. Joe and I were always archrivals. He gave me more trouble than any pitcher in the league.

Though the area where the ball had struck me was extremely sore, it didn't hurt enough for me to be asked to be taken from the lineup. But the pain got progressively worse.

Finally, on August 12, I succumbed to the pain. I had tried to hide it and keep on playing but I couldn't. It was too overpowering. We'd won only four of fourteen games over that period. Danny knew I was in pain and used me sparingly. In fact, I started only six of those fourteen games.

Slowly, the second-place Phillies were gaining on us. They were the surprise team of '75. We hadn't expected them to challenge us, but they stayed on our tail for quite some time. They had a fine club. They were led by a group of talented young players—third-baseman Mike Schmidt, outfielder Greg Luzinski, shortstop Larry Bowa— and veteran Dick Allen. Their pitching staff was anchored by former twenty-game winner Steve Carlton.

Luzinski, known as the Bull, Schmidt and Allen were the Phil's power men. Though the Bull and Schmidt were relatively young and inexperienced at the time, they could hit with anyone.

Allen was a crafty veteran who broke into the majors the same year I did. Dick was known for massive home runs and controversy. He began his career with the Phils, where he was immediately hailed as a hero. But he eventually received the tag of a trou- blemaker, when Bob Skinner, who was managing Philadelphia at the time, resigned because of a squabble with him.

Tags stick, and Dick quickly became a dartboard for the press. I don't think there was any doubt that he and Skins didn't get along, but we all have our personal conflicts. Skins may have resigned, but Dick was made to carry the burden of the conflict around his neck for the rest of his career.

The Phillies traded him to St. Louis, who traded him to Los Angeles, who traded him to the White Sox and a manager named Chuck Tanner, who doesn't believe in tags, only talent. Tanner gave Allen a free rein. He trusted and understood Dick. He didn't judge him by what all the controversial, newspaper-selling stories said. As a result, Allen had his finest years while with the White Sox.

As an example of how misread he was, let me cite for you this example. Dick, like many players, didn't like to speak with the media. Who would, after all they had done to his reputation? So Dick liked to avoid them in any way possible. The press usually interviewed players during batting practice. So Dick asked Tanner if he could work out early each day, on his own schedule. Tanner, who had no reason to mistrust him, said yes.

Dick never shorted Tanner. He appeared at the ball park early each day to work out. By the time the other players and the media arrived, Dick was already in the clubhouse. Seeing Dick remain in the clubhouse while the other players took batting practice, the press got the impression that he was lazy. That's what they reported and that's how his tag and bad reputation began to circulate. Tags begin because of misunderstanding, a lack of knowledge, and they spread through the sports sections like wildfire. Once released, tags are never retracted. It only takes one media person to start a bad reputation. There are thousands of good sports writers throughout the country. But if only one decides to pursue a personal vengeance against a player, the player's reputation is ruined immediately. Other newspapers across the country, who don't contest the authenticity of the story, will use the piece because it's controversial, and within three days a player will have a national reputation that he'll never be able to shake. And it can all start with one little writer who was holding a grudge.

Because of the great seasons Dick had with the White Sox, his return to Philadelphia in 1975 was welcomed. He was one of the most feared hitters in the game at the time.

My injury was diagnosed as a cracked rib. I missed eighteen games with the injury. Over that time we played below .500 baseball. The Phils tied us for first place on August 18. They stayed within one and a half games of us for the next four days. But they didn't have enough fire power to keep pace and we eventually lengthened our lead. Finally, on September 23, we clinched the pennant with an 11–3 victory over the Phils.

We were still a loose, crazy Bucco team, even though some of the names had changed. Dock was sent to the bullpen, Blass was out of the majors. They'd been replaced by other players equally as crazy—Reuss, Rook and Spanky. Danny kept the team loose by limiting meaningless restrictions and rules and instead amplifying confidence. It's easier for a team to have a good time on the field if they have a good time in the clubhouse, too.

Dave was the team's most pleasing surprise. Though he was still learning, he led the team with 25 homers and 101 RBIs. He was on the verge of stardom even though he hadn't used even half his potential. He was still working on that. I still met him at the park each afternoon and worked with him on the finer points of his game.

The fiercest rivalry in the National League was renewed when we met the Reds in the championship play-offs. The Reds were favored to win the Series. They beat us by convincing margins, 6–3 and 6–1, in the first two games. Our offense was stale. I scored the lone run in the second game.

We had our backs to the wall for Game Three, down two games to none and rookie John Candelaria on the mound. Candy—or Foots, as I called him because of the huge size of his feet—had joined us in June from the Pirates' AAA team in Charleston, West Virginia. He pitched well during the year and compiled an 8–6 record with a 2.75 ERA.

But we didn't expect him to pitch the way he did against the Reds. Looking back now, I should have known Foots would come through for us. He was one crazy individual who thrived on pressure. The added tension made pitching more of a challenge for him.

Candy was a loosey-goosey type of guy who always had a prank to play or a joke to tell. He was a kid at heart. He saw everything as a toy. Life for Candy was a game and he played it well. He just overflowed with enthusiasm when he pitched, which almost meant certain death for the Reds during the play-offs.

Foots was dazzling against the awesome hitting attack of the Reds. His sinkers, curves and fastballs mowed down the Reds' hitters one right after the other. John struck out fourteen batters in only seven and two-thirds innings. An average of one strikeout per inning is considered excellent. Candy averaged almost two.

Though Candy allowed only three hits, we lost the game 5–3. Even the Reds and their manager Sparky Anderson couldn't believe that they'd beaten us with the way Foots had pitched. But that's the way 1975 went.

I was again in consideration for the MVP. Though I'd hit .295, with 22 homers and 90 RBIs, I wasn't the favorite. My old buddy Joe Morgan of the Reds, who hit .327, with 17 homers, 94 RBIs and 67 stolen bases, was a shoo-in.

At the time, I had become quite disgruntled with the award anyway. I felt that I had had five great seasons in a row and hadn't been honored with the award in any of those years. Thus, before the voting even took place, I stated that I wouldn't accept the award even if it was offered to me.

I even began to wonder if I had been overlooked for a racial reason. Only five blacks in the last fifteen seasons had been chosen for the award and I felt I had good enough statistics to have won the award at least once.

Joe, who eventually won the award, laughed at my frustration. He thought I was funny. I cooled down and just thanked the Lord for all that he had given me. It would have been nice to win the award, but obviously the Lord had other plans for me. I accepted not winning the award as exactly that.

But something I found hard to accept was the firing of the Gunner and his partner Nellie King. KDKA was the Pirates' TV and radio affiliate. For some reason, a higher-up in KDKA didn't like the Gunner. Thus, he was canned at the end of the season.

The city was shocked. His life was thrown into total disarray. He never even felt it coming. The reason given for his release, which I found to be incredible, was that his rating had slipped. He was the city of Pittsburgh's number-one son. He was loved by everyone in the organization and in the stands.

We as players enjoyed the Gunner's stories and antics. He was a constant flow of motion. He dressed to be absurd. He usually wore bright, summery colors, with a $500 pair of Gucci shoes and no socks. And he was a brave man not to wear socks with his ugly ankles. "It's gauche to wear socks with Gucci," he used to tell me.

Being forced to leave the Pirates broke the Gunner's heart. He'd become an institution with the team. No announcer would ever be a bigger hype for Pirate baseball than the Gunner. He invented the Green Weenie, a green plastic hot-dog-shaped object he'd lead the fans in shaking at the opposition. Such behavior was supposed to spur bad luck for Pirate opponents. He'd draw thousands of women to the games with his Ladies' Nights. And he thrilled the fans with his "babushka power."

Pirate fans loved Bob and he loved being their announcer. There was no job better suited to such a flamboyant personality as his. The only time I ever saw the Gunner depressed was when he was fired. To him, he'd just fallen from Heaven. He'd not only given his time to the job but also his heart.

A few other players and I led a parade through the streets of Pittsburgh to show support for the rehiring of the Gunner. Over ten thousand fans turned out. But nothing turned out for Bob, who eventually was forced to leave the city in search of another announcing job.

A job in baseball is unlike most other jobs. In baseball, you're asked to give your heart, not just your time. The game doesn't pay its nonplaying employees well, especially when they're asked to work upwards of one hundred hours a week. I really think Bob would have worked for free if he had to, he loved the game that much. Being around the players, the game, and receiving an opportunity to offer his views on the sport to an attentive audience were his reward, not the paycheck at the end of the week.

That's how baseball people live. They live for the game and not for the money. No one could possibly pay such loyal employees enough to cover all their time and effort. But they're paid, and paid in full. They feel the thrill of each home run and each win and die with every loss. That's the baseball fan, that's the major-league employee, and that was Bob Prince. Even something as precious and gentle as a friendly game of baseball isn't immune from politicking.

Pirate fans screamed for the return of Bob, but their requests fell on deaf ears. To them, he was a legend, a true representation of something they loved, Pirate baseball. He even made losing streaks fun.

The bicentennial year of the United States, 1976, was a revolutionary year for baseball. To begin with, the players walked out on strike again. Spring training was delayed. Marvin Miller was revolutionizing the labor structure of the major leagues. Finally, on March 18, Bowie Kuhn ordered the players back to camp and the walkout ended.

Around the same time, pitcher Andy Messersmith was testing his right to become a free agent. Messersmith eventually won his case, and baseball would never be the same again.

Until this time, major-leaguers had been given absolutely no rights at all. The owners were in total control. Baseball was a monopoly. Players were left to the mercy of the owners. They couldn't negotiate with any club other than their own unless they had been released from bondage by their present club. Players had no leverage, no bargaining power. They were mere pawns in the owners' game of chess.

But Messersmith changed all that. His court decision opened

the gates for players. It freed them from the bonds placed on them by the owners. They were allowed to become their own bosses. There would be bargaining and bickering between owners over players. The salaries would steadily rise. The balance of power no longer belonged to only the owners. The players now had a piece of the pie.

Thus, in the spring of '76, Messersmith became the first free agent in baseball history, a revolutionary year. He also became the first free agent signed when he contracted with the Atlanta Braves the following April.

The dress of every player in the majors also changed in '76. In observance of the nation's bicentennial, the players were asked to wear specially designed bicentennial hats. They looked more like caps than hats. They had raised sides and were encircled by three horizontal stripes. The teams' insignia was stitched on the front.

Our caps were black with gold stripes and a gold "P" in Gothic lettering on the front. They were a tremendous hit with the fans. The caps were selling like hotcakes on a cold morning. In fact, our fans, both in Pittsburgh and across the country, liked the caps so much that we kept them as our official cap at the end of the season, while other towns went back to their original hats.

We were a confident, cocky group of hitters in '76, who loved to bang the ball. We had built a name for ourselves as the Lumber Company. Posters featuring Sangy, Rennie Stennett, Hebner, Scoop, Zisk, David and me were printed and distributed everywhere in Pittsburgh. We loved our reputation. We wanted opposing pitchers to dread pitching against us.

Dave, who was slowly becoming the leader of the Lumber Company, had his own T-shirt printed. It read: If You Hear Any Noise, It's Just Me And The Boys Boppin'. He wore the shirt proudly. He, more than anyone, enjoyed the reputation of the Lumber Company.

The Phils were favored to beat us out for the pennant in '76, but such talk only fired us up even more. We were ready for '76. Brown had made only one major move in the off-season. He had traded rookie second-baseman Willie Randolph, Brett and Dock, who had been creating all types of disturbances in the clubhouse, to the New York Yankees for pitcher Doc Medich, who was supposed to be the frontline stopper we desperately needed.

We began the season by winning most of our games, unusual for the Pirates, who are known as notorious slow starters. We were in second place in late May, four and a half games behind the Phils, when disaster struck.

It all started on May 24. I drove home to our house in east suburban Pittsburgh after the game that night. We'd lost a 4–2 decision to Woodie Fryman and the Expos. But that wasn't the disaster. I knew how to handle losing a game.

When I arrived home Dolores began complaining about a severe headache. I calmed her down and turned on the late movie. After the movie, she still had the headache. She told me that she felt like something had burst in her head. She took a few aspirin and we went to bed.

As we lay there, Dolores began to groan uncontrollably. It was obvious that she was in terrible pain. I decided to drive her to the hospital. She was admitted for tests immediately. I waited nervously in the lobby of the emergency room for her to reappear. Finally a few hours later, a nurse wheeled Dolores back out to the lobby. They hadn't found anything wrong with her. I was relieved.

The nurse began wheeling Dolores out to our van when it happened. Dolores had a seizure. The nurse spun the wheelchair around and headed back into the emergency room. I waited more nervously than ever in the lobby.

Further tests were run and a blood clot was discovered in Dolores's brain. I stayed at the hospital through the entire night and into the next day waiting for the prognosis, but no decisions had been made. Finally, the doctors told me that I should get some rest and that they'd call me when they made a decision on what to do.

I was too nervous to rest, I drove to the ball park instead. I had been up all night. I'd explained the situation to Danny, and he scratched me from the starting lineup. I hadn't been in the clubhouse long when one of the doctors telephoned me. He said they'd have to operate immediately or we might lose her.

While Dolores was in the operating room, I waited nervously for results in the lobby. As I sat there, I began thinking of all the good times we'd had, all the things we'd done together, and the things we hadn't done. The mind plays funny tricks on you at a time like this. I started thinking all types of strange thoughts. What if she pulls through but isn't all right? Will she live? If she doesn't, what will I tell the kids? How could I live without her?

Finally, after two and a half hours, she was wheeled out of

surgery. It scared the hell out of me when I saw her. There were needles and tubes entering her body everywhere. There were pumps, pushing fluids into her body. She was being kept alive by machines.

I slept at the hospital the next two nights, though I took time out to do my job. On my first night back in the lineup, I responded with a single and a triple. Then on the following day, I hit a home run.

The day after that, the team left on a road trip to Chicago. I stayed home. For the first time in my life, I was struggling to concentrate on my game. It had all been so natural before. But then I'd never had to handle anything like this. I kept drifting slowly back and forth between my thoughts of Dolores and what was happening in the game.

She was partially paralyzed. I was overjoyed when she moved her toes one day. The better she got, the better I got. I began feeling a little better when she telephoned me one day. That was a big step in the right direction.

But over this period of time, my game had tailed off considerably. My mind wasn't on the field. I couldn't stop thinking of Dolores and the kids. I had to be strong not only for myself but also for them. I had to convince them that everything was going to be all right. I had to be more of a father than I had ever been before.

I spent most of my free time with either Dolores or the kids. We bound together tighter as a family than we'd ever been before. I know our constant love and attention helped speed up Dolores's recovery. I had never experienced anything like this before. I was a rookie looking at my first major-league curve ball. But I just prayed a lot and let the Lord do his work.

Dolores's recovery was slow and so was my climb back into the game. I never fully got my mind back into baseball until the end of the season. We'd fallen approximately fifteen games behind the Phillies by then. The reason for our poor showing was said to be our lack of offensive production, which meant Dave and me. My reason for a lack of production was obvious but Dave's wasn't.

Though he was still hitting a considerable amount over .300, his home-run and RBI totals had dropped slightly. He was never criticized for the slippage, but people did wonder what had happened to the extra dozen homers and a handful of RBIs. What most fans were unaware of was that Dave was suffering from some ligament damage in one of his knees. A knee injury makes it hard to do anything.

But back to my problem. I want the people of Pittsburgh to know how much I appreciated their love, patience and understanding in my time of need. Each fan understood my situation. I'd also like to thank the media, who conveyed my situation correctly. Never was I booed. My problem was always taken into consideration when I stepped to the plate. Pittsburgh is a loving town. They're understanding and patient with their athletes. Again, I thank the fans of Pittsburgh for their cards, prayers, patience and love.

Not even Foot's no-hitter on August 9 versus the Dodgers got the team going. But the potential was still there. All that was needed was a spark to get us under way.

Finally, in late August, the spirit returned. We were fifteen and a half games behind the Phils entering the game on August 25 when we began to make our move. We ran off ten straight wins to pull within six and a half games of the Phils on September 4. The key was our pitching. Our starters were unbeatable. Over the course of the ten games, they hurled seven complete games.

After our win streak was broken with a 1–0 loss to Fryman and the Expos, we flew home for an important three-game series versus Philadelphia. The first two games were scheduled as a Labor Day doubleheader. We swept the series and pulled within four and a half games. Our pitching had been the key again, holding the Phils to only four runs in the three games.

We won only two of our next five games and were six games back of the Phillies when we met for two games on the 15th and 16th. Again, we swept the Phils, who had won only six of their last twenty-two games. Their lead was sliced to four games. We won our next game in New York, while Philadelphia dropped a 4–3 decision to the Cubs. We were within three games of first place.

But that's where the magic stopped. We'd won eighteen of our last twenty-two games. We got no closer. We slumped at the end of the season, winning only seven of our last sixteen. But we had given them a scare. If we had kept up our rapid pace or had been in a better position when we started our run, we would have won the pennant. But we didn't and instead finished the season in second place, with a very respectable 92–70 record.

This year, 1976, marked the end of an era in Pirate history. On September 30, Joe Brown announced that he was retiring. He said that he wanted to spend more time with his wife and family. But Joe also saw a shift in the balance of power taking place and he wanted no part of it. Messersmith's court case was going to change the entire complexion of the game. The owners were bound to lose their grip on the game. In Joe's eyes, Pandora's box had been opened. Yes, he wanted to spend more time with his wife and family but no, he wasn't equipped to handle what the future of baseball was about to bring.

It was a very tearful moment for Joe and the entire organization. Joe had been more than a general manager to me, he had been a friend. He tried to be everything I needed. He was strict when he had to be and complimentary when I needed some encouraging. Joe had helped me get to where I was.

But the changing of the guard didn't stop there. Danny, who had been a close friend of Joe's since they'd met in the Pirate farm system in 1951, retired shortly after his old friend did. Danny had pushed his heart a bit too far the last few seasons. He said he was retiring because of health reasons, but that was only part of it. He'd stayed on as our manager at Joe's request, and now, with Joe gone, there was really no reason for Danny to stay any longer.

Danny had lived for the game. Because of his heart condition, he had risked his life for the game. Over the last few seasons, he had not been in the best of health. Without baseball, there was no joy in his life. Baseball people are like obsessive gamblers who can't back away from the roulette wheel. They live from game to game, season to season and championship to championship. The game is their spark for living. Take it away and they fail to exist any longer.

On December 2, at the age of fifty-nine, Danny died from a stroke. He had lived for the game and died without it. But a very big part of him still lives today in all of us who played for him. Through his confidence, patience and friendship he'd given us two World Championships and four Eastern Division Titles. Danny had been created for baseball.

Another Bucco also passed away after the season. My teammate and friend Bob Moose was killed in an auto accident on October 9. I was sitting in a hotel room when I heard the news over the television. I saw Bob's picture appear on the TV screen. At first I thought, What has this crazy guy done now? Then I heard the news. I couldn't believe it. The year mounted to one of death and tragedy for me.

And the game still rolled on. Baseball survives everything and falls prey to no one. It's the love of its fans, players and employees that keeps it going. One generation passes the reins to the next and somewhere down the line that generation will turn over the reins to another generation and so on. But the game is held together by love. That's the reason its employees work thousands of hours for very little pay. And that's the reason its players survive the road trips and the seven months of grueling play. Baseball people love the game, and they don't allow it to die with them either. They pass their knowledge and expertise along to the next generation. Baseball is a lot like life.

In this case, the next generation was Harding "Pete" Peterson and Joe O'Toole. The pair had worked closely with Brown for a considerable amount of time. Pete had begun as a player. When his playing career was over, he became a field manager and was later hired as the Bucs' minor-league director and then as their scouting director. Like Brown, he'd made baseball his life. Joe had trained him personally. During '76, Joe had slowly handed over the reins of power to Pete. Joe's retirement was foreshadowed by the continued appearance of Pete in the clubhouse. He also began to travel with the team, which is unusual for any major-league scouting director. So we basically knew the move was coming. The owners of the Pirates, the prestigious Galbreath family from Columbus, Ohio, named Pete as the Bucs' vice president in charge of player personnel.

Basically Pete and O'Toole split Joe's duties. Along with Pete's new position came one for Joe, who was named as the Pirates' vice president in charge of business administration. Pete was expected to handle the playing end of the club, while Joe was responsible for the business portion.

Like several of the other employees in the Pirate organization, O'Toole had been weaned on baseball. He was born in the Oakland section of Pittsburgh, the home of Forbes Field. He began as a kid by parking cars around the stadium and slowly progressed to a position as the Pirates' mail boy and eventually caught the attention of the Galbreaths, who took a liking to him. He worked his way through the ranks of the organization before being appointed as Brown's assistant in 1956. From that point, Brown taught O'Toole how to handle the administration of the organization, and this training was eventually instrumental in landing him his new position in '76.

Pete, who was responsible for all Pirate trades, was known as a wheeler-dealer and didn't waste any time before he made his first move. Just into the off-season, Pete traded Sangy to the Oakland A's for Chuck Tanner, their manager. What a way to start a career, trading a catcher for a manager! But Pete knew what he wanted and he went out and got him. Chuck had also been recommended by Danny, which weighed heavily in Pete's decision to acquire his services.

I was happy as a pig in slop when I heard the news. Though I'd never met Chuck personally, I'd heard some very complimentary things about him. He was enthusiastic, open and honest with his players. Like Danny, he didn't believe in a lot of rules. He only believed in having fun and winning ball games. He trusted his players and treated them like men. There was also a saying that circulated around baseball about him. Like the players, Chuck also had a tag. It read: If you can't play for Chuck Tanner, you can't play for anybody.

Besides rescuing him from the terribly inconsistent owner of the A's Charlie Finley, the move also brought Chuck home to New Castle, Pennsylvania, which is only forty-five miles north of Pittsburgh. Chuck, who had lived in New Castle all his life, grew up as a Pirate fan. The marriage of Tanner to the Pirates seemed great for all parties concerned.

The press began calling Chuck the Two Million Man, for they felt that his local influence would bolster the Pirates' usually low annual attendance figure to around the two million mark.

Pete kept wheeling and dealing. He acquired whatever players Chuck wanted no matter what the cost. On December 10, he acquired Rich Gossage and Terry Forster, two young fireballers from the Chicago White Sox, for Richie Zisk. Both had played under Chuck when he was White Sox manager. They were his type of players. They were rough competitors who played hard. Winners, Chuck termed them. He planned to use both in the bullpen, which gave us a potent leftie (Forster) / rightie (Gossage) combination.

The next "winner" the Bucs acquired was Phil Carner of the Oakland A's. According to Chuck, Phil was a franchise player. Though his individual statistics were far from overwhelming, Phil's expertise did not show up in the box score. He was a gutsy second-baseman, whom Chuck planned to use at third base to replace

Hebner, who'd gone the free-agent route and signed with the Phillies.

Phil was a hard-nosed, steelworker's type of player. The fans related to him immediately. They nicknamed him Scrap Iron. But the Bucs had paid dearly to acquire Garner. Pete gave the A's six players for Phil. He'd lost most of our top prospects from our farm system in the deal. But Chuck always says that you trade whatever player or players you have to to acquire a "winner." Pete believed in his new manager's philosophy and did just that.

Chuck's optimistic outlook on life and enthusiastic personality bred life in our club. He was also a very innovative leader who rarely managed by the book. He created whatever results a situation necessitated, whatever way possible.

Chuck saw an opportunity to change the entire style of baseball and win some games for the Pirates at the same time. Chuck injected speed as a permanent offensive threat into the game. Besides Taveras, we also had a young Panamanian center-fielder named Omar Moreno on the club. Omar was the fastest man in baseball. In the outfield, he covered the ground of three outfielders, and on the base paths, he was a blur. Just the sight of him at first base wreaked havoc in a pitcher's mind. Chuck planned to bat Taveras first and Omar second. He'd use them as the table setters. Their job was to force the action. This was the first time in the history of the game that base-stealing ability became a consistent factor in a team's success.

To make room for Omar, Chuck moved Scoop to left field. We still had the potent bats, but now we also had the speed. An innovator, Chuck titled our new plan of attack "Lumber and Lightning."

Where Danny had calmed us down and made us more patient players, Chuck sped us up and forced the action. Like our new manager, we became fiery, fighting, hard-nosed individuals who loved to play good old country baseball.

We started the season off quickly but again found ourselves behind the Phillies in the early going. We then ran off sixteen wins in seventeen games in late April and early May and were in first place by three and a half games on May 11, with a 20–7 record. We remained in the top spot until the end of May, when we went into a mild skid. But Chuck never let our heads droop. He believed in us. We became fighting mad.

On July 9, Buster infuriated the Phils' powerful Mike Schmidt when he hit him with a pitch. Buster, never one to back down from anyone, exchanged words with Schmidt as the Philadelphia slugger strolled to first base. The next thing I saw was Schmidt charging the mound. Both benches emptied, but not before Buster got in a few good punches. I tried to play the peacemaker. I separated as many fighting players as possible.

But I forgot all about my passive ways later in the game, when Tug McGraw of the Phils threw a pitch at me. I charged the mound, the first time I had ever done that in my career. As a team we were mad. We weren't going to allow anything to stop us. We came back from a four-run deficit to score four in the eighth and one in the ninth and win 8–7. I still remember what Scoop said about our outing: "If the adrenalin on our bench had been water, everybody in Pittsburgh would have drowned." Our fans loved it.

Though it brought us closer together as a team, unfortunately fighting had its drawbacks. The major drawback was injuries. I was the first casualty. Early in August, I was sitting the bench with an extremely painful left elbow. I figured that I had hurt the elbow during our melee with the Phils. On August 5, I was on the disabled list with a pinched nerve in my left elbow. Eventually, I had to undergo surgery to relocate the ulnar nerve in my left elbow to its proper place.

But the Bucs kept on fighting. On August 6, Taveras charged the mound to get at the Reds' Joe Hoerner. Then, on August 11, Scoop charged first-base umpire Bruce Froemming after being called out on an appeal play. Scoop almost ran over Froemming. On August 13, our catcher Ed Ott, who had been a wrestler in high school, body-slammed New York second-baseman Felix Milan. Milan had initiated the fight by stuffing a baseball in Ed's face. The Troll, as we called Ott, was the wrong person to make an enemy of. Though he eventually played in Japan, Milan's career in the majors probably ended with Ott breaking his collarbone.

Some fans referred to us as the berserk Bucs. Our fans loved it. Unfortunately, we still weren't winning enough games to catch the Phillies. What we needed was more consistent action on the field and less in the boxing ring.

We gave the Phils a good run for the pennant, but they finally clinched it on September 28. We finished in second place, with a

96–66 record. Our ninety-six wins represented our most victories since the '71 championship team had won ninety-seven. But we still finished five games behind Philadelphia.

Dave paced the team that season by winning his first batting title. Bill Robinson, whom we'd acquired from the Phils in April of '75, took over my spot at first base and led the team, with 26 homers and 104 RBIs. Foots paced the pitching staff with a 20–5 record. Goose Gossage was our leader in the bullpen, with 26 saves. But even with all that fire power, we weren't good enough to beat the Phils.

A few of us entered the off-season with some very important decisions to make. Gossage made his decision to go the free-agent route and signed with the New York Yankees for a substantial amount of money. I was also eligible for free agency, but I never opened myself up to the market. I didn't want to play for any team but Pittsburgh. The city was my home. I loved the people and my teammates. I really saw no reason to go anywhere else, no matter how good the money. You might say that I was like a big old oak tree with my roots planted in Pittsburgh. I didn't want to be anything but a Bucco. I let it be known that if I was traded, I would retire immediately. Being home in Pittsburgh meant more to me than any amount of money I could ever earn.

I worked out that entire off-season on a Nautilus machine at Steel City Nautilus in Pittsburgh. My left arm had lost almost all its strength. The Nautilus helped to restore it to full strength.

But the press still hounded me about retirement. They felt that after two consecutive disappointing seasons, I'd call it quits. But they were looking at my age—thirty-six, soon to be thirty-seven—and not my ability. I knew I still had the talent, I just hadn't had the opportunity to prove it in the last two seasons. I swung a hot bat in '77 until the fight with Philadelphia. I fielded all their inquiries but I didn't listen to any of their accusations. I still had faith in myself and that's what mattered. I knew I could come back.

Pete also had a few big decisions to make. How to better a Bucco team that won ninety-six games in '77? Pete traded Scoop, who had hit 135 homers for us in the last eight years, to the Texas Rangers, of the American League, and acquired someone whom he thought to be a championship pitcher, Bert Blyleven. The Rangers also gave us John "The Hammer" Milner, a lefthanded-hitting first-baseman, whom Pete may have acquired as insurance in case I was unable to return. I hated to see Scoop go but I knew Pete was doing what he thought was best for the team.

Bert was showcased by the Pirates to the city of Pittsburgh. Like Bunning, Bert was said to be player who would bring us the pennant. In nine seasons in the American League, Bert won 122 games, with both Minnesota and Texas, mediocre teams at best.

The Bucs signed Bert to a contract that would keep him safe and secure until at least the year 2000. In return, Bert pledged to become extremely civic-minded and the perfect Pittsburgher. Bert was quoted as saying, "The National League is Heaven."

The complexion of the team changed slightly in '78. Scoop was gone, and Hammer and Bert were Buccos. Pete also added veteran pitcher Jim Bibby, a massive 6'5" and 250-pound righthander whom he signed as a free agent that spring. A twenty-year-old pitcher, Don Robinson, also hurled his way onto the club. Don featured a tremendous amount of natural talent and a blazing fastball.

Dave had changed slightly. He reported to camp at 240 pounds, approximately 15 pounds overweight. The press made fun of his extra poundage just as they had done with mine approximately a dozen seasons before. But Dave didn't fight the press, he just worked his way back into shape.

Spring training was interesting as usual. We were up for the '78 season. Dave and Scrap Iron appointed themselves to be responsible for the team's pre-game hype. Phil, the son of a Baptist minister and half Dave's size, was the instigator, while Dave specialized in responses. The two battled daily, much to the delight of me and my teammates. The two would argue over anything from batting averages to skin color to socioeconomic status. Though the two were the best of friends, no one would have known it to walk into our clubhouse. The pair were excellent actors. Their clubhouse antics loosened the troops up before games.

Chuck usually allowed the players to conduct their own hype sessions. He took part only in what happened on the field. All he asked Pete for was winning ball players and he let them do the rest.

We began the season slowly. Nothing seemed to click. When we got good pitching, our hitters didn't hit. When they hit, our pitching let us down. We just weren't performing up to our capabilities as a team.

Entering our game versus the Mets on June 30, we sported a 35–37 record, good enough for fourth place, seven games out of first.

We entered the bottom of the ninth inning trailing by a 6–3 score. But we narrowed the margin to 6–5 when Taveras and Omar scored on Dave's one-out triple. Dave stood only ninety feet away from tying the game. Bill Robinson was the next hitter. Bill popped the ball into short right field, where outfielder Joel Youngblood ran under the ball—two outs.

Dave broke from third. He raced toward the plate with the potential tying run. Youngblood took only one step and rifled the ball toward home. His throw was perfect. It arrived to Met catcher John Stearns slightly before Dave.

Dave, sensing his impending fate, slammed his 6′5″, 225-pound frame into Stearns. It was a massive collision, like two freight trains running full speed into each other. Stearns reeled backward but held onto the ball. Dave lay face down on the ground grasping the area under his left eye. We lost both the game and Dave.

He was rushed to the hospital, where his injury was diagnosed as a fractured cheekbone. The injury infuriated Dave. He grew meaner and more determined. The injury had shaken him up. He was out to show the world he was indestructible. After surgery to repair the fracture, he was asked when he expected to be back in the lineup. His answer: "I'm the toughest man in the world. I can see, so I can play. There's no man alive who can say that except me."

Dave loved to challenge himself. That's how he got himself psyched. Though Pittsburghers relate more to modest athletes, they respected Dave for his determination.

I believe that race horses are a lot like baseball players. With horses, you do the best of everything for them. You feed them the best grains and hay, make sure you hire the best trainer and employ the winningest jockey, then you let them run. From that point forward, you have absolutely no control, it's all up to the horse. The trainer may have chosen his training schedule and the jockey may be there to guide the horse along, but that's all you can do. The rest is up to the horse. All you can do is hope that he'll show the type of potential you think he has.

Dave's Kentucky Derby was 1978; he ran and almost won. When lesser players would have been out of the lineup for months, Dave returned to the team after missing only eleven games. He was armed with two different masks, one for batting and the other for base running, to protect his cheekbone. He was ready to play.

On the scoreboard:

M JULY 11 IN SAN DIEGO WILLIE STARGELL
HIT HIS 302ND CAREER HOME RUN OFF OF
JE ARLIN TO LEAD OFF THE FIFTH INNING FOR
PIRATES. WITH THIS HOME RUN WILLIE BECAME
HE ALL - TIME PIRATE HOME RUN SLUGGER
SURPASSING RALPH KINER WITH 301.
ONGRATULATIONS WILLIE AND MANY MORE !

PIRATES

AT BAT

SP RP
43   PADRES
      PIRATES

Joe Brown and I at a pre-game ceremony commemorating my 302nd career homerun. We all wore
a ''21'' patch that season as a silent tribute to our deceased teammate Roberto.

Above: I owe a large part of my success to Joe Brown, who helped me both as a player and as a person. Here he is with his lovely former secretary at the Pirates, Jean Donatelli.

Right: My roomie, Doc Ellis, and teammate Jim "Mudcat" Grant show off their mod apparel in front of Pirate City. Doc was not only my roomie but also a very close friend. *(Charles W. Carroll)*

Below: What was that saying that former Pirate slugger Ralph Kiner always said? "Home-run hitters drive Cadillacs while singles hitters drive Chevies." Here I am immodestly photographed with my Rolls-Royce. *(Gene Page of Photographic Infinity, Holmes Beach, FL)*

Above: Chuck rushes out to greet the troops after a big victory in 1978. From right to left: Foots, Rennie Stennett (behind me), me, Joe Lonnett (behind Ed Ott), Ed Ott, Don Robinson, Rook and Chuck. *(Louis Requeña)*

Right: Matt Alexander scores another valuable run. Almost all the runs that Scat scored either tied or won a game for us. *(Rich Wilson)*

Below, right: Joe Coleman played a valuable role for us in '79. Though his contributions rarely surfaced in the box scores, they did show up in the standings.

Below: Tim Foli exemplifies his gutsy style of play as he bowls over Cardinal catcher Ted Simmons.

Chuck is all wet but also all happy after winning the National League Pennant in 1979. *(Rich Wilson)*

Dog triumphantly leads the Buccos to the clubhouse after we defeated the Reds in the 1979 National League Play-Offs. *(Pittsburgh Post-Gazette)*

Jim Rooker showed the nation what he was made of when he out-dueled the Orioles' Mike Flanagan in Game 5 of the '79 Series to take us back to Baltimore for the remaining two games.

Foots and I in an unusually serious moment on the mound during the Series.

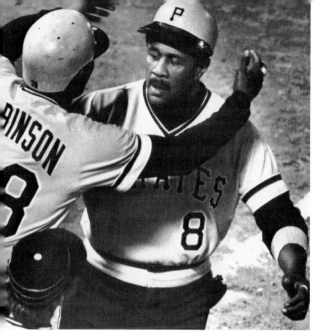

Bill Robinson greets me at homeplate after I hit the Series-winning blast in the sixth inning of Game Seven of the '79 Series.

Dave and Teke. A World Series trophy is a wonderful thing to behold.

THE 1979 BUCCOS. (Dog and Dave Roberts are missing from the photo.)

First row, from left: Steve Nicosia, Batboy Steve Hallahan, Batboy Steve Graff, Phil Garner and Ed Ott. *Second row:* Ed Whitson, Trainer Tony Bartirome, Coach Al Monchak, Coach Harvey Haddix, Manager Chuck Tanner, Coach Bob Skinner, Coach Joe Lonnett, Jim Rooker, and Enrique Romo. *Third row:* Grant Jackson, Rennie Stennett, Matt Alexander, Manny Sanguillen, Tim Foli, John Milner, Mike Easler, Dale Berra, Lee Lacy, Rick Rhoden and Traveling Secretary Charles Muse. *Back row:* Bill Robinson, Bert Blyleven, Omar Moreno, Dave Parker, John Candelaria, Jim Bibby, Kent Tekulve, Willie Stargell, Bruce Kison and Don Robinson.

Dave and I in a funny moment . . .

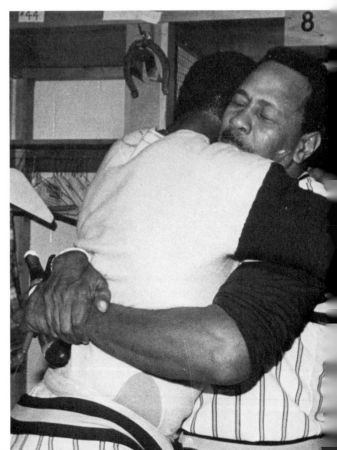

. . . and in a sentimental moment.
(Rich Wilson)

I always said that when it was time to retire I would know it and I would just tip my hat to the crowd and walk away. It may not have been that easy, but yet I want to thank the fans, fellow players and baseball people everywhere for the chance to say goodbye.

My first job after my retirement from baseball, as a narrator for the Eastman Philharmonia. That's conductor David Effron in the background. *(Chris Quillen, Eastman School of Music)*

I never saw any player as determined to succeed as Dave. Combine that with his natural ability and he was awesome.

He returned in mid-July. But he wasn't immediately productive. In fact, he slumped after his return. I could see that he was frustrated. He wanted to lead the Buccos to the pennant. He had the magic but had misplaced the wand.

This was one of those times that Dave needed a pat on the back. Sometimes a person can't fully understand a situation because of his close proximity to it. That's what it was with Dave. I simply explained to him what I saw. He was weak from the surgery and his timing had fallen off slightly over the lay-off. I told him to be calm and patient. His chance would come.

Dave listened to me, and soon afterward he was on top of the game once again.

After dropping a doubleheader to the Phils on August 6, we were written off as dead by Pittsburgh's leading baseball writer, Charley Feeney of the *Post-Gazette.* His prediction was logical, because no one could have imagined an ending like the one we had planned.

Dave wouldn't let the Buccos give up. A player felt ashamed if he didn't give all he had after playing next to David and his fractured cheekbone. Dave was responsible for our turnaround. He was named the National League Player of the Month for both August and September, the first player to ever be so named for two consecutive months. His enthusiasm was contagious.

Scrap Iron hit two grand slams on two consecutive nights, September 14 and 15, to lead us to victory both times. Though they argued plenty, the two were extremely close friends. Dave's enthusiasm especially affected Gar.

Our win streak was being compared with the New York Giants' miraculous comeback of 1951, when they defeated the Brooklyn Dodgers in the last game of the season to win the pennant on a ninth-inning homer by Bobby Thomson. We always knew we were good enough to match the Phils, but we needed someone like Dave to lead us.

It all started on August 13, when we won the final game of a four-game series with the Phils. It was our only win of the series. We were 52–61 at the time, in fourth place and ten and a half games back of Philadelphia. We won thirty-four of our next forty-five games, while the Phillies played below-.500 baseball over the same period. Again, Dave led the team with his bat and enthusiasm.

We entered the crucial four-game, season-ending series with the Phils on September 29. We were as high as the sky. We'd won twenty-four consecutive games at home. We needed to win all four games to win the pennant. The Phils were floundering at the time. They appeared ripe for the picking, but yet they only needed one win to clinch.

We were scheduled to play a doubleheader on Friday night to open this series. Approximately twenty thousand fans were in the stands at the beginning of the first game, but the crowd slowly swelled to over forty thousand as the excitement mounted.

In the first game, we entered the bottom of the ninth with the score tied 4–4. Then the magic struck. Ed Ott led off the inning with what appeared to be a routine fly ball to right center field. Phils' right-fielder, Bake McBride, who'd called for the ball, caught sight of approaching center-fielder Garry Maddox in the corner of his eye. McBride shied away from the ball, not wanting to collide with Maddox. But Maddox had heard McBride call for the ball and had no intention of trying to catch it. The ball fell between the two fielders.

Ott, who was closing in on second base when the ball fell to the ground, headed for third. Maddox picked up the ball and fired it toward third-baseman Mike Schmidt, who was standing on the base. The throw was way wide. Schmidt lunged for the ball but missed it. The ball rolled into the Phillie dugout. Ott scurried around third to score, and was met by a jubilant group of teammates at home plate. We won 5–4 and were still alive.

The second game matched Steve Carlton, the ace of the Phils' staff, against Buster. The Phils jumped off to a 1–0 lead in the second on Greg Luzinski's solo home run. We tied the score at 1–1 with Buster's solo homer in the fifth.

The game remained tied going into the bottom of the ninth. We were confident. We knew we would win. Our slow start hadn't tainted our image of ourselves. We believed in ourselves—that was the key.

With the crowd cheering wildly behind us, we loaded up the bases against Carlton with no one out. Dave was the lead runner on third base. Dave knows how to win. He does it not only with his bat but also his glove, his arm and his base running.

Warren Brusstar was brought in to relieve Carlton. Intent on winning, the forty-five thousand fans roared in support of their Buc-cos. Three Rivers was rocking. On fire with the entire situation, Dave began playing with Brusstar's already nervous psyche. The stadium seemed to shake. The dugout vibrated. Most of us were standing up.

Dave began forcing the action at third base. He jumped to and fro trying to distract Brusstar's attention. Then came the play of the game. Brusstar looked to catcher Bob Boone and got the sign. He stepped onto the pitching rubber. He began his windup. Just then Dave faked a dash down the line. Brusstar stopped in the middle of his motion. "Balk," the umpire called.

Dave ran wildly down the base line and jumped on home plate, landing into the open arms of his teammates. The fans roared with approval in the background. We showed our fans what we were made of that night. It's amazing what twenty-five guys can do to-gether when they all put their minds to it. Our team had gusto. We believed in one another and we believed in ourselves. We didn't see any reason why we couldn't win the pennant. We had that much confidence.

We were so confident after those two wins that we would have played both the third and fourth games of the series that night. We weren't tired. We were psyched and we didn't want to lose our magic.

We couldn't wait for the next game to begin. Most of us would have been content just to leave our dirty uniforms on and party all night. I didn't think I could fall asleep. It would take me the remain-der of the weekend to come down.

The third game of the series pitted rookie Don Robinson, a mature 14–6, against the Phils' Randy Lerch. We opened our scoring in the bottom of the first when I took Lerch deep for a grand slam. The Phils had scored one run in the top of the first. But it seemed that whatever they did we matched or immediately outdid. We took each run they scored as a challenge.

The Phils came within one run when Lerch hit solo homers in the second and fourth innings. Then Luzinski gave the Phillies a 6–4 lead with a three-run homer in the sixth. The Phils added four more runs in the eighth on Hebner's bases-loaded triple and Schmidt's sacrifice fly.

Going to the bottom of the ninth with the score 10–4, we defi-nitely had our work cut out for us. But we still believed in ourselves.

We weren't about to back down to even a six-run deficit into the bottom of the ninth. We were fired up.

The Troll led off the inning with a single. The crowd roared. We scored four quick runs, and with only one out, Bill Robinson was on base. I was standing at the plate. We trailed 10–8. Ron Reed was the pitcher. This was the type of situation I'd dreamed of as a boy, it was almost a déjà-vu. But Reed's blazing fastball was much harder to hit than any bottle cap tossed softly in the air.

I stepped to the plate thinking only one thing—home run. I was going to be guessing, swinging as hard as I could into the space where I thought Reed would throw the ball. The season had come down to an educated guess. But I guessed wrong and struck out.

With two out and Robinson still on base, Garner grounded out. The Phils won the game and the pennant.

But we weren't losers. It was only that we had started winning too late and the season had been too short. Yet all my enthusiasm immediately turned to depression. I found myself on the bench crying. For the first time in my career I hated to see a season end. It wasn't only the fun of the pennant race that I would miss but also my teammates. We'd become very close. It's difficult to describe how we felt about one another. But it would suffice to say that we didn't have to think about caring about each other, we just did. That's what a Bucco is—a very close, sincere friend first and a teammate next.

"We were the Buccos, World Series Champs, the best baseball team in the world. But more important, we were a family."

7

THOUGH THE CLUB had the same quiet confidence the '71 team had, I hoped we wouldn't be picked to win the pennant—and we weren't, the Phils were. Good, because I wanted to sneak up on them. I also knew that being picked anything less than first would fire up the troops. They loved being the underdogs and always played better when they had something to prove.

The 1979 season began pretty much as '78 had ended. Gar and Dave performed their daily argumentative ritual in the clubhouse. We were a loose, confident, almost cocky club. Dave started the season wearing his protective mask.

Our home opener against the Expos was cold and windy, but a good crowd was on hand just the same. We lost in a squeaker, 3–2. Dave went 0-for-4 and committed an error. He was booed, the result of negative publicity concerning him and his new contract.

Dave was now the highest-paid player in the game, baseball's first million-dollar-a-year major-leaguer. His contract was a direct result of his fantastic year in '78. He'd won the batting title with a .334 batting average, in addition to hitting 30 homers and driving in 117 RBIs. He was easily the finest player in the game.

I also had a fine season in '78; I batted .295, hit 28 homers, had 97 RBIs, and was named as the National League's Comeback Player of the Year. But my season didn't even compare with Dave's. It was he who led our late-season revival. His courage and enthusiasm led the rest of us. At that time, Dave was the finest ball player that I had ever seen take the field.

That's why I felt he deserved the big contract. I pushed him in that direction. I felt a million-dollar-a-year contract would revolutionize the entire salary structure of the big leagues and I felt that Dave was the one who most deserved the money. During the weeks of negotiations, Dave kept me abreast of all the important facts and figures.

Finally after some intense meetings, Pirate owner John W. Galbreath okayed a five-year, $5 million agreement for Dave. The contract included a substantial signing bonus and several years of deferred payments, revolutionary moves in the field of major-league contracts.

Dave was definitely setting a trend for other major-leaguers. Unfortunately, he wasn't ready to handle the pressure of being a trend-setter—the death threats, the hate mail, the prank telephone calls, the boos. The baseball world wasn't ready for a million-dollar-a-year black baseball player.

The criticism began almost immediately. Though most sports writers favored the signing of Dave, most were stunned, insulted by the money he was given. Most wouldn't earn in a lifetime what he would be making in a year. He immediately became a punching bag for frustrated media people.

Dave reported to spring training two days late. He had had strep throat and had stayed in Pittsburgh to recuperate. The press began slinging criticisms right from the beginning, though initially Dave handled them quite well.

They cut him to ribbons every chance they were given. Because of the bad press he received, Dave was forgotten as a baseball player and thought of as only a millionaire. That's why he was booed on opening day. The negative publicity had begun to work on the fans' minds already.

Initially, Dave didn't allow the negative press to hamper his style of play. He led the team to a 7–6 victory over the Expos the very next day. He won the game in typical Dave Parker fashion, by bowling over Expo catcher Gary Carter with the winning run in the ninth inning.

But even with Dave in overdrive, the rest of the team was stuck in first gear. Jerry Reuss, who'd been sent to the bullpen, was dissatisfied with his new role and wanted to be traded. Pete, tired of listening to Jerry squawk, shipped him off to the Dodgers for Rick Rhoden, a pitcher on the disabled list with arm trouble.

Like Dave, shortstop Frank Taveras was also taking a lot of heat from the media and fans. His play was definitely affected by the adverse conditions. Finally, after a game that we lost because of one of his fielding errors, Pete peddled Frank to the Mets for shortstop Tim Foli.

The trade was a good one for both clubs and both parties. As I said, Frank had fallen victim to the pressure of the fans and the media. He definitely needed the change. Going to the Mets gave him a second chance.

In Timmy we acquired an average hitter with a good glove. Tim's only defect was that he was a hothead. He'd been known as a dirty player, a fight-starter and a rabble-rouser. This was the reason for his nickname, Crazy Horse.

But by the time we acquired him, Timmy had taken a new lease on life. He'd become a born-again Christian. Though he was still a little crazy, as a Christian he tried to save all his craziness for the playing field.

He was also still a fierce competitor when we got him. He had been a bench player with the Mets. As with Frank, the trade gave him new life. Chuck planned on using Timmy as our starting shortstop.

There was a definite place for Timmy with us. We needed a good defensive shortstop, and that's all we expected from him. We didn't want him to try and do anything outside his range of ability. We expected him to field balls that were hit to him and turn double plays. That's it. If he'd do that for us, he'd become one of the most valuable guys on the club. Each of us had a role to play, and that was Timmy's.

Though I got off to a fast start in '79, I bruised my hip in the early going and had to be replaced by John Milner at first base. The Hammer responded well. In fact, the writers began referring to me as Wally Pipp, the Yankee All-Star first-baseman who disappeared after yielding only one game to a young Lou Gehrig.

Hammer was a comedian with a unique sense of timing, both for jokes and home runs. Ham had hit seven grand slams in his career, second on the club only to me. He literally carried us through the first month of the season by hitting .469, with 4 homers and 13 RBIs in only fourteen games in April. Before becoming a Bucco, John had been used exclusively as a starter. He was a reserve player with us. He adjusted to his new role quite well.

The team was still sputtering as late as early May. That's when I decided to have a talk with them. I kicked all nonplaying personnel out of the clubhouse—trainers, coaches, Hully and Chuck. I knew if I could get my teammates' engines running, we'd have a good chance to win the pennant.

My speech was simple. I reminded the guys that our slow start in '78 had cost us the pennant. I told them to become more consistent—never too high, never too low. I told them to keep their minds in the gray area in between. Then I told them to just go out and play some good old country baseball, and most of all, to have fun.

We began playing good old country baseball shortly after. We won sixteen of our next twenty-six games. And, may I add, in very exciting fashion.

On May 9, in a game against the Braves in Atlanta, we scored seven runs in the top of the seventh to defeat the Braves. We'd overcome almost every obstacle imaginable to win the game: bad calls by the amateur umps, who were there because of a strike by the regular umpires, beanball battles and bench-cleaning brawls.

But the conflict only served to heighten our fire. Chuck, third-base coach Joe Lonnett, Rennie Stennett and Dave were all thrown out of the game. The rest of us simply picked up where they left off. Timmy drove in four runs, as did Hammer, who hit the eighth grand slam of his career in the wide-open ninth. The Braves may have gotten the calls, but we won the game.

On May 16 in Three Rivers, Mike "The Hitman" Easler hit a solo home run in the thirteenth inning to defeat the Mets, 4–3. Mike was the happiest Bucco on the team. He'd survived ten grueling years in the minor leagues before finally getting his chance with us in '79.

Easy had been known as an all-hit, no-field player. He'd been a consistent .300 in the minors, but no big-league team was willing to take a chance on him defensively. But Chuck, who never read tags anyway, liked the way Easy hit the ball and decided to give him a chance.

Easy was born to hit. And when he wasn't swinging a bat, his favorite pastime was talking about hitting. He was a natural. To him a good afternoon meant extra batting practice or some instruction on how to hit to the opposite field. The Hitman accepted his role as a bench player. He was just happy to be in the major leagues.

Easy's homer got us going. We won our next six games. Over that period, we hit fourteen homers, five of which were mine. At the time, we had needed someone like Mike to pick us up.

On May 29, in the midst of another six-game win streak, we reached the .500 mark with an 8–0 win over Chicago. We were playing inspired baseball. The press began comparing us with the '60 Pirates. Like the Team of Destiny, we ruled the later innings. We'd intimidate our opposition in the early going and squash them with our stingy relievers and powerful bench from the seventh to ninth innings, just as the team did in '60. We didn't mind being compared with such a great team. In fact, we were flattered.

Their comparisons made me think of my second season in the minors, 1960, when I was at Grand Forks. I'd followed the Pirates' progress all through the later months of the season and into the World Series. I dreamed of being on a team like that. I felt a slight tingle run the length of my spine when I realized that my dream had come true.

Bucco Bill Robinson, whose performance was basically overlooked in the complexion of the entire season, led us in the early months. Bill led the team with nine homers in both May and June and nineteen in the entire first half.

He was another one of our players who accepted his role as a utility man. He backed me up at first, shared left field with Hammer and pinch-hit regularly. Whenever he was inserted in the lineup, he produced. He wasn't a selfish player. He did what Chuck asked of him and never worried about individual glory. Like Timmy, Bill was a born-again Christian.

There's one fact about Bill that I'll always remember: how his most productive day of the season always fell on his birthday. If there had been such a thing as a designated birthday player, Bill would have certainly been it. In '79, Bill celebrated his thirty-sixth birthday with a game-winning homer and a game-saving catch versus the Mets on June 26, his B-day. We won a total of thirty games in May and June. We couldn't have won half that many without Bill.

We couldn't have been as successful without Dave either. But obviously some of the fans didn't agree with me. Dave was hitting over .300, with 10 homers and 42 RBIs entering the game on June

24 versus the Cubs at Three Rivers. It was Bat Day, one of the Bucs' biggest give-away days on their newly revamped promotional schedule.

Forty-three thousand fans were in attendance. One of those envious, Parker-hating fans ruined the day by throwing his bat at Dave in right field. Fortunately, the fan missed, but the whole incident shocked Dave. Though the bat thrower was captured and charged, the incident only bred attention for a senseless act. The fan never gave any reason for throwing the bat at Dave. We all just took it for granted that he was jealous of Dave's million-dollar-a-year contract.

We were locked in second place at the end of June but still a considerable distance from first. That's when Pete pulled off the deal of the century by acquiring Bill Madlock from the San Francisco Giants on June 29. In conversations at the beginning of the season, I told Pete and Chuck that I thought we could win the pennant if we acquired both Timmy and Bill.

Like Timmy, Bill—nicknamed Mad Dog, which we soon shortened to Dog—came to us with a bad reputation. The press called him a selfish ballplayer with a bad temper. Again they were wrong, and Chuck knew it. He wanted Dog because he was a natural third-baseman and he could hit. He'd already won two batting titles.

Dog had been out of position as a second-baseman with the Giants. He was happy that Chuck wanted to move him over to third. And Gar was happy too that Chuck was going to switch him back to his natural position, second base. Everything seemed to work out best for us.

The entire city was happy with Timmy and Dog. Soon after Dog's arrival, we became the best show in town. It felt good to see fans lined up at the ticket windows, fighting for the best seats. It was good to know that the people of Pittsburgh were behind us. We liked playing in front of the larger crowds. Like every team, we needed our fan support. We played hard so we'd make our fans happy and they'd keep coming back.

Our momentum was flowing like water at the end of the first half. Seven and a half games out of first place going into the second game of a doubleheader versus Cincinnati on July 8, we caught fire for four straight wins and six of our last seven before the All-Star break.

After taking back-to-back, one-run decisions against Cincinnati and Houston, we took on the toughest pitcher in the majors—J.R. Richard of the Astros—on July 11. J.R., pitching in the Astrodome, the toughest home-run park in the majors, held us totally intact through six innings. He looked devastating. He'd allowed only three hits entering the seventh.

But that's when Dave and I got things rolling. J.R. made his first mistake of the game with Dave at the plate. He threw Dave a low slider, which he drove 430 feet into the right-center-field stands. That tied the score at 1–1.

I was the next batter—Richard's second mistake. I did what few men have ever done in the Astrodome. I hit an opposite-field home run, 430 feet into the left-center-field stands, a massive shot. Hammer followed my homer with a triple off the left-center-field wall. We went on to score two more runs that inning and won the game by a 5–1 score.

We struck quick. We were a devastating offensive team. We struck fast and hard. We never felt overmatched in any game, no matter whom we were playing or who was pitching. We were the Buccos.

We were within striking distance at the All-Star break with a 46–39 record, whereas we were only 40–41 at this time the previous year. We all realized the importance of being in the pennant race far earlier than we had been in '78.

Dave was the National League's starting right-fielder in the All-Star game. He was also named the M.V.P. His throwing arm had won him the award. His two strong throws to home plate nailed two American League base runners. If they had scored, the A.L. may have won. But because of Dave, the N.L. won, 7–6.

We picked up right where we had left off before the All-Star break. We won our next seven games in a row and ran our win streak to nine consecutive victories. We moved to within one game of first place before losing four straight.

Dave was slumping at the time. Even a city as beautiful as Pittsburgh has fair-weather fans. They're the ones who infuriate a player the most, booing when you're down and cheering when you're up.

I began watching Dave in batting practice during that time, trying to isolate his problem. I couldn't have chosen a better time to discover a solution. The Phils were due in town next. I noticed that Dave was holding his hands too low. I kept reminding him to keep them up. He listened well.

We opened the weekend series with a doubleheader versus the Phils on a Friday night, August 10. We were in second place at the time, one game behind the surprising Expos. Three Rivers was buzzing. Forty-five thousand fans were in attendance. The atmosphere reminded me of the season-ending weekend series versus the Phils in '78. Buster and Phillie starter Dick Ruthven battled to a 3–3 tie through six innings. The game then became a battle of the bullpens. Their ace Tug McGraw, a cocky lefthander, was on the mound. We countered with Enrique Romo, our fiery Mexican righthander with a million pitches.

The Phillie hitters were as baffled by Enrique's repertoire of pitches as he was with the English language. Enrique was a newcomer on the team. We'd acquired him from Seattle in the off-season. He had the longest hair on the club. He sent his long black locks flopping on every pitch, resembling a charging Comanche. But no one could charge him with not having any talent. Enrique frustrated the Phillie power boys with his off-speed curve balls, his off-speed screwballs, his off-speed sliders and his quick little fastball.

While he held the powerful Phillies hitless over the last three innings, Dave broke out of his slump with a three-run homer in McGraw's first inning of relief. The fans ooohed and aaahed as Enrique baffled the Phillies and cheered when we moved within half a game of first place with our 6–3 win.

The crowd was buzzing like a beehive for the second game. But big Jim Bibby never allowed the game to get exciting. He shut down the Phils on five hits and one unearned run. The combination of Enrique's off-speed pitches in the first game and Bibby's blazing fastball in the second game transformed the Phillies into schizophrenic hitters. They had no idea if they were coming or going.

But the Expos hung tough and we only gained half a game by sweeping the Phils. Our victories were more than a pennant race for us, though. We were out to prove something to ourselves. We'd been held down by our cross-state rivals three years in a row. We wanted out from beneath their thumb. We wanted to win the pennant.

And win we did. Thirty-four thousand fans were in the seats at Three Rivers the next day to watch Foots pitch a masterful 4–0 shutout over the Phils. He didn't do it alone. Though Foots was like a kid off the field, he was a man on the mound. He was as fierce a competitor as I'd ever seen. Even his chronic bad back couldn't keep him out of the rotation. He pitched in pain each outing, but he also pitched with effectiveness. At times, I could see the pain written across his face as he released the ball toward home plate. He grimaced like someone had just stabbed him in the back. But he went as far as he could each game, which usually meant until Kent Tekulve time.

Teke had been our ace reliever since Gossage took the free-agency route. Most fans expect relievers to be mean, burly, afraid-of-nobody types. Teke was the complete opposite.

He was 6'5" and 175 pounds in spring training and worked down to about 145 pounds by the end of the season. When he faced the Phils that weekend, I'd say he weighed in at about 162. He kept his weight down by pitching in over ninety games a season. He looked like Ichabod Crane turned major-leaguer. But he made the opposition look even worse.

His underhand delivery was the key. He would have been the worst batting-practice pitcher in the history of baseball. It was difficult to hit even his bad stuff. Teke was that good. He was also the nicest guy on the team. He was down-home and simple. He looked at home in a bowling shirt.

Candy, or Foots, who was as crazy as anyone I'd ever met, and Teke made an odd-looking duo. Foots prided himself on his elegant style and his shining fleet of Mercedes cars. Teke resembled your average Joe. But together they were untouchable. The odd couple combined for four shutouts in seventy-nine. Foots controlled the opposition for the first six or seven innings, or until his back gave out, and Teke held them the rest of the way.

But even with our third straight victory over the Eastern Division champs, we weren't able to wrestle first place away from the Expos. We were still half a game behind as we entered our Sunday twin bill versus the Phils.

The Phillies started their stopper Steve "Lefty" Carlton in the first game. We countered with Bert Blyleven. By this time, the Phillies were frothing at the mouth. This was make-it-or-break-it time for them. If we beat their best pitcher and went on to defeat them four straight games, their spirit would surely be broken.

The Phillies stormed out to a quick 8–3 lead. The forty-six thousand fans in the stands were down. Chuck inserted veteran pitcher

Joe Coleman. We'd recalled Joe shortly after the All-Star break to serve as our long relief man. Joe had definitely seen better days. A former twenty-game winner, he was said to be a better golfer than pitcher at this point. But Joe had guts. He shut the door on the Phillies in the fifth and sixth and gave us some time to regroup for a comeback.

When Joe was removed from the game, we were down 8–7. The crowd was right back in it with us. Catcher Steve Nicosia led off the eighth with his fourth hit of the game, a double. Steve, or Nic, was a rookie, but to see him play one would have never known it. He played like a twenty-year veteran. He was also the best storyteller on the club and handled pitchers with the control of a den mother. He knew what he was doing behind the plate—strange for a rookie —and our pitchers trusted him and often confided in him.

I followed Nicosia as a pinch-hitter. My infield out advanced him to third. Timmy then scored him with a single, and the game was tied. Our fans were going wild. They couldn't believe we'd come back, and neither could the Phillies, who desperately began looking for a way to stop us.

They tried McGraw again. Teke had held them scoreless in the top of the ninth. We were still tied 8–8 going into our half of the inning.

Outfielder Lee Lacy, who was in search of his fourth World Series ring, singled for us with two out in the bottom of the ninth. Lee had been specially inserted in the lineup that Sunday to face Carlton. Besides being a righthanded hitter, Lee was also the most successful hitter in baseball against Carlton. He was also fast. He stole second to move into scoring position.

Dog was intentionally walked. Then reliever Kevin Saucier responded to the cheers of forty-six thousand Pirate fans and walked Scrap Iron, loading the bases. That's when Phil's manager Danny Ozark called for McGraw.

Chuck countered with one of the most questioned moves in the history of baseball: he pinch-hit Hammer for Nic, who was 4-for-4 on the day. Some of us thought Chuck was nuts. First of all, he pinch-hit for our hottest hitter. Then the pinch-hitter he sent to the plate was lefthanded, as was McGraw. Hammer was placed at an immediate disadvantage. Not sensing what we thought to be a mistake, the crowd cheered uncontrollably.

But Chuck was our manager for several reasons. One reason was that he knew baseball better than any of us. He proved it when Hammer rocketed McGraw's first pitch into the right-field seats for a grand slam.

Our fans went berserk. The electricity of the whole situation filtered through each of our bodies. Some of us jumped, some clapped, some danced, some hugged each other, but all ran to home plate to greet Hammer. Hammer glided around the bases like he was walking on air. We were all at home plate to lift him onto our shoulders and carry him into the clubhouse. No fan in his right mind was going to leave before the second game.

Hammer symbolically broke the backs of the Phillies with his grand slam that day. Never had I been on a team so spirited. The Phillies played the second game in a daze. We'd broken their spirit. They had no idea how to beat us. We'd beaten their top starter and their top reliever and outscored their best offensive threats.

We captured the second game by a 5–2 score. Omar Moreno and Scrap Iron drove in two runs, and Dog drove in the other. The Expos had also lost that same day, which meant that we moved into first place by a game and a half. We were in the pennant race and much earlier than the year before.

Later that evening we left for Chicago to begin a week-long road trip. I was worried about a letdown. I knew the Cubs had the potential to damage us in the standings, and playing in Wrigley Field can make even the worst clubs look like champions.

That's exactly what happened for Chicago. They instantly jumped on Rook for seven runs. Chuck brought in Joe Coleman, our official mop-up pitcher. Joe's initial job was to hold the Cubs intact until we could mount a comeback. When he wasn't able to do that, he asked to stay in the game.

If Joe stayed on the mound and finished the game, we could rest our other relievers for another day. But the Cubs didn't make it easy for old Joe. Everything he threw to the plate they hit back at us twice as hard. My fellow infielders and I did all that we could do just to stay alive. Balls that were hit to the outfield chiseled pieces of brick off the old Wrigley Field wall. I felt like I was in a shooting gallery. I wished I'd worn a chest protector.

But the story here does not deal with pitching ability, it deals with sacrifice. Joe was obviously at the end of his career when we acquired him. Once in his career as a Detroit Tiger, he had been a great pitcher, a twenty-three-game winner in 1973. But Joe never allowed his ego to stand in the way of his role as a player.

Joe stood out in the boiling Chicago sun embarrassing himself so that our more valuable relievers could save themselves for another game. The Cubs clobbered Joe for thirteen hits and nine runs in his five innings pitched. I'm sure he was embarrassed by his outing, but he'd done what was best for the team. He'd sacrificed himself. We had little chance to win that game. So Joe took our beating for us in hopes that the pitchers he saved could be used in a winning effort on another day.

I'd always liked Joe, but I really respected him after Chicago. His effort epitomizes what it takes to be a member of a winning team—sacrifice.

Not all of us can be home-run hitters or Cy Young Award winners. Some of us have to contribute in a different way. And it's the players who sacrifice themselves that make a good team into a great team. Tim Foli batted second behind Omar most of the season. Timmy took strikes, hit to the right side of the infield, laid down bunts, anything he could do to help his speedy teammate steal a base or move into scoring position. Timmy gave himself up at the plate for the betterment of the team. Omar led the league with 77 steals and scored 110 runs in '79, but he couldn't have done so without Timmy.

We all have roles to play and the quicker we accept those roles, the better we'll be. That was the key to our team's success in '79. We all accepted and fulfilled our roles. None of the bench players were jealous of Dave's or my spot in the lineup. They just contributed whenever or however they were needed.

Let's take, for example, second-baseman Rennie Stennett and pinch-runner Matt Alexander. At one time, Rennie had been one of the finest second-basemen in baseball. A converted outfielder, he was just coming into his own when he broke his ankle in a game versus St. Louis in 1977. He was batting .336 at the time, only a few points behind Dave's league-leading .343 average.

Rennie never fully recovered from the injury. His range was severely hampered and his production at the plate dropped significantly. Since we acquired Dog and Gar had moved over to second base, Rennie was relegated to the bench. I'm sure the demotion hurt at first, but Rennie rebounded well.

I remember one game in which we entered the bottom of the ninth down by a substantial number of runs. Somehow we forged our way back and tied the score. Rennie had already left the dugout and walked back to the clubhouse. He was in the middle of a shower when Chuck called for him to pinch-hit. Rennie couldn't believe we'd come back from so far so fast.

He threw on his uniform, ran up the runway to the dugout, grabbed a bat from the bat rack and hurried to home plate. He delivered with a walk. That's where Matt "The Scat" Alexander entered the game.

Scat was our designated pinch-runner. He was also our barber, a profession he planned to take up full-time when his playing days were over. He was forced to accept a limited role as a pinch-runner even though he was a talented athlete. Like all our guys, he sacrificed his personal feelings for the team and made himself into the best pinch-runner in the game.

He had great natural speed, but he still worked daily at his technique as a base runner. He studied pick-off moves, worked on getting good leads and practiced running the bases. When the game edged its way into the later innings, when he knew his services might be called for, Scat worked on a rigorous routine of stretching exercises in the runway, practiced his lead-offs and ran to loosen up his legs.

In this particular game, by the time Rennie stepped up to home plate Scat had been loose and ready for fifteen minutes. Rennie had done his job, and now it was time for Scat to do his.

Scat bolted from the dugout to take Rennie's place at first base, and we informed Rennie that he could now go back to his shower. From there Scat made things happen. He stole second base. The catcher's throw was wild. Scat got up and headed toward third. The outfielder, who'd backed up the play at second, threw wildly to third. Scat scored easily and we won.

Scat appeared in only forty-four games in '79, thirty-five as a pinch-runner. But he scored sixteen runs, most of which had either tied or won a game for us. Though he was too talented to be only a pinch-runner, he accepted his role for the best of the team, as did Rennie.

Every player on every team must make sacrifices. Without players like Joe, Rennie, Scat and Timmy, we would never have even entered the pennant race. These players' statistics never drew an accurate account of their total value, but each of us knew and felt what they had done as Buccos. Being a good team player means being whatever type of player your team needs.

We left Chicago after winning only one out of our three games and headed for a four-game series in Philadelphia, where the Phils were itching to burst our bubble, since we'd embarrassed them only the week before.

We entered the first game of the Friday night doubleheader in first place by a game and a half. As had become routine in our match-up, the Phils jumped off to a quick lead. We tied the score to move the game into extra innings.

Sixty thousand Phillie fans cheered as Bud Harrelson's check swing was mistakenly called a ball. The umpire had goofed in a critical situation. Harrelson should have been called out. Maybe the umpire was growing weary. After all, we were in the twelfth inning, the game had been delayed by rain and it was nearing eleven-thirty at night.

This bad call cost us the game when two pitches later Harrelson hit a line drive past Dog at third to score Phillie Bake McBride. Though we were furious with the umpire's poor call, we didn't allow our frustration to inhibit our game; in fact, we used it to enhance our play instead.

We took the field for the second game slightly before midnight. We were even more fired up than we had been for the first game. The Phillies had just wounded a big bear.

Buster and Teke pitched masterfully, and the troops provided just enough offensive support to win. At 1:30 A.M. we entered our clubhouse with a 3–2 victory. It was one of those nights when we should have slept in our uniforms. We couldn't wait for the next game to begin.

We arrived back at our hotel at approximately 2:00 A.M., caught a few hours of sleep and headed back to the ball park. Our game was scheduled for a 2:15 P.M. start. We were NBC's Game of the Week. Don't let anyone tell you that players don't care about being on TV. Big crowds and national attention always make a player's heart beat just a little faster. We also wanted to prove to the nation that we were the best baseball team in the country.

Rook got bombed again. The Phils scored seven runs almost instantaneously. Chuck brought in Coleman, who held the Phils to only one run in two and two-thirds innings. The funny thing about the whole game was that we were behind 8–0 to the defending divisional champs as we entered the fourth inning and we still felt we were going to win.

But while Joe somehow held the floodgates shut, and while NBC switched their viewers to the backup game, and while several Pirate fans back in Pittsburgh got disgusted and turned off the game, we started our comeback.

We held the fifty thousand Phillie fans in awe when we scored five runs in the fifth and drew to within three of the lead. Omar had led off the inning with a homer. Though the homer only narrowed the gap to 8–1, many of my teammates and I felt we would win the game because of it. Omar's homer was what we had needed to get us started.

We were unstoppable from that point forward. While NBC executives fumbled for the switch to put our game back on the national circuit, we scored four more runs in the seventh to go ahead 9–8. Not the crowd, the Phillies or the national TV audience could believe what we had done.

The Phils sent their top reliever, McGraw, to the mound to put us in our place at the conclusion of the seventh. But Ed Ott's grand slam off the Phillie reliever in the eighth was the final nail in Philadelphia's coffin. We added one more run in the ninth, and Teke staved off a Phillie rally half an inning later. We won 14–11. We'd shown ourselves, the Phils and the entire country who was the best team in the nation.

We all scurried up the runway to our clubhouse. There was plenty of celebrating to be done. But just as the last player entered the clubhouse, the Hitman, whose base hit had put us ahead for good, reached up and turned on his stereo tape player. Mike must have pre-set the tape. The disco tune "Ain't No Stoppin' Us Now" began pulsating throughout the room. It seemed so natural, everybody began singing. Chills ran up and down my spine as I sang along with my twenty-five teammates, my friends, my family.

By this time we had become known as the Family. The title wasn't my invention. Joe Brown had begun calling us the Pirate Family back in the '60s. It was only the personality of our club that finally made our title known throughout the country. But it did exemplify how we felt about one another.

The guys called me Pops, a name Dave Parker came up with. I liked the name but I never let on. I really enjoyed being the kingpin of such a fine group of guys. Besides hitting home runs, I took it upon myself to serve as entertainment and morale director too. I organized the team parties and some of the practical jokes and handed out Stargell Stars.

The Stars were an idea I picked up from a friend, Sid Litzer. While at Sid's home, I noticed a large quantity of small rose-shaped stickers. I asked Sid what they were used for. He told me that they were his own personal way of rewarding good deeds. He didn't always give them to someone he knew. He just handed one out to anyone he thought deserved one.

That's when I was struck with the idea for my stars. I think everyone deserves to be told their effort has been appreciated, especially on a ball club, so I had the Stargell Star designed. They weren't anything fancy, only little gold stars with some stickum on the back, but their meaning was everything to me. They were an outward show of my appreciation for a job well done. In that way, they were a much-needed pat on the back, a team handshake, an extension of my heart.

Though they gained their popularity through the team, they weren't designed exclusively for team members. In fact, the first star I handed out was to an airline stewardess. I don't recall where I was flying to, but there was an older lady a few seats in front of me who obviously had never flown before. She was extremely nervous and at times even nauseous.

If it weren't for one of the young stewardesses aboard, she may not have made it through the flight in one piece. The young stewardess spent the entire flight with the first-time flyer, talking with her, joking with her, comforting her in any way possible. I was so touched by the stewardess's effort that I pasted a star on her lapel as I left the airplane.

Though I don't think she knew who I was or even what the star represented, I just wanted her to know that I noticed what she had done for the first-time flyer.

From that point forward, I gave out the stars whenever an appropriate situation presented itself. Again, they weren't reserved for players. I handed them out to bat boys, trainers, coaches, office personnel and fans. But I only handed them out when I felt a person deserved one. I never cheapened their value.

I even hesitated when Senator Ted Kennedy asked me for one at a banquet once. Mr. Kennedy was in Pittsburgh campaigning for the presidency at the time. The reason I hesitated was not that I didn't think Mr. Kennedy deserved a star. I just wasn't sure if he was the candidate I wanted to give one to.

Ed Ott, the Troll, was in charge of keeping my stars, which eventually became even more popular than autographed balls. They were also as hard to acquire, because I only gave them out at chosen times and to deserving people. That's why I left Ed in charge of guarding them.

He was easily the toughest Bucco on the team. No one, not even Dave, messed with the Troll. Though he was only about 5'10" and 185 pounds, Ed knew how to use every ounce of his weight. His body-slamming of Milan a few years before stuck in all the players' minds around the league. No one challenged the Troll.

Ed was a feisty catcher who prided himself on his plate-blocking ability. He loved collisions and he designed his own individual plan of defense. Instead of taking a base runner straight on, Ed always attacked a player from his flank. Ed would drift up the third-base line a few feet and await the throw home. Then he'd blast the base runner from the side instead of taking him straight on. Ed guarded my stars with the same ferociousness with which he guarded the plate. With Ed's help, I kept the meaning of the stars from being cheapened.

To represent how we felt about each other, I chose a theme song "We Are Family" by Sister Sledge. It wasn't only the song's title that appealed to me but also the lyrics. I first heard the song during a rain delay and once I listened to the lyrics, I knew the song was for us.

I asked Joe Safety, who was our director of publicity, if there was any way the song could be played during the games. By this time, our theme of a family had begun to spread. Our fans were not only hungry for a pennant but also hungry to contribute. "We Are Family" gave them the opportunity they longed for. It became the most popular song in Pittsburgh.

Safety had the song played during the seventh inning stretch at our home games. The crowd would clap in unison. They felt very much a part of our team, as they rightly deserved to be.

The song not only brought us and the fans closer together but it became a rallying cry for the city as well. We were all one—my teammates, our families, the fans, the city, everyone. Pittsburghers all moved to the same beat. We all pulled for each other, we all shared in one another's sorrows and celebrated one another's victories.

No song represented how I felt about Pittsburgh more than "We Are Family." Ever since I had put on a uniform for the Pirates in 1959, I had grown more in love with the organization, the players and the city each day. By my thirty-eighth birthday, in '79, living there and playing there meant everything in the world to me.

What our theme song stressed was unity, not just unity in the clubhouse but also in the community. And that's also what it bred. As the tales of the team traveled throughout the Pittsburgh area, more and more fans came to our ball games.

What I saw when I looked up into the stands before each game was much the same as what I saw in our clubhouse each game day. I saw all kinds of people from all different places, representing all religions, racial backgrounds, socioeconomic groups and political beliefs, getting together at a ball game. I saw people sit down next to each other as strangers and part as friends. I saw those thousands of different people unite each game in the singing of "We Are Family." I saw love, affection, caring, the way things could always be if we'd all drop our grudges and prejudices and just decide to get along.

Looking up into the stands and seeing all this happen made me realize just how beautiful and powerful a group of individuals can become. Their togetherness was contagious and bred even more fire and enthusiasm from our play.

But we were contagious, too. I looked in our dugout and around our clubhouse and I saw unity, I saw love. We were twenty-five guys who bonded together to fight a battle. Alone we would have perished but together we were champions.

We knew what job we had to do, and we relied on one another to get it done. We respected everyone. But together we feared no one. We were one another's strength, one another's guidance. The fans gained strength and guidance from us, and we from them. That's what "We Are Family" represented. It stood for the Pirates, it stood for Pittsburgh, it stood for unity. It stood for what the Lord wanted the world to be like and what Heaven was supposed to be.

I must admit that there were thousands of fans throughout the country who thought that our camaraderie, my stars and "We Are Family" was only some kind of publicity hype to elevate our attendance. But let me tell you firsthand, our feelings for one another were as genuine as a sunset. You could see it in our eyes. You could feel it in our hearts. You could hear it in the clapping and cheering of the fans. You could see it in the faces of Pittsburghers every day. Believe me, it was real. Just ask any of our opponents. They'll back me up.

The love we all possess was alive in Pittsburgh in '79 and it's alive in each one of us today. All we have to do is quit harboring bad feelings against our fellow man and start spreading a little more love into the world.

Love was the basis of our family and it should be the basis for each of our lives every day. If it were, the world would be a much happier place.

The enthusiasm inspired by the team, the fans and the city pulled us even closer together and perked us up at the right moment. We won three out of four games in that weekend series in Philadelphia. We headed home in first place two and a half games ahead of the Expos.

But we weren't the only ones fighting for a pennant. After six consecutive wins, the last three in Philadelphia followed by a three-game sweep over the Padres at home, the always tough Dodgers beat us two games in a row. But our magic hadn't left, it had only been put on hold.

We went into the bottom of the ninth in the third game with the Dodgers locked in a scoreless tie. But "Happy" Hooton had held us to only five hits, while Foots had held them to four before leaving in the eighth for a pinch-hitter. Teke took over on the mound for us.

The fans grew anxious as rain clouds hovered overhead. Hammer hit a one-out double, and Bill Robinson, the next batter, struck out. Dog stepped to the plate. The crowd looked above them at the darkening sky. They prayed for a game-winning hit that would save them from getting drenched. That's just what Dog gave them.

Dog drilled Hooton's first pitch deep to left center field. As the ball crossed over the outfield fence and Dog raised his fist in joy and Hammer jumped around on home plate and Hooton bowed his head in disbelief, the clouds burst open. Dog's homer had not only won the game for us but also started a downpour. Strange, but we had so much confidence when we were together that we even thought we could control the weather.

The power even surfaced in Dave Roberts. Dave had been the

forgotten man in the Madlock trade. He was a thirty-four-year-old lefthanded pitcher. The Pirates were his sixth major-league team. He was called a throw-in in the Madlock deal and appeared to be on his way out of the majors when he joined the team. But the atmosphere even rejuvenated old Dave Roberts. It didn't improve his velocity or movement on the ball but it did make him a happier person and a better pitcher.

Dave became our resident spinner of oldies. Since about a half dozen of us were in the thirty-four-and-above age bracket, we'd all grown up on the same music, the Drifters, the Beach Boys, the Temptations, etc. Dave carried a box of cassette tapes of oldies wherever we went. In our more mellow times, my older teammates and I would gather around Dave and his tape player and harmonize for hours. We even entertained a few planeloads of people during the course of the season. Dave was obviously the happiest he'd ever been in his career. And happiness breeds conviction and a willingness to work.

Dave really showed us what he was made of in a game in San Diego. The press were calling our second swing out West our do-or-die trip. Eastern clubs always had a tough time beating the California clubs out West. The consensus was that if we had a successful road trip and arrived back in Pittsburgh in first place, we'd have a good chance to win the pennant. Several Eastern division clubs had died on road trips to the West Coast and buried their seasons along with them. We were leery but also fired up for the challenge.

Our first stop was San Diego. The Padres beat us 3–2 our first night in town, but we'd gone down hard. In our next game the following night, we refused to go down at all.

We and the Padres battled to a 3–3 tie after nine innings. From that point forward both teams dug deep into their benches and bullpens. As the game carried on, we began running out of players.

In the sixteenth inning the Padres loaded the bases with nobody out. Dave Roberts was our lone reliever left in the bullpen. Chuck called for the thirty-four-year-old lefthander. Almost any kind of hit would have scored a run for the Padres. Dave's pitching had to be picture perfect.

Old Dave gutted-up the pressure. He had fire in his eyes. He pitched like a twenty-five-year-old rookie and struck out three Padres in a row. There is a time and a situation for every player on a championship team, and this was Dave's finest hour. Things didn't get much easier. In the seventeenth, with a runner on third and two out, Dave intentionally walked two batters to get to pitcher John D'Acquisto. Dave's first two pitches were out of the strike zone. He turned to look at second base, where Padre base runner Dave Winfield was standing. Winfield lifted a hand to his throat and gave Dave the "choke sign." He shouldn't have done that. Dave was now more intense than ever.

His next pitch was ball three. What was left of the Saturday night crowd—now the Sunday morning crowd—roared. But in another gallant effort, Dave threw three straight strikes past the Count and got out the inning.

We eventually went on to win the game in the nineteenth on Timmy's two-out double. Dave was credited with the most well-deserved win of his life. Dave was another great role player for us. As with Joe Coleman, his better years were far behind him, but he gave us whatever he had left whenever we needed it. He was one of the many drops of glue that bound our team together. I'll never forget that night in San Diego or our hero of the evening, Dave Roberts.

We were due to leave San Diego the next day, and after more hours spent packing than sleeping we were back out on the field versus the Padres the next afternoon. Buster was our starting pitcher and also our best hitter. Buster knew how to pick his spots. He always pitched his best with the season on the line and he hit pretty well in such situations, too. He pitched seven innings of one-run ball against the Padres and hit a grand slam in the second inning. We won handily, 9–2.

After two wins in three games against the Dodgers, we flew to San Francisco, home of the windy, cold and unruly Candlestick Park, for a four-game series. We won the first game of the series and entered the second game, which was also the first game of an afternoon doubleheader, on a three-game win streak. My two homers made it four straight but not before some of the craziest baseball managing I'd ever seen.

We entered the ninth with our 5–3 lead. Buster had pitched seven innings and had given up all three Giant unearned runs. Teke, who relieved him in the eighth, was still on the mound in the ninth. Then came the strangest but most effective strategy I had ever seen used by a major-league manager. Needless to say, Chuck was an innovator.

With one on and two out, Chuck called time and walked to the mound to talk with Teke. Leftie Grant "Buck" Jackson was warmed and ready in the bullpen. Darrell Evans, a lefthanded power hitter, was the Giants' next batter. It seemed logical that Chuck would call Buck in from the bullpen to pitch to Evans.

Chuck took the ball from Teke and waved for Buck. Then Chuck said, as serious as a heart attack in the third stage, "Teke, you're going to left field." Teke, who looks funny just walking, was as surprised as anyone. To look at Teke, it would be hard to believe that he could catch anything with the exception of the common cold. And in this situation, with the tying run at the plate? I fought to hold back my laughter. Even though I realized that Chuck wanted to keep Teke in the game to face the second hitter, Clark, if Buck failed to get Evans out, I couldn't quite picture Teke in the outfield, unless he was lying on the grass sunning himself.

But he began on his way to the outfield. He passed Hammer, who was on his way into the dugout. Ham shook his head. He knew he wasn't the best defensive outfielder in the league, but being replaced by Teke was hard for him to accept.

As Teke strolled to the outfield, he very professionally picked up a few blades of grass and tossed them into the air to check the direction and velocity of the wind. Omar hurried over from center field to offer advice on how to catch a ball. Teke laughingly shrugged him off. He took up a position in the outfield according to coach Al Monchak's instructions and set himself for the pitch.

Buck knew that he had to keep the ball away from Evans, which meant he'd probably hit the ball to left field. If Buck pitched him inside, he'd be giving him too good a pitch to hit. I ran the situation through in my mind. I looked out to left field at Teke and started to laugh. Chuck was one crazy manager. Seeing Teke as an outfielder, I understood why he'd chosen to be a pitcher.

Well, all happened as planned with the exception of one thing. Buck threw the ball on the outside part of the plate. Evans went with the pitch and drove a fly ball to left field. There was Teke positioned perfectly. I started to laugh again. He waved his arms like a spastic pelican. Little did he know that there wasn't a fellow player for thirty yards that needed waving off.

Teke narrowly moved a step, lifted his glove in the air and followed the ball into his mitt. That's what we didn't expect. Usually after a win, I was filled with uncontrollable relief. But in this instance, I was filled only with uncontrollable laughter. The entire team bypassed Buck on the mound and ran out to left field to congratulate Teke on his miraculous catch, knowing that any catch for Teke was a miracle. After that bit of strategy, I knew who was at the heart of our team's craziness: Chuck.

With the toughest part of the road trip, Teke's appearance as an outfielder, behind us, we swept the two remaining games and headed home with a six-game winning streak and in first place by three, one and a half games over the Expos.

But as some of my least experienced teammates discovered, a club must play nearly perfect baseball to win a pennant. That fact emerged immediately. We won six of our next nine games (a .667 winning percentage) and blew a three-and-a-half-game lead to drop into second place behind the red-hot Expos.

At this time the Canadians were winning games in even more amazing ways than us—winning runs scored on wild pitches, on balls bouncing off seams in the astroturf, etc. They definitely had magic in their wands at that time.

But we had plans of changing their luck when we flew north of the border for a crucial two-game weekday series on September 17 and 18.

The fans of Montreal make up for their lack of baseball knowledge with their enthusiasm for the game. The Expos, who were perennial cellar-dwellers until '79, had always been supported well by their fans, no matter what place they were in.

Though we could see them developing, '79 was actually the year the Expos came together as a team. With the help of a few key trades and some talented young players who had been raised in the Expo farm system, the Expos built one of the best teams in baseball. Our major advantage over the Expos was our experience. Most of our players were older than the Expo youngsters and had lived through a few pennant races before. The only experienced veterans in the Expo starting lineup were Dave "A.C." Cash, who'd been acquired by Montreal in a trade, and former Red slugger Tony Perez.

But the Expos didn't allow the pennant pressure to affect their play adversely. In fact, I believe it bettered their game. The Expos were a gutsy team.

And so were their fans, who cheered with every pitch. Fifty-four thousand fans were in attendance for the first game of the series, amazing for a Monday night in a hockey town. But like Pittsburgh, Montreal considered itself a winning city, and its fans felt like a part of the action. They were the most jovial fans in the league. They danced, sang, ate, drank and cheered loud for their Expos. Though their reactions often gave them away as first-time baseball fans, they remained terribly enthusiastic just the same.

They all stood and applauded each time the Expos had any type of rally going or every time they thought the Expos should have a rally going. Some fans remained on their feet the entire game. They even gave standing ovations to long, foul balls as if to say "Good try." The backing of their fans made the young Expos a super team.

But we were in Montreal to prove that we were the finest team in the league. As expected, the Expos didn't make it easy for us. We sent young Don Robinson to the mound against their finest pitcher, Steve Rogers.

Don—or Man-Mountain, as he was sometimes referred to because of his large size—was only twenty-two years old but he was as mature and confident as anyone in the league. Don was a native West Virginian who spoke with a slight twang. He'd been a high school football and baseball star in his home town, Kenova, and had married his high school sweetheart.

Though Don was from a tiny town planted in the West Virginia hills, he loved big-city ways. When he wasn't with his beautiful wife Rhonda or at the ball park, he loved to go to the dog track, horse races or wherever one was permitted to place a bet. Don was a natural-born gambler.

To look at his background, one would have guessed that the crowd in Olympic Stadium that night, almost fifty-five thousand, would have shaken the young man. Heck, fifty-five thousand was several times the entire population of his home town. But someone should have told the Montreal fans that big crowds always brought the best out of Donny. The more noise they made, the better he pitched.

Donny was one of those unique individuals who thrived on emotion and pressure. Without either ingredient, he was no better than an average pitcher. But with both present, he was one of the finest pitchers in baseball. I suppose that's what made him such a good gambler.

I would not have liked to be batting against Donny that night. The excitement I saw in his eyes would have alone scared me away from the plate. The louder the Montreal fans yelled, the harder he threw. His blazing fastball and snappy curve eventually quieted the crowd with a 2–1 Bucco victory.

In the course of his incensed play, Donny, an excellent hitter, also scored the winning run of the game in the fifth inning after he singled, advanced to second on Timmy's base hit and was driven home by Dave. With Donny's pitching and hitting and a few timely base hits by Dave, we moved back into first place with a one-game lead.

But our win hadn't burst Montreal's bubble. The Expo fans came out in droves for the second consecutive night. The fans started drinking, dancing and cheering hours before game time. The noise intensified with every pitch of every inning. The more ale that flowed into their cups the more noise ran out of their mouths.

But the noise level didn't affect either starting pitcher. Buster started for us. He was easily our best September pitcher. Like Donny, Buster thrived on pressure. It always seemed to bring out the best in him, and this was the reason for his lopsided winning record in the later months of the season.

Bill "The Spaceman" Lee was going for the Expos. Lee, though a fine pitcher, had become known as much for his liberal, Timothy Leary type of philosophy, as he had for his curve ball. The crowd wouldn't affect Lee's game either way. He was immune to several human emotions. That's why they called him the Spaceman.

We racked the Spaceman for three runs in the top of the first, which made the Expo fans cheer even louder. They wanted to see their team come back, which they did. The Expos scored two runs in the third and one in the sixth. We went into extra innings with the score tied 3–3.

Now we get down to what my role was with the '79 team. At the age of thirty-eight, I wasn't blessed with great speed, and my throwing arm had seen much better days. I was responsible not only for the team's morale but also for a good portion of their home runs. I was supposed to be the big popper in the lineup, the guy all the pitchers feared, the one who was constantly placed in the position to drive in the big run and usually did. I accepted that as my role much as Joe Coleman accepted his long relief role and Scat accepted his pinch-running role. Hitting home runs in key situations was how I could most help the team.

The Lord blessed me with highly unusual pop in my bat while

he blessed other players with different talents. It's the proper blend-
ing of these talents that makes a successful team. And it was our
players knowing their roles and playing within their limitations that
made our club the great team that it was. No one expected me to
whirl my thirty-eight-year-old body around the base paths and steal
bases. I was expected to hit home runs and trot slowly to home plate.

Preparation was the key to my success as a timely hitter. Hours
before the situation arose for me to drive in the winning run, I was
running thoughts through my mind on what to expect. I thought
about each of the opposition's pitchers, what they threw, how fast
they threw, where they threw it and how often. I also used batting
practice to try various methods of hitting I planned to use against
the other team's scheduled starter and their top relievers. I'd practice hitting outside pitches the opposite way and pulling inside
pitches to right field.

By the time the situation arose for me to produce, I was ready.
I'd thought everything out in advance. It also helped that I loved to
hit with men on base and with the game on the line. I guess I
practiced that, too, back in my window-breaking days in the projects. Like Donny loved to pitch in front of huge crowds, I loved to
hit with men on base. It was my role and I'd become one of the best
in baseball at it.

Though I hit only .222 in September, I still did my job by hitting
8 homers and driving in 18 runs—that was my job anyway, not
hitting for average. I hit 4 game-winning homers in September, one
of which came in the eleventh inning versus the Expos in our extra-
inning game on the eighteenth. It was a two-run shot off of Dale
Murray at 1:46 in the morning. He hung a forkball, and I was expecting it. We won 5–3 and moved two games in front of Montreal in
the standings. We had again quieted the Expo fans but failed to stop
Montreal's momentum.

It seemed that we were the only team in baseball who could
beat the Expos. Right after we left town, they began winning again.

We arrived in Philadelphia around 6:00 A.M. after our flight
from Montreal. We had a late afternoon doubleheader with the
Phils, which meant that we had to report to the ball park at about
three o'clock in the afternoon. It was our typical series with Philadelphia. We never needed a reason to get ourselves up to play the
Phillies. The natural rivalry was always there. But by this time, they
were playing the spoilers instead of the champions.

As usual, they jumped off to a large lead, 6–1, entering the top of the eighth inning in the first game. Mike Schmidt's grand slam in the seventh inning was the big blow. But we still chattered on the bench about coming back to win. And in the next two innings we did.

We scored three quick runs off McGraw in the eighth and then began to light him up again in the ninth. Rawly Eastwick was finally brought in to relieve the Bucco-beaten McGraw. But the new pitcher didn't stop our fun. We just kept banging. The big hit of the game was Sangy's two-run triple with two out in the ninth inning.

Sangy was thirty-five years old at the time. I'd seen him rise to a superstar status as a Bucco and eventually fall to the role of a pinch-hitter. But he accepted his job well. He'd had his day in the sun. He was just another valuable yet hardly noticed cog in the Pirate machine.

After twelve years in the majors, Sangy hadn't lost an ounce of his enthusiasm for the game. He was still the smiling Panamanian, and Pittsburghers loved him for what he represented. He spoke in mixed English and Spanish, and though his diction wasn't always correct his meaning was clear, for he spoke from the heart.

We'd reacquired Sangy from Oakland before the '78 season and it was obvious that his year away from Pittsburgh hadn't changed him one bit. He was still loosey-goosey, a free-swinger, afraid to fly in airplanes and known as "Smiley." It was a pleasure to know and play with such a talented ball player and such a genuine human being.

The Phillies were even better in the role as spoilers than they had been as champions. They defeated us the last two games of the series and we fell one-half game behind the hungry Expos.

In fact, we found ourselves still half a game back of Montreal four days later, on September 24. We knew that we'd have to beat them ourselves since no one else seemed to have the ability to do so. Fortunately for our pennant hopes, we had them on our own turf for a four-game weekday series. It was a battle for first place. This was a chance to break their spirit, just as we had done with the Phils a month before.

But by this time, we'd developed a deep respect for the Expos. They were a lot like us. They never gave up. They just kept coming back. We wanted to win the pennant, but if for some reason we couldn't, I believe our guys would have started rooting for Montreal.

As usual, we played come-from-behind ball the first game. The Expos had taken a 2–0 lead early in the game. But as had become our style, we thrilled the forty-eight thousand hometown fans with our last-minute heroics. Bill Robinson's three-run homer in the sixth gave us all the runs we needed to win. We let Teke do the rest, shutting down the Expos in the last three innings to preserve our 5–2 win.

But we hadn't broken the Expos' spirit. Although we took a quick 6–2 lead into the sixth inning of the second game, they refused to die. They may have even caught us off guard. We never expected them to hang tough. They played the Bucco brand of catch-up baseball in the second game, beat us 7–6 and recaptured first place.

We entered our Tuesday night game in second place. To be in first place when the Expos left town, we had to win the last two remaining games. But we were in a better position than any time before. We'd seen the Expos at their best. I think the Lord had used their comeback win the night before to serve as a good kick in the butt for us. We may have become slightly overconfident after the first game.

Well, even if the Lord hadn't staged the Expos' win for that purpose, it sure worked to our benefit. We were extra hungry entering the final two games. They belonged to us.

I hit a two-run homer in the first inning on the 25th, to spot us a 2–0 lead. But the feisty Expos tied the score a few innings later. It was my turn again in the fourth. I did my job, I played the brute, I spotted us a 3–2 lead with my second homer of the evening. The thirty thousand fans in the stadium stood and applauded until I walked from the dugout and took my curtain call. I was overcome with emotion. Tears filled my eyes.

We wound up winning the game 10–4 but we hadn't beaten the Expos, only outlasted them. We won because we scored more runs after nine innings of play. We were back in first place. But they weren't beaten yet.

It was Buster's turn the next night. As I stated before, he was our money pitcher. He proved it that night as he limited the heavy Expo hitters to only one run and seven hits, while we pounded their pitching for fourteen hits and ten tallies. Again, a large crowd, over forty-two thousand, was in the stands to see us perform. We were the best show in town and also the best team in the division—by one and one-half games, to be exact.

But the race wasn't over yet. Our magic number was four, which meant that we needed any combination of our wins and the Expos' losses to equal or exceed four before we won the pennant. We were defeated by the Cardinals at Three Rivers on the 27th. The Expos were rained out. Our lead was narrowed to one game.

The next day Jim Bibby, the underrated work horse on our staff, blew the ball by the Cubs for a 6–1 win. Bibbs was the strongest man on our team. He'd been a slow starter. His career had been held back by a few years in the military and injuries early in his career. But like the team he played for, he kept coming back.

Chuck used Bibbs in all types of situations, splitting his time equally between starting and relief. Bibbs never let us down in either role. Though he had the strongest arm on the team, he accepted what Chuck asked him to do. Some major-leaguers allow their ego to get in the way of their productivity. But Bibbs didn't have an ego. He just had a lot of size, strength, guts and enthusiasm.

His win lifted his record to 12–4, lowered our magic number to two and gave us a two-game lead over the Expos, who lost to the Phillies, with two games to go.

We entered our game the next day looking to put pressure on the Expos. If we won, the Expos would have to win their last three remaining games.

But I personally sent our pennant hopes into the last day of the season with my throwing error in the thirteenth inning.

Here's how we lost. The Cubs' Mick Kelleher singled and went to second on a sacrifice bunt. The next batter hit a lazy ground ball to Dog at third, who looked Kelleher back to second and threw over to me at first. Then came the play and the boo-boo of the game.

After Dog's throw, Kelleher decided to force the action. He took off for third. Dog's throw landed squarely in my mitt. I gunned the ball back to third. The ball carried over Dog's outstretched glove. While Timmy and Dog ran to the sight of my errant toss, Kelleher scored. We lost 7–6.

Of course, the press gathered around my locker looking for my version of the play. All that I told them was that I expected Dog to run a down-and-out pattern and instead he did a buttonhook. They seemed confused by my humor.

But I redeemed myself on the last day of the regular season. I upped our lead to 3–0 in the fifth inning versus the Cubs with my solo home run. Buster and Teke did the rest. We won 5–3, while the

Expos lost to the Phillies. At 4:19 that Sunday afternoon, we were crowned Eastern Division Champs.

We celebrated with one eye on our bottles of champagne and the other on our archrivals, the Reds, whom we'd have to beat in the play-offs. But I was so happy and so proud of what we had accomplished as a team, an organization and a city that tears of joy stained my face. I think I was the only Bucco that cried. My teammates were too busy cheering to do much else.

Though several of my teammates weren't Buccos the last few times we'd been defeated by the Reds in the play-offs, I still felt the rivalry deep inside. Some of the Pittsburgh fans remembered our past performances in play-off action against Cincinnati and felt we didn't stand a chance against the revamped Big Red Machine.

But my teammates and I had different plans. We weren't afraid of anyone. We respected the Reds as Western Division Champs but we weren't intimidated in the least. We didn't care what had happened in the past.

We were the same old Buccos and we played our usual brand of comeback baseball. We were tied 2–2 with the Reds in Cincinnati for Game One after nine innings. Both Foots and Tom Seaver of Cincinnati had pitched well. We finally won in the eleventh inning. As usual, the troops set the table for me and I played the brute. My three-run homer won it for us. Again, I didn't consider myself anything special. It was simply my job to hit home runs, drive in runs and win ball games. I was no better than any of my other teammates and I was no more important. My role was simply much more glamorous and brought me much more attention than the others, that's all.

Game Two was quite similar to Game One. We went to extra innings tied 2–2. This time it was Dave's role to play the brute. His base hit in the tenth scored Omar from second. Donny, who was now working as a reliever because of arm troubles, shut the door in the last inning. We went back to Pittsburgh with a 2–0 lead in the series.

It's always great to be home, but when I saw the cold, wet weather that greeted us, I began second-guessing myself. Game Three was delayed a significant amount of time because of rain, and almost eight thousand fans who had bought tickets failed to show. But there were still over forty-two thousand fans in the stadium when the game finally began.

Bert Blyleven, who owned the meanest curve ball in the majors, was slated to start for us, young Mike LaCoss for them. Bert was one of the few Dutch-born players in the big leagues. He was also devoted to his craft and an extremely hard worker.

Bert could have outrun any major-leaguer in an endurance race. He trained by running mini-marathons in the off-season. During the regular season, you could set a clock by Bert. He was at the ball park early every day running his self-timed laps. Bert was devoted.

He was also fascinated by statistics. He liked to watch his career totals grow. Earlier in the season, Bert had asked to be traded because he wanted to pitch more often. Rather than lose a fine pitcher like Bert, Chuck decided to schedule the starting rotation around him.

But nothing ever seemed to jell for Bert. He was our hard-luck pitcher extraordinaire. We never scored any runs for him. On the other hand, we scored runs in droves when Bibbs pitched. I realize that it was just a coincidence, but Bert was willing to try anything to break his spell of bad luck.

Once before one of his starts, crazy Bert charcoaled his face black and slipped on Bibb's jersey, in hopes of drumming up some offensive support. The troops erupted into laughter when charcoal-black Bert was standing outside the clubhouse door to greet us as we stepped off the team bus.

But because of his hard luck and some personal problems, Bert's two seasons with the Bucs had been no laughing matter. He hadn't become the caliber of player the team had traded Scoop for two years before.

Most of us were awaiting the time when all Bert's potential would come together in one show of brilliance. In Game Three it happened. Bert mesmerized the tough-hitting Reds. He was nearly unhittable. I drove in three runs with a solo homer in the third and a two-run double in the fourth.

But the most exciting action of the day happened during the seventh-inning stretch, when "We Are Family" was played for the crowd. We were well ahead, 6–1 at the time, when Pam Nicosia, Nic's wife, began leading our wives up to the concrete platform behind the backstop. The twenty-five or so young women, clad in black and gold, waving pennants, banners and whatever, led the crowd in a premature victory celebration as "We Are Family" blared in the background.

The national network announcers called the performance bush but I realized why the wives had done it. Even more than their men, they needed a release. They were tense. They were as much a part of our effort as anyone, but unfortunately their contribution often went unnoticed. All they wanted to do was release all the joy and worry they had stored up inside. They just needed to take a deep breath of fresh air.

No one can fully understand what a wife of a major-leaguer has to go through. First of all, she must love her man enough to stick with him through both the good and bad times. Being a major-leaguer isn't like your normal 9-to-5 office job. Players' pay is a reflection of their performance. A player could have a few bad days in a row and find himself on a plane to the minors. So a major-leaguer's wife must suffer through the slumps, losing streaks and injuries with him. She must be his crutch and his strength when he is down.

Second, a major-league bride sees her husband only between road trips and in between games. Thus, if she is also a mother, she may need to play the father too. Major-leaguers aren't the most attentive fathers, for they're rarely at home.

It seemed that every time I went on the road, something would always go wrong at home. Dolores was constantly left with flooded basements, feuding kids, etc. I remember once when one of my daughters was hit, but not injured seriously, by a school bus. That was a tragedy in the Stargell household, and Dolores was left to cope with it alone. I was on the road with the team.

So I was all for what the wives did. They were every bit as much a part of our effort as any of our players. They deserved a little of the spotlight.

The Reds bowed out of the play-offs 7–1, only two innings after our wives' exhibition. I was named M.V.P. for the play-offs. But most important, we were on our way to the World Series.

None of us had seen the Orioles play but we'd all heard that they had a great team, much like the '71 squad. They had combined fine pitching with powerful hitting to easily outdistance their Eastern Division opponents.

What we did hear a lot about was the Baltimore fans, who were supposed to be the loudest in the American League. They were led by the local fans, and adopted as mascot Wild Bill Hegy, a tall, beer-gutted, flannel-shirt-sporting, cowboy-hat-wearing cheerleader. Bill's claim to fame was leading the Orioles' fans in the spelling of O-R-I-O-L-E-S by assuming a variable number of positions with his lopsided body. The Baltimore fans loved it.

Chuck chose Buster, our best late-season pitcher, to start Game One of the World Series. It was a wet, cold night in Baltimore. I believe the game would have been called were it not a World Series game. But there was too much money, time and effort already put into the game to call it because of the weather.

Unfortunately, Buster's forte was not cold, wet-weather pitching. The Orioles jumped on him instantly for five runs in the first. I think we were all a little bit cold, or at least our early play hinted that we were.

But we'd been down many more runs before and later in games to give in. We fought and we scratched but we still came up one run short. We lost Game One by a 5–4 score.

Game Two was another tight battle. We went to the top of the ninth tied 2–2. Ed Ott was on second base with two out when Chuck picked Sangy to pinch-hit against the Orioles' Jim Palmer. With two strikes on him, the thirty-five-year-old, smiling Panamanian sliced the ball to shallow right field. Right-fielder Ken Singleton fielded the ball cleanly while Ed rounded third. Singleton's throw was accurate, but first-baseman Eddie Murray mistakenly cut it off. Ed scored. Sangy dedicated the hit to his fallen amigo Roberto.

Teke held the Orioles, who I'm sure had never seen anything like his delivery before, hitless in the bottom of the ninth. We'd gone ahead on a scrappy play by a former wrestler and a professional pinch-hit by an aging former superstar. And our win was preserved by an underhand-throwing, scarecrow reliever. What a combination. We headed home tied one game apiece with Baltimore.

The fans had been shoehorned into Three Rivers for Game Three. But what we gave our fifty thousand fans was not a typical Bucco performance. The Orioles were a good team. I don't think any of our guys would deny that. They pounded Foots and Romo for eight runs while their crafty Scott McGregor held us to only four.

Game Four went basically the same way. We weren't ourselves. I don't know why but we weren't. We were leading 6–3 going into the top of the eighth. Then the floodgates broke open. Not even

Teke could force them closed. We lost 9–6. I don't know why we looked so terrible. Maybe the Lord was setting us up for one of our patented comeback finishes.

Whatever the reason, our confidence never swayed. The saying around the clubhouse was: We're going back to Baltimore for some of those good crabs. We never talked about losing the Series. That wouldn't have done any good. Sure the deck was stacked against us, but we still expected to win. We just leaned a little more on one another.

Some of the national media began calling us chokes. That, combined with the fact that Chuck's mother had just passed away the morning of the game, inspired us. We wanted to win the Series for Chuck and we wanted to prove to the country that we were the best. At times, negative publicity can inspire a team. We had articles posted all over the clubhouse. They all said in their own individual ways that we were choking. What Winfield's choke sign had done to Roberts in that extra inning game in San Diego these articles were now doing for us. We felt possessed to win. It was just like being in the fifth inning in Philadelphia and behind 8–0 and still feeling we were going to win. Because of the cohesiveness between my teammates, the fans and the city, the Buccos' confidence never let down.

All of us respected and loved Chuck dearly. He stayed strong at all times. No one would have ever known to look at him that Sunday afternoon that he had just lost his mother. We knew where Chuck's heart was but we also knew where he was. His decision to stay and ride the storm out with us was an inspiration. We were higher than at any time in the Series.

Though we never doubted any of Chuck's decisions, not even sending Teke to left field in San Francisco, the media questioned Chuck's choice of Rook as the starting pitcher for crucial Game Five. There was some validity to their inquiries. After all, Rook had been our most inconsistent starter during the season and had finished the season with a poor 4–7 mark. His mound opponent was Baltimore's ace pitcher Mike Flanagan, a twenty-game winner.

Statistically, it looked like a mismatch. But Chuck took into consideration factors not everyone considered. First of all, Rook was a good cold-weather pitcher. Buster, whom he replaced in the rotation, wasn't. And the Lord knows it was cold in Pittsburgh that day. Second, Rook had guts. A match-up such as this would only bring out the best in him. Rook was an intimidating pitcher. He'd serve as an inspiration for the team on the mound. We all felt secure in Chuck's decision, as we always did. Rook was ecstatic about the decision. He felt as if he'd been given a second life, resurrected from the bullpen.

Much to the surprise of our national television audience, all worked just as Chuck had planned it. Rook was phenomenal. He mowed down the Orioles with ease. He gave up only one run and three hits over five innings before giving way to Bert.

At this time, Rook was the hero of the Series. But like all of us, he simply did what was expected of him. Chuck had asked him to keep us close for five or six innings. He gave us a phenomenal five. Rook, as much as anyone, represented the inspiring style of a Bucco. He was tough and crazy, and he loved life, his teammates, the game and a good challenge. Every successful play from this point forward was an inspiration for us. But we owed our turnaround to Rook.

Bert picked up where Rook had left off. He made the Birds look like minor-league hitters. While Bert held them intact, we pulled away. We scored two runs in the sixth, two in the seventh, and three in the eighth and won by a 7–1 score. We were on our way back to Baltimore for some more crabs.

Game Six was a continuation of the Pirate odd-couple series, featuring Foots and Teke. Foots was his usual masterful self for six innings, allowing six hits but no runs. It was now his tag-team partner Teke's turn. Jim Palmer was pitching a good game at the same time. The score was 0–0 when Teke entered the game. It was essential that he hold the Birds down.

We finally got our engine running in the eighth inning, thanks to our spark plug and good lead-off hitter Omar Moreno. Omar—or the Antelope, as he was sometimes called, because of his blazing speed—was what made the Bucs go. He was a severely quiet individual, who would much rather respond to an inquiry with a nod than a phrase. But he was loud on the base paths. His presence would often drive our opposing pitcher nuts. Omar would do almost anything to distract a pitcher's attention away from the Pirate hitter at the plate. His antics made us better hitters, and his speed made us a better team.

His defense also gave us an excellent defensive outfield. It didn't matter who Chuck put in the outfield to flank Omar, even Teke, as long as the Antelope was in center. Because of Omar's speed, there was never any gap between him and the other outfielders. Balls rarely rolled to the wall for an extra base. Omar covered ground like a race car.

It was only fitting that as our spark plug, he get us started in Game Six. With one out, Omar singled. Timmy followed with a base hit. Omar advanced to second. The Antelope sped around third with the game-winning run as Dave's sharply hit ball bounced off second-baseman Rich Dauer into right field.

Teke did his job and held the Birds to only one hit in the last three innings. We added a few more runs for insurance but really didn't need them. We won 4–0 and were on our way to Game Seven.

We used the same tactics to prepare for Game Seven that we used to get ready for every other game. Gar and Dave led a rousing mock argument in the clubhouse. We were loose. Gar had done everything Chuck could have asked for. He'd pounded Baltimore pitchers for eleven hits in twenty-one at-bats, played good defense, helped psych us up before the games and served as an inspiration on the field.

Though Gar was listed as only 5'10" and 177 pounds, really more accurately 5'8" and 160 pounds, he had a heart as big as an elephant's. He was the "winner" that Chuck had pushed Pete to trade six players for. His style was also conducive to Pittsburgh victory. He was gritty and tough and had plenty of guts. His Yosemite Sam mustache distinguished him from anyone else on the club. Phil was as colorful as any Bucco character and he was also the most underrated player in the Series.

We entered the seventh game with a huge amount of confidence. We knew that if we all just did our jobs, we'd win. It was as simple as that. Bibbs was our starting pitcher. He did his job by holding the Orioles to only one run in four innings.

Donny relieved Bibbs and allowed only one hit and no runs. Buck Jackson was our next pitcher. He was also our most experienced pitcher. As an Oriole, Buck had pitched against us in the '71 World Series. Buck was our teacher in the bullpen, our wise old reliever.

Buck knew just about everything there was to know about pitching. He not only knew how to throw several different pitches but also knew how to set hitters up. Buck was also far and away the best card player on the team. I'd once seen him study the individual styles of some players in a poker game, ask to be dealt in for one hand and walk away with a fistful of money.

That's how Buck worked as a pitcher. He studied the style of opposing hitters innings before he was called into a game. Then he'd fleece them for all they had, just as he did in a poker game. When the game was over, he'd usually leave with either a save or a win.

Buck did his job by holding the Birds hitless for almost three innings. During that period, I was called on to do my job. We entered the seventh inning, trailing by a 1–0 score. Bill Robinson was on base. Leftie Scott McGregor was pitching for the Birds.

He started me off with two fastballs high and tight. That meant only one thing to me: he was setting me up for the breaking ball away. I decided to wait on the breaking ball, which meant that I'd have to hold up my swing just slightly. If I got too anxious and swung too hard, he'd make me look like I was swinging a toothpick instead of a war club.

I'd borrowed Sangy's bat for the occasion. It was narrower at the end and would allow me to get around quicker on the leftie McGregor. I laid back awaiting the breaking ball. I guessed right. There it was. I waited just long enough to pull the ball but not so long that I'd overswing. I got the fat part of the bat on the ball and drove it high in the air to deep right field. Singleton, their right-fielder, faded back to the fence, braced himself and leaped, half his torso outstretched over the wall. The ball angled into our bullpen, slightly behind his glove. It was a home run. We took the lead, 2–1. Like my teammates, I'd done my job.

Now it was up to the gangly Teke to do his. The Orioles loaded the bases with two out in the eighth. Eddie Murray, the Orioles switch-hitting first-baseman, was the batter. He'd been our nemesis in the early going, but he was now on an 0-for-20 streak. Being a lefthander, he was supposed to be natural trouble for the right-handed Teke. In fact, that was Teke's tag—he couldn't get lefthanders out.

Like Chuck, Teke didn't believe in tags. He got Murray to pop out to Dave in right field to end the inning. We added two more runs just for good measure in the top of the ninth. Teke shut down the Orioles in the bottom of that same inning.

Yes, we were crowned World Champions but most of all we were a family of friends and fans. That's what had gotten us there and had made the year so rewarding. I was named M.V.P. for the Series but I wished I could have broken the trophy up into a million little pieces to share with all the fans in Pittsburgh, the radio and television announcers, our wives and kids, the people in the front office, the ushers, the ground crew, my fellow players, the trainer Tony Bartirome, Hully, everyone associated with our effort, for we together were responsible for winning the Series, not me alone. We won, we lived and we enjoyed as one. We molded together dozens of different individuals into one working force. We'd shown the entire world what could be done by exchanging all one's prejudice and grudges for the love of one's fellow man. We were products of different races, were raised in different income brackets, believed in different Gods and religions and had varying political beliefs. But in the clubhouse and on the field we were a family.

We had Sangy, a smiling Panamanian; Roberts and Coleman, schooled veterans on their last leg in the majors; Rooker, the intimidator; Gar, the winner; Dave, the instigator; Scat, the legs; Omar, the tablesetter; Donny, the gambler; Teke, the stopper; Easy, the Hitman; Romo, Mr. Variety; Dog, our missing link; Lacy, the utility man; Nic, the mature, storytelling catcher; Hammer, Mr. Grandslam; Timmy, Mr. Sacrifice; Bill Robinson, our leader in the first half; Buster, Mr. September; Bibby, Mr. Versatility; Buck, who always played his cards right; Dale Berra, Yogi's son, who'd fill in when we needed him; Bert, the talented Dutchman; the Troll, our wall behind the plate; Foots, the great endurer of pain; Stennett, who forgot his role as a starter and did whatever was asked of him; and myself, the Brute.

There were also some nonplayers who were every bit as important as any of us on the field. Harvey Haddix, the pitching coach, who steadied a sometimes shaky group of hurlers; Joe Lonnett, our third-base coach, who'd throw batting practice until his arm went numb each day; Bob Skinner, our batting instructor, with an eagle eye for defects in our swings; Al Monchak, our Russian first-base coach, who helped each one of us at some point during the season defensively; Chuck, the leader, the inspiration, whatever we needed; Tony Bartirome, our trainer, who kept the clubhouse loose with an interesting mixture of practical jokes; Hully, the Judge, who made our lives much easier by just being around; Charley Muse, our traveling secretary, who made spending months on the road a livable experience; our wives, our kids, our families, our crutches and our strengths; the fans and people of Pittsburgh, the inspiration to keep going on when times were tough.

We were the Buccos, World Series champs, the best baseball team in the world. But more important, we were a family.

"The bat is gone, but the smile remains."

8 LIFE IS ONE BIG TRANSITION. We're constantly aging, maturing and bettering ourselves. It's how we handle these transitions that determine how happy of a life we live.

Myself and the Buccos went through a rash of changes in 1980. First of all, I reported to spring training a year older. For a youngster one year either way may not make much of a difference. But for a thirty-eight-year-old major-leaguer soon to be thirty-nine, the change was drastic.

Though my upper body strength remained relatively unaffected and my bat remained lightning quick, my knees had gotten progressively worse. After all the operations they'd undergone, all the material between their bones had been extracted. I had a bone-on-bone situation, no cartilage, no ligaments, nothing. My bones scraped against each other with every step I took. They'd also become arthritic and they stiffened up immediately if they weren't kept in constant motion or out of cold weather. But I wasn't depressed over what was happening to my body. I knew that just like everybody else I'd someday grow old, but I didn't expect to still have as much enthusiasm for the game at such a late age. I found myself in a race with Mother Nature to play as much baseball as I could before she forced me to stop.

I was still young at heart. I was still excited by spring training and I still horsed around with the guys. Oscar Wilde once said, "The tragedy of old age is not that one is old, but that one is young." That's how I felt. I was still very young inside even though my body was aging quickly on the outside.

Some of my friends suggested that I should have retired after '79. They thought such a season would have been a great ending for my career. But in my heart, I wasn't ready to retire. A major transition like that needs to be mentally prepared for and I wasn't ready yet.

My life had also gone through several other changes by this time. Because of our dramatic performance in the World Series, I was a more popular and sought-after figure than I had ever been before in my life. There were thousands of requests for appearances and interviews. Everybody wanted to find out what I was really like. I welcomed the extra attention. Everyone likes to tell others about themselves, their ups, their downs, about their family and their upbringing. I also saw this as an opportunity to share my simple philosophy of life with the folks.

But the best part of all the added attention was being able to meet hundreds of new, interesting people. I find all people I meet interesting in their own individual way. People intrigue me. There's nothing I find more interesting or stimulating than a new friend. The added attention offered me the opportunity to meet hundreds of new folks. The entire experience was exhilarating.

But it was tiring, too. I was so bombarded by speaking appearances and interviews that after only three months into 1980 I was run completely ragged. Writers and radio and TV reporters seemed to spring from everywhere. I was constantly on camera or behind a microphone.

That didn't bother me during the off-season, but once I arrived at spring training and had a rigorous routine of workouts scheduled each day, the interviews began to get in the way. Each reporter tried to take a new angle on my life. They were never satisfied with one another's stories even though they asked basically the same questions and wrote the same words. But I realized that they all had jobs to do and I tried to be as patient with their repetitive questions as possible.

After a while, I began to feel obligated to answer their questions each day even if I wasn't going to be present. I felt it was part of my job. That's why I wrote the answers to a routine interview on a piece of paper and tacked it on the spring training clubhouse bulletin board when I was scheduled to be out of town on business one day. My responses read:

1. Yes, I am 38 and I'll be 39 on March 6.
2. If everyone stays healthy, we do stand a chance.
3. I'll play in as many games as I can.
4. Yes! Other clubs have helped themselves. Otherwise, they'll finish like they did last year.
5. Kison and Stennett will be missed from the family. It will give others a chance to prove themselves.
6. I'm not tired from all the traveling this winter, so I don't see any setbacks.
7. You have a good year (hit .300).

But although the added exposure had highlighted my image around the country, it had limited my popularity with Dolores. We were going in totally different directions. Change sometimes hurts. The change I was going through cost me a marriage and a lovely wife.

Dolores had been everything to me for so many years that I hurt very deep inside when we separated. I still have a tremendous amount of respect for her, and the love we shared will never be replaced. But we weren't the same two people we had once been. She was going to the left and I to the right. Sometimes you lose a large part of your past when you're forced to surrender to your future.

Our separation hurt both of us immensely and I'm just glad that we've been able to remain such close and dear friends. She still owns a piece of my heart that I know I'll never get back.

The team had gone through a transition period also. Buster and Rennie had both gone the free-agency route. The Hitman won a starting position in left field. Dave Roberts was traded, Joe Coleman was released, and we added B.J. Solomon, Rod Scurry and Andy Hassler to our pitching staff.

But in the biggest change of all, we forgot about our own reputation as a slow starting team and ran off an 11–5 record in April, good enough for first place. I must admit that the club did it mostly without me. I bruised my left thumb early in the month and was out of the lineup for seven games. I finally returned and swung the bat with authority until I pulled a hamstring running to first base on June 19. Mother Nature was beginning to force the situation. I had just had my finest game of the season only six days before, when I tore into the Houston pitching staff for four hits in four at-bats, including two homers and five RBIs. But because of the injury, I was limited to pinch-hitting duty for the next twenty-three games. Finally, I was placed on the disabled list and missed another twenty-one games.

Though I still wasn't off the disabled list, the Pirates held a special ceremony for me in between games of a doubleheader versus the Dodgers on July 20. With all the outpouring of the fans' love, I found it hard to hold back the tears. The team had flown in my Mom, Dad and Percy. It was a real family gathering. I carried a towel around my neck to wipe away my tears.

But the ceremonies were slightly tarnished after a fan threw a flashlight battery at Dave in right field during the first game of the doubleheader. Such occurrences had become commonplace throughout the league since the bat-throwing incident in '79. Dave's name was left out of the lineup for the second game.

I felt partly to blame when he asked to be traded shortly after. He began referring to himself as "a player without a home." I wish I could have helped him more, for I had lived through similar circumstances early in my career.

Dave wasn't the first major-leaguer ever to have a fan throw something at him. It happened to me several times throughout my career. It got so bad at one time that I had to wear a helmet out to first base just to protect myself.

I remember several times when fans would throw chips of ice at me. They were the worst. The chips' sharp edges would dig into my skin. They hurt worse than anything. I recall several times walking back into the dugout after the end of an inning with a bloody neck. I was sometimes an irate fan's favorite target. During the course of my career, I saturated many a towel with my blood after being struck by an object thrown from the stands.

But I learned very early in my career never to complain. That would only alienate myself from the good fans and enlist more support for the bad ones. I took my licks as part of my job. I never complained and thus my situation never got half as bad as Dave's.

Unfortunately, Dave decided to take another approach. He decided to turn against all our fans because of one bad apple. What

Dave did was infuriate all our fans because of his reaction to that one who threw the battery. He became a chronic complainer. In his own defense, he attacked the fans, the city and the club. I realize that what happened to Dave was wrong, but the situation was only made worse when he turned against our fans because of it. Sometimes people must accept what they cannot change. Too bad Dave never followed that philosophy. His life would have been much happier if he had.

As a result of Dave's reaction, more irate fans emerged. Throwing incidents became daily news in whatever city Dave and the Pirates played at. His car was also constantly attacked in the parking lot. His story made good copy and sold newspapers. Thus, his exploits were reported on a daily basis. And because of the bad press he received, a deeper and deeper hole was dug for him each day.

But even with all the confusion Dave and his situation created, the team still played exceptionally well. We were in second place, only a game and a half out of first, when we met the Phils for a four-game weekend series in Pittsburgh on August 8. We won the first game 6–5 and cut the Expos' lead to one game.

By the time we swept all four games from the Phils, we were tied for first place with Montreal. We moved into a one-game lead by beating the Mets 2–1 the next day.

But one day later, on August 12, Steve Henderson of the Mets drove a line drive past me at first. I dived for the ball but missed it. The ball rolled into the corner and slid past Easy, who was playing right field. Henderson, running all the way, just beat Scrap Iron's throw home for an inside-the-park home run.

The 3–1 loss stopped our win streak at eight games, slid us back into a tie for first place and eventually put me on the disabled list. I'd injured my knee diving for Henderson's ball. My body couldn't take the licks the way it used to. Mother Nature was telling me something again.

On August 21, I was placed on the disabled list and underwent arthroscopic surgery on the knee soon afterward. I had originally planned to rejoin the team in the second week of September for the pennant race. But under the advisement of the surgeon who operated on my knee, I stayed on the disabled list the remainder of the season.

But even without me, the Buccos seemed destined to win the pennant. Over one stretch, they lost eight consecutive games at

Three Rivers and moved back into first place. The pennant was theirs for the taking, but they just didn't have the horses to take it.

Since both Dave, who was also suffering from a bad knee, and I were out of the lineup, the team needed another big bopper, which unfortunately they didn't have. The team won only nineteen of their last forty-nine games and finished in third place behind the Phillies and Expos.

In the beginning, I traveled with the team while on the disabled list but I eventually became saddened and decided to remain in Pittsburgh. This was a very difficult time in my life. I was struggling with the reality that my body could no longer do what I wanted it to do. I desperately wanted to help the team but couldn't. I was hurt and frustrated. I was beginning to feel old.

At first the thought bothered me. In fact, I told some reporters, who constantly hounded me about retirement, that I couldn't see going through another season like this. From that point forward, my retirement became the major topic in each town we entered. I was getting weary of answering all the same questions, which I had no specific answer for anyway. "Is this your last year?" "When are you going to hang it up, Willie?" "Do you think you'll be in a Pirate uniform next season?" I think the questions were part of the reason I decided to stay home instead of traveling with the team. I simply wasn't sure what to do at the time.

But after a great deal of thought, I realized one thing: I didn't want to leave the game after a season like 1980. I still had the enthusiasm. I shrugged off all the questions about retirement and decided to return for another year.

While Pete worked on rebuilding the Buccos, I worked out daily at rehabilitating my knee. My surgeon from Lansing, Michigan, Lanny Johnson, said that my upper thighs needed strengthening. He prescribed bicycle riding.

After undergoing surgery in the off-season, Dave also worked on a rehab program. The big story in the newspapers was about how much weight he'd gain while on crutches. But Dave got extremely serious about his career. The fans in Pittsburgh had shown a great deal of concern for his situation. In fact, over a dozen people telephoned the Pirate front office to say that they had thrown the battery at him in July. Obviously, only one of them could have thrown it. But the others were calling simply to make him feel better so he'd change his mind and stop asking to be traded.

Their efforts must have worked, because Dave later in the season told the press that he wanted to stay in Pittsburgh. Like all of us, Dave simply needed to be told that he was appreciated. It's tough when a player plays through injuries, hustles all the time and gives his team 150 percent on the field and all he receives is criticism. Dave just needed to know that he was wanted.

He spent the majority of the off-season in his Florida condo, where he dieted on fruits, vegetables and fish while running and working out daily. His slim, trim appearance at the beginning of spring training surprised just about everyone. And he also surprised everyone by reporting on time, the first time that he had done so in three years—in fact, he reported early to training camp.

Both Dave and I looked and felt ready for the season, but I fell out of the race almost instantly. I'd progressed to jogging on my knee. One of my favorite pastimes was to go running with my dog. On one of those occasions, I twisted my knee in a hole. I was back at square one again. I immediately flew to Lansing, Michigan, to visit Dr. Johnson. As usual, the press began talking about my retirement again. But I was bound and determined to play this season out.

The fans began to worry. The Buccos still needed a bopper. Dave wouldn't be enough alone. He'd need support. That's when Pete traded Ed Ott and minor-league pitcher Mickey Mahler to the California Angels for lefthanded, power-hitting first-baseman Jason Thompson. I wasn't insulted by the trade. I knew that Pete had to do what he felt was best for the team. But I was as surprised as anyone when Pete tried to peddle Thompson to the Yankees only thirty-five minutes after he'd acquired him. Fortunately, Baseball Commissioner Bowie Kuhn vetoed the Bucs' trade with the Yanks, and Pittsburgh ended up with Jason, who immediately became a very reluctant Bucco.

Unlike his teammates, Jason was a quiet, introverted player. He rarely spoke but when he did say something, it was usually complimentary. But anyone could tell that he was harboring some very confused feelings inside. He simply didn't know if the Pirates wanted him or not. No one in an official position had notified him either way and it wasn't his style to ask.

While I began the season sitting on the bench waiting for my knee to heal, Jason began slowly at the plate. In the beginning, he didn't seem to be the power hitter the Bucs needed. He looked at too many pitches and swung at too few.

234

But Chuck was extremely sympathetic to both our cases. He kept me glued to the bench early in the season when the weather was cold. He knew that I would only hurt my knee worse playing in such cold weather. Because of my knee, I was also having a difficult time pivoting at the plate, but Chuck was more than accommodating.

Though Jason was performing poorly, Chuck still showed all the confidence in the world in his ability. That's what makes Chuck such a super manager—he's always on your side, no matter how bad you're going. He never applies undue pressure, he only injects needed confidence. But even Chuck couldn't turn Jason around in the early going.

I was slightly frustrated with my injury situation at this time. What was killing me was that I still had plenty of enthusiasm for the game, but I was unable to do anything on the field to express it. It's tough being patient at times, especially when a player must sit in the dugout and watch his last few playing days go by without him.

Around this time, I told the press that my next injury would be my last. Of course, that quote sold newspapers. I began to wonder when I should retire.

I remember what Danny Murtaugh said the first time he retired in 1965. When he left the team at that time, he was suffering from heart problems, and he said that he wanted to retire while he could still walk in the garden and smell the roses. What he said made sense to me. I began running what he had said over and over again in my mind. Like Danny, I also wanted to be able to walk when I left the game. I wanted to be able to go to the park each day and play with the kids.

Retirement is a difficult subject for anyone to face, especially when one considers oneself a kid trapped in an old man's body.

But things started looking better for me as the season ran on. Though I saw action only as a pinch-hitter, my knee had improved significantly. Finally, in the beginning of June, Chuck began using me as his regular first-baseman in place of Jason, who was still in a slump.

It took a few at-bats to get myself back into the swing of things, but once I did, it was just like old times. I began scalding the ball, and the team began to pick up momentum right along with me. I hit .368, or 7-for-19, in five starting assignments between June 2 and

10. We won five of our eight games over that stretch. We were playing like the Buccos of old.

But then players' counsel Marvin Miller called for a players' strike against the owners over a new contract. The strike stopped everything in its place. It was the worst possible thing that could happen to both me and the team. It robbed me of valuable playing time and the Buccos of their momentum.

Unfortunately, the great game had become a big business, one of the reasons Joe Brown had decided to resign as general manager. Both sides were too worried about money and not enough about the game. Me, I always thought about the game and talked about money later. My production was always first on my mind, not the dollar sign.

None of us thought the strike would last as long as it did, and most of us had originally hoped that it wouldn't happen at all. But when we were ordered to walk off the field, it was a very realistic slap in the face for idealists such as me.

Like always, I decided to make the best of the situation. I began enjoying short summer vacations with my kids, and for the first time in over twenty years, I spent July 4 at home. I'd forgotten how beautiful summer could be.

I also used the time to undergo more treatment on my knee, which still hadn't fully healed. I began an herb vitamin diet during the strike that my knee responded to almost instantly. The time off also helped my knee. By the middle part of July, I was feeling real healthy. I was ready to begin playing ball. I'd enjoyed the time off and all the days I'd spent with my kids and now I was ready to take to the diamond again. I had a good feeling about both me and the team.

The length of the strike defied belief. I never thought we'd play again. But finally the strike ended and I was the first one back in the clubhouse. I felt just like a rookie at my first spring training. It was good to see all the troops again and it was especially good to be back on the diamond. It filled the empty spot in my heart that had been left vacant during the lonely days of the strike.

Within a few days and after a couple of exhibition games, we were ready to play. After a long deliberation, Bowie Kuhn decided to split our normal season into two halves. The Dodgers and Phillies were declared winners of the first half, which ended on June 10, the day the strike began. The second season was slated to start on August

10, right after the annual All-Star game. All the games in between the two dates were canceled. They were forgotten. Thus, not every team in each division would play the same number of games in either half season. It was a strange arrangement, but I believe Kuhn did the best with what he was given.

We were scheduled to reopen with the Expos in Montreal on August 10. Because of my fine showing at the end of the first season, I was in the starting lineup. I was excited to be playing again. But all the enthusiasm in the world couldn't hold my aging body together. Mother Nature assured me of that in my second at-bat of the game.

It was a simple injury but very painful. I stepped out of the batter's box to run out a routine ground ball when I heard something pop. It was my heel. Though it was only a twinge in the beginning, it got extremely painful later on. I finished up the game, but the heel swelled like a balloon afterward. I could no longer pull my shoe over it. I had to be satisfied with slippers. I was also having some trouble with my shoulder.

I termed my heel and shoulder problems "Dizzy Dean injuries." Dean was a legendary pitcher in the thirties and forties. Once during his career he injured his foot but continued to pitch by simply adjusting the rest of his body to compensate for the injury. That's exactly what I had done with my bad knee. I had changed both my running and throwing so as not to injure my knee further. My heel and shoulder injuries were the result of my adjustment.

Since I'd said I'd retire rather than go on the disabled list again, the press swarmed around me looking for a retirement date. My head was saying retire but my heart was saying no.

I began contemplating all my alternatives at this time. I wasn't sure what to do. I was growing tired of the constant aches and pains. My life revolved around pain. In fact, I followed a very strict routine to rid myself of much of it each day. After the game each evening, I'd go home, pour myself a glass of white wine, soak in my Jacuzzi and watch a little TV. After a combination of the wine and the hot massaging water loosened up my body enough to sleep, I'd go to bed.

I'm normally an early riser, and in the morning I'd begin a whole new routine. I'd climb out of my water bed and jump into the Jacuzzi again. I'd turn on the TV for entertainment. My favorite show was Phil Donahue, so I'd usually try to schedule my whirlpool around that.

After that, I'd head for the sauna I have on the second floor of my house. After a considerable amount of time in there, I'd begin riding my stationary bike. Some mornings I was so stiff that I even had to take a second dip into the Jacuzzi. This routine was what kept me going the last few years of my career. If it hadn't been for my Jacuzzi, sauna and bike, I might have had to retire years earlier. The routine usually took me to late each morning to complete. But as I said, it was the only way I could keep my aging body functioning.

While I was contemplating retirement and soaking my old tired bones in my Jacuzzi each day, Jason began hitting like a pro. Though he was only hitting in the high .180s through August, he finally caught fire on September 6.

Until that time, he'd been deathly silent. But anyone could tell by just being around him that he was bothered by something deep inside. Finally, he released it all. He told Dan Donovan of the *Pittsburgh Press* everything. What had hampered Jason's performance for so long was the fact that his feelings had been hurt by Pete's effort to retrade him to the Yankees.

About an hour after Jason spoke his piece to Donovan, he had his finest day of the year, with four hits, two doubles, a home run and four RBIs versus the Padres. From that point on, Jason hit well over .300. Releasing his frustrations had done the trick for him. He simply needed to clear his mind.

Jason's turnaround played him into a starting role, while my injury glued me to the bench. But I wasn't jealous of Jason one bit. In fact, I'd been rooting for him all year long. He began doing what I'd hoped he'd finally do. The first-base job was his. That was something I was going to have to accept. It was the only position left on the field that I could play. If I wanted to stay in baseball, I'd either have to become a full-time pinch-hitter or go to the American League and become a designated hitter.

I really didn't like either idea. I'd always prided myself on being a good all-around player. That had always been my dream. I'd also sworn off the idea of ever becoming a DH years before. But becoming a pinch-hitter didn't sound appealing to me either. I didn't know if it was worth all the frustration and pain just to be a pinch-hitter. I wanted to contribute, and being a pinch-hitter wasn't my idea of enough of a contribution.

As you can see, my struggle with my decision to stay or leave was a very complicated one. I didn't like the idea of a limited role, but I also didn't like the idea of going out on such a poor season. I had dreams of leaving after a full 162-game campaign, not a makeshift split schedule specially designed for a strike season.

I was swaying between my two options for quite some time before I finally made a decision—or should I say, someone made the decision for me. Near the end of the season, it was obvious to my teammates that I was struggling to make a choice. Several players had asked me to return for another season. The press was nipping at my heels the entire time. But it wasn't until Dave asked me to stay that I decided to return for one final year.

"Pops," he said, "I wish you'd hang around for another year. I need you to help me work through a few things."

Dave and I had grown extremely close over the years. I'd helped him as a ball player. I'd watched him rise to a superstar status, make himself a millionaire and eventually fall slave to his success.

At the time, I thought Dave could use my help. He was a victim of constant attacks from both the fans and the media. He wasn't taking the pressure very well.

But I must admit that it was good to hear him ask for my help. Since he'd signed his new contract, he'd shied away from my assistance. He was afraid to ask for help. He felt that since he was the highest-paid player in the game, no one could teach him anything. He had an image to uphold. Dave stopped leaning on friends. He tried to do it all alone. At times, he even became aloof.

Dave's request for me to stay was what kept me with the Bucs in '82. I was willing to suffer through another season of injuries and pinch-hitting duty for him. After I made the decision and the announcement during the winter of '81, the pinch-hitting role didn't sound that bad. In fact, I was excited by the challenge of it all.

Life is one big change after another. We have to learn to adapt to enjoy all that it has to offer. The past is for memories. The future is for living.

The Buccos had changed significantly since '79. Buster and Rennie had left immediately after the season to take advantage of the free-agent market. Scat and Joe Coleman had been released. Dave Roberts had been traded. Ed Ott had been dealt for Jason. Bert, after demanding to be traded, and Sangy were sent to Cleveland. Gar, who was in his option year and had squabbled with Pete over a new contract, was traded for second-baseman Johnny Ray. Buck was dealt to Montreal at the end of the '81 season for a player to be named later. Hammer was also sent to the Expos but for first baseman Willie Montanez. Rook went to the broadcast booth. Timmy was the last to go. He was traded to the California Angels for sensational young hitter Brian Harper. Timmy's trade made room for young Dale "Yogi" Berra at short.

As you can see, the total complexion of the club changed before my final year. But baseball is built around change. To a major-leaguer, change is a constant part of life. You must rationalize being traded, released or sent down, and even if you are fortunate enough not to fall victim to any of these three, others on your team may, which keeps faces around you from becoming too familiar. And as in life, the sooner one accepts a change, the easier the transition will be and the less time will be wasted grieving.

We used to be a loud, crazy bunch in '79. The fans always knew when the Buccos were coming—they could hear our team bus blocks away. We were known as fun-loving, boisterous ball players. That had been our trademark. We just loved being together and having a good time.

After an uneventful '81, Pete did plenty of wheeling and dealing. Several of the components of the crazy '79 crew were gone.

Like all the Bucco teams I had been a member of, the '82 Pirates enjoyed each other's company, though in a very quiet fashion. There weren't any complaints filed against us by airline personnel or passengers. They were Buccos but with a different style than the '79 bunch. They were a confident, professional club that sported plenty of young talent at every position.

Our main weakness was our starting pitchers, an essential link, and thus we started off '82 as we had ended '81, at or near the bottom of the division. Finally, Foots and Donny, who both had suffered arm injuries the year before, came back to lead the staff in early June. The other components fell into place alongside them. We were the best team in the division from that point forward. Unfortunately, we were too far behind when we started to catch the league-leading Cardinals.

I felt as though I was becoming less and less of an influence on the performance of the team. I was only a late-inning pinch-hitter. I rarely made any starts. I was no longer the conductor of the orchestra on the field. That role belonged to Dog, whom Chuck was priming as the new Pirate team captain.

To say the least, Dave was infuriated with Chuck's choice. He'd felt that he should have been appointed captain. At one time, he'd been in line for the post, but with all the hassles Dave constantly placed himself in, Dog was chosen instead.

With all that was happening, I wasn't feeling as useful to the team as I had once felt. I didn't feel that the troops listened to me the way they used to. Several had signed long-term contracts and felt insulted when someone offered them advice. Big contracts had changed the attitudes of several players toward the game. Some wouldn't listen to or take advice from anyone.

One of those players was Dave. Though I'd stayed around in '82 mostly for him, he never asked me for help. He ignored me when I offered advice. He was under a tremendous amount of pressure. But instead of leaning on a friend when he needed help, he withdrew into a shell. As a result, he had no one to turn to for help. His situation worsened by the hour. All the negative publicity had shamed him, defeated him. He was in a no-win situation. He played the game out of hate and revenge instead of love.

There was nothing I would have rather done than throw my arms around Dave and console him. I could see he was suffering.

Dave had been made a sacrificial lamb. Since he was the first million-dollar-a-year player, he was crucified for all the others that would come after him. He was the one who opened the gate, so he was the one they stoned. I had expected his contract to revolutionize baseball's salary structure but I had never expected it to ruin him.

Over the years, everyone forgot that Dave Parker was a human being. He was treated like a nonhearing, nonseeing, nonfeeling being. But Dave was human. That's why he hurt so much when the media blasted him or the crowds booed him. It took a while but he eventually began to react violently in defense of himself. Which, of course, only fed the anger of the fans even more. While he longed for the affection and respect of the fans, he was also chasing them away. I wished by staying on another year I could have helped him more.

But when he turned his back on me, I turned to the younger players on our team who were hungry for knowledge. Like everyone, I needed to feel as if I was important, needed.

As I mentioned much earlier, one of those players was rookie second-baseman Johnny Ray. He wanted to hear all that I had to say and I was glad to help him with anything, anytime, anywhere.

Johnny gave me the opportunity to utilize the vast amount of knowledge I'd stored through the years. I was an encyclopedia waiting to be opened.

About that time, I began to realize where my future was taking me. Not with all the worldly old veterans sporting hefty contracts but with the youngsters in professional baseball, the minor-leaguers. I had a wealth of knowledge to share and they were more than ready to listen. The Lord was pushing me in that direction. That's where my future lies, with the youth of today. I had my chance to make life better and now it is their turn to do what they can with it. They are my future, my chance to live again.

The more I thought about it, the easier it became for me to walk away from the game. I finally gave in to Mother Nature, who had been telling me that for years. She had finally won and convinced me that it was time to leave. There wasn't a muscle or bone in my body that didn't hurt.

It was definitely time for me to step aside and allow some young stallion to take my place. And it was also time to use my influence elsewhere than on the diamond. Times like this happen to everyone. I wasn't being demoted, only transferred to another area of interest where my experience would be more valuable.

Life is change. When we were kids, we had to progress from grade to grade and from school to school, leaving friends and memories behind each time. When we grew older, we graduated from high school, and often had to leave our friends, our memories and the security of our parents forever. The transition wasn't always easy but we did it just the same.

From that point forward, our lives change rapidly. Some of us go to college, some to work, some get married. Our lives deal with pluses and minuses, changes that we have to learn to adapt to. When the Lord closes one door, he always opens another. It's a shame if we allow ourselves to beat on the closed door behind us while turning our backs on the open door in front of us.

I didn't beat on that closed door. I gladly walked through the open one instead. And while I did, I began to think of what all my wonderful accomplishments had done for me. I thought about what baseball had given me. It had taught me to be understanding, patient and nonjudgmental, and to be myself. It gave me friends, happy times, a glorious twenty years, a prosperous living and a dream come true.

Baseball had not changed me as a person, it only refined my talents and exaggerated my qualities. It gave me an opportunity to show the world what Willie Stargell was really like.

That's what I thought about as I prepared to leave. I just thanked the Lord for such a wonderful career and such a satisfying life. It's always difficult to leave something or someone that you love behind, but it is part of living to do so. We must learn to adjust to the constant changes in our lives to enjoy living. Flexibility is the key to a happy existence.

The Lord has separate plans for each one of us and he doesn't wait for anyone. He forces changes and drags us along life's path. If you're flexible, you'll enjoy the journey. If you're not, you won't. It's as simple as that. We need to have enough faith to believe that what the Lord is doing for us is right. I'm just glad that he gave me over twenty thrilling years in professional baseball. I'm also thankful that he gave me 1982, one more year to smell the roses, feel the excitement of a pennant race, bow to a few more crowds and cry with a few more old friends.

To me, baseball has always been a reflection of life. Like life, it adjusts itself to trends, fads, wars, depressions and disasters. Like life, it survives everything.

I knew the game wouldn't crumble when I left, but I was overwhelmed by the number of people who turned out to see me off. The days held in my honor throughout baseball were the happiest yet saddest days of my life. I was thrilled to know that I had touched so many lives but I was sad when I had to say goodbye. Memories of home runs, strikeouts and exciting wins, losses and events flashed before my eyes on my last trip into every National League park. I soaked a towel that I'd drape around my shoulders for the sole purpose of drying tears each time I was asked to say a few words or take a final bow in front of a stadium full of fans.

It was a very difficult time for me, but I had to move on to other challenges and adventures. It was also someone's turn to take my place at first base, in the lineup and in the peoples' hearts. To me, baseball had been a long train ride, and this was just my stop to get off and change trains while someone else got on.

I leaned on my family and friends for support. They're what made my life so special. They're the basis of my happiness. I knew that as long as I had them, I would always be happy.

With this understanding, the transition was made much easier and I'm happier now than I've ever been. My bones and muscles don't ache. I've given up my relaxing routine of Jacuzzis, steambaths and bike riding. I'm no longer on the road half the year and I'm with my family almost every day. I no longer feel the tension of baseball, I only reap the joy of working with its young people.

The key to remaining flexible during a transition is to never allow the changing circumstances of your life change you. In that respect, I can honestly say I'm happiest. I'm still the same old loving guy who awakes each morning with a gleam in his eye and lives his life for all the beauty it has to offer. I'm still the smiling project kid, the minor-leaguer, major-leaguer, All-Star, MVP, with a bat firmly planted in his hands. The only difference now is that the bat is gone —the smile remains.

DEDICATION

IT'S THE PEOPLE YOU MEET ALONG THE WAY THAT MAKE living fun. Thus, this book is dedicated to all my teammates, whether in the minors or majors, for it was because of them, along with my managers, coaches and baseball fans everywhere, that my career was such a blessing.

Eduardo E. Acosta, Gary Aldrich, Gary Alexander, Matthew Alexander, L. Eugene Alley, Mateo R. Alou, Rodolfo Arias, Antonio R. Armas, Anthony Asaro, David R. Augustine, Robert S. Bailey, C. Douglas Bair, Eugene W. Baker, William Baker, Charles Barrett, Ross Baumgarten, Robert Beall, Franklin Beattie, Robert Belinsky, Rafael Belliard, Dale A. Berra, John Berry, Kurt A. Bevacqua, James Bibby, Joseph Blasko, Stephen R. Blass, Rikalbert Blyleven, Frank Bork, Donald J. Bosch, Dorian Boyland, Ronald Brand, Kenneth A. Brett, Nelson K. Briles, Charles Brinkman, Frank L. Brosseau, Preston Bruce, George S. Brunet, Stephen Brye, James P. Bunning, Forrest H. Burgess, Thomas A. Butters.

Ernie Camacho, Fred D. Cambria, James A. Campanis, Duncan Campbell, John R. Candelaria, Christopher J. Cannizzaro, Bernardo Carbo, Donald E. Cardwell, Paul Carmine, Frank D. Carpin, Clay Carroll, David Cash, Alfred Chavez, Clarence N. Churn, Robert Clear, Roberto W. Clemente, Donn A. Clendenon, Eugene A.

Clines, Francisco Coimbre, Joseph Coleman, Richard C. Colpaert, Donald Corella, Delmar W. Crandall, Victor Cruz, J. Bruce Dal Canton, Victor J. Davalillo, Richard Davis, Ronald E. Davis, Lawrence C. Demery, Libo DeRorio, Thomas A. Dettore, James Dickson, Miquel A. Dilone, Richard Doepker, Sammy Drake, Don R. Dyer, Michael A. Easler, Michael L. Edwards, Lawrence L. Elliot, Dock P. Ellis, Faust, Timothy Foli, Terry J. Forster, Lawrence C. Foss, Earl C. Francis, James L. Fregosi, Eugene L. Freese, Doug Frobel, Woodrow T. Fryman, H. Eugene Garber, Philip M. Garner, Clarence Gaston, John R. Gelnar, Joseph C. Gibbon, Patrick Gillick, David J. Giusti, James Gleason, Charles F. Goggin, Jesse L. Gonder, J. Fernando Gonzalez, Richard M. Gossage, Alex Grammas, James T. Grant, Richard Gray, Fred A. Green, Reginald Grenald, Thomas Griffin, Richard M. Groat, Cecilio Guante, Juan Guerra.

Thomas Haake, Dale Hackbart, Harvey Haddix, Jerry Hairston, David Hamilton, Reginald Hamilton, James Hardison, Gary Hargis, Brian Harper, Charles O. Hartenstein, Andrew Hassler, Ray Hathaway, Richard J. Hebner, Thomas V. Helms, William R. Henry, Jacinto Hernandez, Ramon G. Hernandez, Charles J. Hiller, Donald A. Hoak, Alfred W. Holland, William Holt, Arthur H. Howe, Julio Imbert, Rodger Irvine, Frank Jackson, Grant D. Jackson, Leonard Jackson, Jesse Jefferson, John Jeter, Juan A. Jimenez, Manuel E. Jimenez, Robert D. Johnson, Sanfrid Johnson, Rex D. Johnston, Odell Jones, Tim Jones, John Kelly, Ronald Kent, Donald Kildoo, Clyde King, Edward L. Kirkpatrick, Bruce E. Kison, Ronald L. Kline, Charles Kolarkowski, Gary A. Kolb, George F. Kopacz, Al Kupski.

Leondaus Lacy, John A. Lamb, J. Rick Langford, Lorenzo Lanier, Vance Law, Vernon S. Law, Mark Lee, Robert Lee, Miguel Lemoine, Charles Leonard, Donald G. Leppert, Lenny Levy, James Little, Larry Littlejohn, John Logan, Alberto Lois, Robert Long, Joe Lonnett, LeRoy Luketich, Alvin D. Luplow, Gerald T. Lynch.

Kenneth E. Macha, Bill Madlock, Michael Mahler, Louis A. Manqual, Nicholas Maras, Louis S. Marone, R. James Marshall, Jose Martinez, John Mason, C. Dallas Maxvill, David May, Jerry L. May, Milton S. May, Fred Mayberry, William S. Mazeroski, Alvin O. McBean, Darrell McCall, Samuel E. McDowell, William McEnaney, Orlando J. McFarlane, Edmond McKay, James M. McKee, Gerald E. McNertney, Larry McWilliams, George F. Medich, Mario A. Mendoza, Gene E. Michael, Peter J. Mikkelsen, John Milner, Albert

Miranda, Chester Mitchell, Henry Mitchell, Al Monchak, Guillermo Montanez, Edward Montgomery, Robert R. Moose, Omar E. Moreno, Joe Morgan, John G. Morlan, James Morrison, Paul Moskau, Manuel R. Mota, Albert Muench, Danny Murtaugh, Edward Napoleon, Sam Narron, Calvin A. Neeman, James L. Nelson, Steven Nicosia, Randy Niemann, Donald Nipp, Wayne Nordhagen, Nelson Norman, Frank Oceak, Thomas O'Connor, William O. O'Dell, Albert Oliver, Diomedes A. Olivo, Adalberto Ortiz, Don Osborn, N. Edward Ott.

Jose Pagan, James V. Pagliaroni, David G. Parker, Thomas A. Parsons, Fred J. Patek, Daryl Patterson, Albert Pehanick, Antonio Pena, Orlando Pena, Hugh M. Pepper, George I. Perez, Pascual Perez, John Pesky, Leslie Peterson, Felix Pizzaro, Juan C. Pizzaro, Elmo A. Plaskett, Paul E. Popovich, John C. Powers, Robert S. Priddy, Harold W. Pritchard, Donald Pulford, Robert T. Purkey, Bill Ralston, Pedro G. Ramos, Willie L. Randolph, John Ray, Curtis L. Raydon, Kenneth Reitz, Jerry Reuss, G. Craig Reynolds, Richard Rhoden, Dennis J. Ribant, David W. Ricketts, Thomas Rinks, David A. Roberts, David L. Roberts, Robert E. Robertson, Don Robinson, William H. Robinson, K. Andre Rodgers, Enrique Romo, James P. Rooker, Donald Rowe, Victor Roznovsky, Gary Rushing, Michael J. Ryan.

Ramon Saba, James M. Sadowski, Peter Sala, Roberto Sanchez, Charles D. Sands, Manuel D. Sanguillen, Manuel Sarmiento, Theodore E. Savage, J. Richard Schofield, Donald B. Schwall, Rodney Scurry, James P. Shellenback, Larry Shepard, Larry Sherry, Donald Shodron, William R. Short, Thomas W. Sisk, Robert R. Skinner, Harold R. Smith, James L. Smith, Robert Smith, Eddie Solomon, George H. Spriggs, Ronald Spring, Renaldo A. Stennett, George Stephanovich, James Stoll, Arthur Strichek, Richard L. Stuart, Thomas V. Sturdivant, Arthur L. Swanson, Chuck Tanner, Franklin F. Taveras, Carl M. Taylor, Kenton C. Tekulve, Emiliano Telleria, Jason Thompson, Peter Thompson, Luis Tiant, Bobby Tolan, B. Lee Tunnell, Hediberto Vargas, Orville I. Veal, Robert A. Veale, Mickey Vernon, William C. Virdon, Osvaldo J. Virgil, Harry Walker, J. Luke Walker, Reginald Walton, Gilbert Watts, Larry West, Eddie L. Whitson, David C. Wickersham, Maurice M. Wills, David A. Wissman, George A. Witt, Wilbur Wood, Thomas Woods, Mel Wright, W. Chris Zachary, Richard W. Zisk.